THOM GUNN

A BIBLIOGRAPHY

KU-821-773

THOM GUNN

A BIBLIOGRAPHY

1940–1978

With an Introductory Biographical Essay by
THOM GUNN

Compiled by
Jack W. C. Hagstrom
and
George Bixby

Bertram
ROTA

LONDON

First published 1979

© 1979 Jack W. C. Hagstrom and George Bixby

"My Life Up to Now" and Juvenilia © 1979 Thom Gunn

Bertram Rota (Publishing) Ltd
30 & 31 Long Acre
London WC2E 9LT

ISBN 0 85400 021 6

Printed in Great Britain by
Robert MacLehose and Company Limited
Printers to the University of Glasgow

C
c

CONTENTS

INTRODUCTION

THE format and most of the procedures followed in this bibliography are conventional and will be obvious to the user upon examination of the listings themselves, but a few comments may prove helpful. In general, we used as a model the second edition of the outstanding *W. H. Auden: A Bibliography 1924–1969*, by B. C. Bloomfield and Edward Mendelson (Charlottesville, University Press of Virginia, 1972). Each section and appendix of the book is preceded by a separate introduction.

We have based all of our citations and descriptions on examinations of the items themselves. Any item which was not examined by at least one of the compilers is annotated, before the description, by the statement "Not seen" in square brackets. Anonymously published items included here have been confirmed by Thom Gunn as having been written by him. A distinction is made and is so indicated among signed, initialed, and unsigned items.

Notes that add details or explanations are liberally used throughout the book and are inserted at points where they are deemed most appropriate. Information included in notes is from a wide variety of sources, but most commonly from examination of the item itself.

No attempt is made to trace systematically the printing history of an individual poem or prose piece, but this is easily done by consulting the index. No attempt is made to identify textual revisions of poems except when individual poems have been either retitled or rewritten in such a way as to result in one or more derivative poems.

Square brackets surrounding a date or a page number indicate that the date or page number do not appear as such. Square brackets are also used in the transcriptions of the title pages and in descriptions of the dust wrappers and covers to describe publishers' logos, devices, *etc.*, that cannot be adequately transcribed *per se*.

Accepted practice is observed when transcribing upper and lower-case letters; italic is used for any sloping type faces. Unless otherwise indicated, the type is roman, and no attempt is made to indicate the size of upper and lower-case letters or the amount of space between individual words or letters. In descriptions of title pages and quasi-facsimile material all printing is in black; colored printing is indicated in square brackets before the relevant words or letters. A vertical rule marks the end of each line, and any specific color or type variation that continues on the following line is indicated again at the beginning of that line.

Designation of colors, although in our experience it is fraught with difficulties and inexactitude, is based on Prof. G. T. Tanselle's article "A system of color identification for bibliographical description" (*Studies in Bibliography*, XX [1967], 203–34). The color numbers for all colors (with a few exceptions when a color could not be matched reasonably) except black, white, gold and silver refer to the ISCC-NBS Centroid Color Charts (National Bureau of Standards [Washington, D.C.], Standard Sample No. 2106). No systematic attempt is made to distinguish among types of cloth or paper used for bindings and wrappers. Wove paper is distinguished from laid paper and, when identifiable, special papers are named. For paper wrappers and dust wrappers, the indicated color of the paper is that of the base (*i.e.* unprinted paper stock). The word "shiny" has been used to describe the whole group of coated papers and glossy (versus dull) printing.

The collation is given by signatures and by leaves for sewn books. Standard notation is used for signatures; since in no case is a book actually signed on the sheets, all signature marks are enclosed in square brackets and are supplied by the compilers. For books that are described as "perfect bindings" (those in which all pages are cut and roughed up at the back or binding edge and held together by an adhesive), since there are no identifiable signatures in the finished book, no signatures marks are supplied and only the total number of leaves is indicated.

The size of an individual leaf is given in millimeters, height preceding width. This also applies to size descriptions of broadsides, labels, *etc.*

In all sections and subsections all items are listed chronologically. In section C, *q.v.* items within a given year are listed preferentially by season, month, and specific date.

Prices of each item at the time of publication are given only for the country in which the book was published. Price changes are indicated when they are known to the compilers.

Publication data are based on information supplied by publishers and supplemented, when necessary by other sources. The phrase "data unavailable from publisher" means that the publisher could not locate the necessary data. In some instances, it is the policy of an individual publisher, for whatever reason, not to make figures available on the number of copies that were printed. This is indicated by the phrase "publisher prefers not to reveal the number of copies printed."

A listing of critical articles, books and dissertations is not included; neither is a list of reviews of the writings of Thom Gunn.

Unquestionably there are errors, omissions, and incorrect data in this book. Our aim has been to be as thorough and accurate as is possible. Any additions and emendations would be welcome and should be sent to the publisher.

Jack W. C. Hagstrom, M.D.
George Bixby

New York City, April 1978

ACKNOWLEDGEMENTS

THE authors wish to thank Thom Gunn in particular. He put up with endless enquiries and without his patience and enthusiasm this book would still not be completed.

We wish to acknowledge the special help provided by the following individuals who in their own way gave us an extra measure of help: The Earl Amherst, M.C.; Mr. B. C. Bloomfield; Prof. Douglas Chambers; Mr. Alan Clodd; Mr. Thomas J. Fleming; Miss Edythe Fuller; Mrs. Darlene Holdsworth; Mr. Charles Montieth; Miss Pat Strachan; and Mr. Robert A. Wilson.

Many individuals, acting in an official or personal capacity, have gone out of their way to be helpful. To all these individuals we express our gratitude. Ms. Judy Addison; Mr. Rolf Aggestam; Mr. Victor Allkins; Mr. A. Alvarez; Miss Carol Anderson; Mr. Michael André; An anonymous British Collector; Audio-Visual Productions; Mrs. Muriel F. Austin; Mr. Anthony Baker; Mr. Jonathan Barker; Dr. Martin C. O. Bax; Dr. Robert Beare; Miss Ingrid Bergom-Larsson; Miss June Bird; Miss Mary Boccaccio; Mr. Stephen Bradshaw; Mr. Richard Brain; Mr. Stanley Bray; Mr. Willis Bridegam; Miss Mary Brodbin; Mr. John Byrne; Mrs. Janet Bystrek; Miss Pat Cassidy; Miss Maxine Cassin; Mrs. Mary Castrataro; Miss Katherine Chatard; Mr. Man Chowdhury; Mr. Ross Claiborne; Mr. Jack Clark; Miss Joanna Clark; Miss A. A. Cleary; Miss Cristiana Clerici; Mr. and Mrs. Douglas Cleverdon; Mr. Richard Cody; Mrs. L. H. Cohn; Mrs. Anne Coleman; Mr. Peter Collenette; Mrs. W. H. Corning; Mr. John Cotton; Mr. J. M. Couper; Mr. Allan Covici; Miss Margaret J. Cox; Mr. Gordon Craig; Mr. Louis D. Dolinsky; Miss D. E. Dorner; Mr. Kenneth Doubrava; Mrs. Sara S. East; Mr. J. M. Edelstein; Mr. Alistair Elliott; Mr. David Farmer; Mr. David Farrer; Mr. William Ferguson; Miss Judith Fiennes; Mr. Ian Fletcher; Dr. Levi Fox; Mrs. Jane Franklin; Mr. G. S. Fraser; Mr. John Fuller; Miss Cristabel Gairdner; Mr. Donald Gallup; Mr. Juan Garcia; Mr. Roger Gard; Mr. J. H. H. Gaute; Mr. K. C. Gay; Mr. Michael Geare; Mr. Bernard Gershenson; Mr. Richard Gilbertson; Mr. James Gilvarry; Mr. Robert Giroux; Mr. David Godine; Mr. Joseph Gold; Mr. Tim Gorelangton; Mr. John Gurnet; Mr. Donald Hall; Mrs. Holly Hall; Mr. Colin B. Hamer, Jr.; Miss Julia E. Hamilton; Miss Ann Harrison; Mr. James D. Hart; Mr. Ronald Hayman; Mr. Geoffrey Hebdon; Mr. R. D. Hewlett; Mr. Brian Hinton; Mr. J. M. Hore; Mr. Michael Horovitz; Mr. Peter Howard; Ms. Olwyn Hughes; Mr. John Huntington; Mr. Nicholas Jardine; Mr. Howard Junker; Mrs. Jacqueline Kavanagh; Mr. Trevor Kaye; Mr. T. H. Kelly; Miss Jean Kempton; Miss Pamela Kent; Miss Judith W. Kimberg; Dr.

ACKNOWLEDGEMENTS

Donald W. King; Mr. David K. Kermani; Dr. Dietrich Klose; Mr. Lee Kresel; Mr. Thomas Kuehn; Mr. John Lancaster; Mr. Andrew Lanyon; Mr. Douglas Lares; Mr. Philip Larkin; Mr. Edward Connery Lathem; Mr. John Lehmann; Mr. Herbert Leibowitz; Mr. Denis Lemon; Mr. Roy Lewis; Mr. Kenneth A. Lohf; Mr. Philip Lyman; Mrs. Angela Maher; Mr. John Mander; Mr. Norman Mann; Mr. Paul Mariah; Mrs. Mary Beth Martin; Mr. William Matheson; Mr. Frank Matson; Mr. Derwent May; Mr. Hans Mayer; Mr. Oscar Mellor; Mrs. S. Melluish; Mr. K. K. Merker; Mr. Floyd Merritt; Mrs. June Moll; Mr. Donald Monroe; Mrs. Margaret Moore; Miss Irene Moran; Mrs. Margaret Mossey; Mr. James McCarthy; Mr. Newton F. McKeon; Mr. David McKitterick; Mr. and Mrs. Julian Nangle; Miss Joan Newman; Mr. J. C. T. Oates; Miss Elizabeth Ogilvie; Mr. Peter Orr; Mr. Geoffrey G. H. Page; Miss Elizabeth Paterson; Miss Diane Pearson; Mr. M. R. Perkin; Mr. John H. Peterson; Mr. Edward Phelps; Mr. J. Richard Phillips; Miss Pamela L. Pickering; Mr. Jan Piechowicz; Mr. Robert M. Pierson; Mr. Neil Powell; Mr. Göran Printz-Påhlson; Mr. and Mrs. James Randall; Dr. T. W. Roberts; Miss Pamela Robinson; Mr. Jeremy Robson; Miss Sandra Roscoe; Miss Elizabeth Rose; Mr. Alan Ross; Mr. Anthony Rota; Mr. Jerome Rothenberg; Mr. R. Röttiger; Mr. Anthony Rudolf; Mrs. Minnie Ruffin; Mr. Y. Sakamoto; Dr. Angus Sampath; Dr. Roberto Sanesi; Mr. Richard Schaubeck; Mr. James Schevill; Mr. Michael Schmidt; Miss Donna Schrader; Mr. C. A. Seaton; Mr. Charles Seluzicki; Mr. Harold Silver; Mrs. Barbara Smith; Mr. Timothy d'Arch Smith; Miss Henrietta Smyth; Mr. Peter Snow; Mr. Geoffrey Soar; Mr. Wallace Southam; Mr. Carlo Volpi Spagnolini; Miss G. Stamford; Mrs. Nina Steane; Mrs. A. B. Stein; Dr. Heinz Steinberg; Mr. Arthur Strange; Mr. C. T. E. Style; Mrs. O-lan Style; Mr. Keisuke Suzuki; Mr. Wesley B. Tanner; Mr. G. Thomas Tanselle; Miss Saundra Taylor; Miss R. M. Thicknesse; Mrs. M. Thomas; Mrs. Nancy Thomas; Miss Sandra Thomas; Mr. Anthony Thwaite; Mr. A. Tillotson; Mr. John Barr Tompkins; Mrs. Carrie M. Townley; Miss Candida Tunbridge; Mr. Roland Turner; Mrs. S. Uberoi; Miss Clair Van Vliet; Mr. Jerry Vaughan; Mr. James Vinson; Mr. L. A. Wallrich; Mr. David J. Walsh; Mrs. P. Watson; Mr. Anthony Whittome; Mrs. Eileen Williams; Mr. Michael Wishart; Mr. Iain Wright; and Miss Juliet Wrightson.

The following libraries and their staffs have provided facilities and reference materials. We gratefully acknowledge their assistance. Amherst College Library, Amherst, Massachusetts; The British Library, London; University Library, Cambridge; Rare Book and Manuscript Room, Columbia University, New York, New York; Humanities Research Center, The University of Texas (Austin); Poetry Library, Arts Council of Great Britain, London; Poetry Collection, Lockwood Memorial Library, State University of New York, Buffalo, New York; Special Collections, The University Library, University of Nevada, Reno, Nevada.

MY LIFE UP TO NOW

ONE day my father, who was a journalist, came home with a dummy newspaper for me. That is, it said *Daily Express* at the top, it was divided into columns, and it even had a space for the Stop Press, or late news. But otherwise it was blank, and there were no headlines or stories or pictures. So I filled it all in with a pencil. I couldn't write words, but I got a lot of satisfaction from drawing pictures and then surrounding them with line after line of scribble. And this is the first creative act I can remember.

My father was the son of a merchant seaman whose family had emigrated from North-East Scotland to Kent some time in the nineteenth century. He was devoted to his job, working for the Beaverbrook press for many years, but eventually, in the early fifties, becoming editor of the *Daily Sketch*, the circulation of which he raised to over a million. He was a man full of charm who made friends easily; I remember in my childhood how exciting the house was on his days off, crowded with his colleagues and their wives— every weekend seemed like a party. But he and my mother were divorced when I was eight or nine, and I never found myself close to him. Neither of us ever invited each other into any intimacy: from my mid-teens onward we were jealous and suspicious of each other, content merely to do our duty and no more.

I was close to my mother and, while I never heard much about my father's family, the history of my mother's formed a kind of basic mythology for me. The Thomsons were Baptists from a village called Echt near Aberdeen. Toward the end of the last century the eldest son went down to Kent to try his luck as the bailiff of a farm. His luck was so good that he sent for his mother and all his brothers and sisters, like Joseph in Egypt sending home for the rest of his family—the parallel cannot have failed to strike the Bible-minded Thomsons—and by the start of this century each of the brothers was established as a tenant farmer in the villages between Maidstone and Rochester, my grandfather Alexander's farm being in Snodland.

They and their families were characteristic country Nonconformists of the time, Baptists on the way to becoming Methodists. They venerated education and despised frivolity—of which the idolatry of Catholics was the most pernicious example. They were pacifists, Keir Hardie socialists, and anti-royalists—the last because they considered the Royal Family not only outdated but corrupt. (They still believe that Mary, the Princess Royal, was "lost in a card game" to her future husband by her brother, George V.) Before World War I, one of my great-uncles went to jail for a weekend for refusing to pay tithes, and briefly became a local hero.

My mother was one of seven children, all girls, and all of a very independent turn of mind. (I am forever grateful that my brother and I were brought up in no religion at all.) She became a journalist, meeting my father in the office of the *Kent Messenger*, but stopped working before I was born in 1929. When I was about four I got lost in Kensington Gardens; a policeman asked me what my mother was like: I described her as "a proud woman". Like her sisters, she was something of a feminist, though the word was not used in those days. At the same time she enjoyed fashion—how her smart clothes and her hennaed hair mortified me when my school friends saw her—but was prepared to give it her own turn. She was once seen at a party wearing an orchid pinned by a brooch in the shape of hammer and sickle. From this distance the combination sounds like a cliché of the thirties, but it wasn't: other women wouldn't have done something so outrageous. I see behind it an impudent and witty proclamation that she wanted to get the best of both worlds, and at the same time I can see the half-rueful self-criticism.

And the house was full of books. When she was pregnant with me she read the whole of Gibbon's *History*. From her I got the complete implicit idea, from as far back as I can remember, of books as not just a commentary on life but a part of its continuing activity.

The first book I read by myself was Louisa Alcott's *Little Men*, and all that stays in my mind from it is the character of Dan, the rebellious boy who is out of place among the pieties of Dr. Baer's model school: I have liked the name Dan ever since. As for poetry, probably my earliest models, after nursery rhymes, were the poems in Arthur Mee's *Children's Encyclopedia*, by Victorians like Jean Ingelow and Charles Kingsley. The books that meant most to me, however, were prose romances—George Macdonald's and John Masefield's books for children, and all the novels of that sensible and imaginative woman, E. Nesbit.

I wrote poems and small stories, but only occasionally, and I suspect that when I did so it was often as much for the approval of adults as for my own satisfaction. But I do remember that when I was eight I once sat down and wrote character sketches of all the boys in my form at school. That was done for myself alone, and the process of rendering them in words interested me, just as much with the boys I disliked or felt indifferent to as with my friends.

I had a happy childhood. Because of changes in my father's job, we moved around the country a lot at first, but finally we settled down in Hampstead, not then nearly as wealthy a place as it now is. It was quiet and rather old-fashioned. I played with my friends on the Heath, fording streams or skirmishing with strange children.

My younger brother Ander (his name was short for Alexander) was a partner in a lot of these games, we being fairly close in age. Early in our lives he and I had been cast in the roles of, respectively, extrovert and introvert, I am sure unfortunately, and so our interests tended to be complementary rather than identical. But we always had a firm friendly relationship, sometimes playing together and as often going our own ways.

At the time of the Blitz we were sent for a year or so to a boarding school in Hampshire. While I was there, my mother asked me to write a "novel" for her birthday. So during siesta every day I wrote in a notebook until it was full. The result was a story called *The Flirt*, curiously sophisticated for a twelve-year-old. It was written in short chapters and illustrated with pictures cut out of my mother's magazines, chiefly *Vogue*. It was the story of the courtship, marriage, and divorce of an aging Lothario known as the Colonel (based, for his physical characteristics, on the cartoonist David Low's Colonel Blimp, with his bald head and white walrus mustache). In an almost wholly female society he is constantly patronised and jeered at, yet it is he who survives at the end, with a new girl on his arm. (Most of the other characters die, the heroine out of simple poverty as the result of having become an unsuccessful prostitute.) One reason for the preponderance of women may be that the pictures from *Vogue* were unlikely to be of men, but because I had far more female relatives than male I knew what such a society was like. And interestingly enough there is a lot of covert sympathy shown by the author for the Colonel, since he (my father? me?), however spineless, remains jovial, slow-witted, and warm-hearted to the end.

I was reading adult books by this time, devouring H. G. Wells, for example, and perhaps already the early issues of *Penguin New Writing*, but I'd be hard put to say what was behind *The Flirt*. This interesting production had no successor, however, and eventually in my teens I became concerned with grandiloquence, under the influence first of Marlowe and Keats, then of Milton, then of Victorians like Tennyson and Meredith. I wanted by then to *be a writer*: the role was all-important, was in fact a good part of the writing's subject matter.

Well, I'm glad I got much of that out of my system relatively early. Meanwhile I was back in London, eying the well-fed and good-looking G.I.s who were on every street, with an appreciation I didn't completely understand. I was back at University College School, a day-school I attended for about ten years (apart from the break forced by the Blitz). I enjoyed being there: it was not very good academically, I suppose, at least during World War II, but it was a tolerant and easy-going school, and the headmaster, C. S. Walton, was an impressive and exemplary figure for me, who covertly helped me through some early difficulties with my father. After my mother's death when I was fifteen, I lived with family friends in Hampstead during the weekdays of the term and with two of my aunts in Snodland during the weekends and vacations. My aunts had a milk-round on which I sometimes helped out, serving the milk out of pails into covered jugs left outside or inside back doors. Then I did my two years national service in the army. Apart from the first ten weeks of basic training, which were at least exuberantly healthy, the two years were largely a matter of boredom, drudgery, and endurance, as they were for most of the rest of my generation. After that I worked in Paris for six months at a job, something of a low-paid sinecure, that a friend of my father's had got for me, and then I went to Cambridge in 1950.

During the whole of this time, from the beginning of 1945 to 1950, I was trying to write novels and poetry, but the results were imitative and dispiriting. I was still copying, of course, as I had earlier been copying on the dummy newspaper, and the imperfections in the copying could have been the beginning of my own real writing. But something was in the way; there was some kind of material that I wasn't able to face up to. I'm not certain what it was: it wasn't simply that I couldn't yet acknowledge my homosexuality, though that was part of it. It was more that my imagination retreated too easily into the world before my mother's death, a world that in practice excluded most of the twentieth century. I read an enormous number of nineteenth century novels in my teens. It was the present that I couldn't deal with in my imagination or in fact. The army, surprisingly, had been of some help, by forcing me into what were for me extreme situations with which it was necessary to cope for the sake of survival. But by twenty-one I was strangely immature, a good deal more so than any of my friends.

My first year at Cambridge changed that, and by the end of it my emotional age had just about caught up with my actual age. In the next two years, 1951 to 1953, I wrote almost all the poems that were to be published as my first book, *Fighting Terms*. In 1952, my first poem to be "published" nationally, "The Secret Sharer", was broadcast by John Lehmann on his BBC program *New Soundings*. I was still influenced by dead writers— especially the Elizabethans—but they were writers I could see as *bearing upon* the present, upon my own activities. Donne and Shakespeare spoke living language to me, and it was one I tried to turn to my own uses. Suddenly everything started to feed my imagination. Writing poetry became the act of an existentialist conqueror, excited and aggressive. (Robert Duncan uses the same image for the poet, that of the conqueror, in *Ceasar's Gate*, but I wasn't to hear of him for several years.) What virtues this collection possesses, however, are mostly to be found in an awareness of how far I fell short of being such a conqueror. Proust and Stendhal as well as Shakespeare and Donne had taught me to watch for the inconsistencies of the psyche.

The image of the soldier recurs in this book, as it does I suppose throughout my work. First of all he is myself, the national serviceman, the "clumsy brute in uniform", the soldier who never goes to war, whose role has no function, whose battledress is a joke. Secondly, though, he is a "real" soldier, both ideal and ambiguous, attractive and repellent: he is a warrior and a killer, or a career man in peace-time, or even a soldier on a quest like Odysseus or Sir Gawain. (I read *Sir Gawain and the Green Knight* at Cambridge, and it took posession of that part of my mind that had wondered at George Macdonald's prose when I was younger and at Browning's "Child Roland to the Dark Tower Came" in my teens.) In a poem called "The Wound", which comes in this book, the speaker is both—at one time Achilles, the real soldier in a real war, and at another time the self who dreamt he was Achilles.

(Perhaps I should here note that when Jerome Rothenberg published *Fighting Terms* in the U.S. in 1958, I had put the whole book through a rigorous revision. Then when Faber and Faber published it in 1962 I *de*revised it somewhat. Several people complained about the alterations in both editions, and I can now see how I was tidying up something I oughtn't to have tampered with. By regularising things so much, I was taking from whatever quality that first book had, a kind of rhetorical awkwardness. I would now reprint it pretty much as it appeared in the first edition, though continuing to omit two minor catastrophes, one, "Contemplative and Active", for being dull, and the other, "A Village Edmund", for being unintentionally comic.)

It was around the time of the original publication of this book, 1954, or perhaps a little earlier, that I first heard of something called the Movement. To my surprise, I also learned that I was a member of it. (Vernon Watkins told me that he had had a similar experience in the early 1940s with the New Apocalypse.) It originated as a half-joke by Anthony Hartley writing in the *Spectator*, and then was perpetuated as a kind of journalistic convenience. What poets like Larkin, Davie, Elizabeth Jennings, and I had in common at that time was that we were deliberately eschewing Modernism, and turning back, though not very thoroughgoingly, to traditional resources in structure and method. But this was what most of the other poets of our age (even many Americans) were doing in the early fifties. When an anthology from a rival group called the Mavericks appeared, it was hard to see any essential difference between the kind of poems that they and we were writing. The whole business looks now like a lot of categorising foolishness.

My poetry was far more influenced by people I met at Cambridge, Karl Miller, John Mander, and John Coleman, and to a much greater extent Tony White, the soul of our generation, who remained throughout his life my best reader and most helpful critic, knowing what I was trying to get at in poems often so bad that it's difficult to see how he divined my intentions. I went to the lectures of F. R. Leavis, then in his prime, whose emphasis on the "realised" in imagery and on the way in which verse movement is an essential part of the poet's exploration were all-important for me.

Also at Cambridge I met Mike Kitay, an American, who became the leading influence on my life, and thus on my poetry. It is not easy to speak of a relationship so long-lasting, so deep, and so complex, nor of the changes it has gone through, let alone of the effect it has had on my writing. But his was, from the start, the example of the searching worrying improvising intelligence playing upon the emotions which in turn reflect back on the intelligence. It was an example at times as rawly passionate as only Henry James can dare to be.

In my last year at Cambridge, I edited an anthology of undergraduate (and some graduate) poetry of the previous two years. It says something about the literary climate in Cambridge at the time: I was not alone in being influenced by the metaphysical poets of the seventeenth century, for example. The prevailing tone is clever, bookish, and spirited.

After I left Cambridge I spent some months in Rome on a studentship (though I came back to Cambridge for the following spring and summer to stay in the Central Hotel). In front of a new notebook I wrote:

> A style is built with sedentary toil
> And constant imitation of great masters.

The master I chose to imitate that winter was the author of these lines, Yeats. Little got finished, as a result: Yeats was too hypnotic an influence, and my poetry became awash with his mannerisms. Of the great English poets he is probably the second most disastrous influence after Milton. The skills to be learned are too closely tied in with the mannerisms.

I found that the only way to get to the United States, where I intended to eventually join Mike (who had had to go into the Air Force) was to get a fellowship at some university. An American friend, Donald Hall, wrote suggesting that I should apply for a creative writing fellowship at Stanford University, where I would work under Yvor Winters, with whose very name I was unfamiliar. I applied, and was fortunate enough to get it, so in 1954 I set out for America, spending my twenty-fifth birthday in mid-Atlantic and landing in New York during a hurricane. What followed was a beautiful year, during which I wrote most of what was to become my second book. I had a room, for fifteen dollars a month, at the top of an old shingled house on Lincoln Avenue in Palo Alto. The eaves stretched down beside the window where I sat at my desk; I could watch the squirrels leaping about on it as I wrote.

I went several times into San Francisco. It was still something of an open city, with whore-houses flourishing for anybody to see. A straight couple took me to my first gay bar, the Black Cat. It excited me so much that the next night I returned there on my own. And I remember walking along Columbus Avenue on another day, thinking that the ultimate happiness would be for Mike and me to settle in this city. It was foggy and I remember exactly where I thought this, right by a cobbler's that still stands there.

But for most of that year I was some thirty miles away down the Peninsula, and the person I had most to do with was Yvor Winters. It was wonderful luck for me that I should have worked with him at this particular stage of my life, rather than earlier when I would have been more impressionable or later when I would have been less ready to learn. As it was, he acted as a fertilizing agent, and opened the way to many poets I had known little of—most immediately Williams and Stevens, whom he insisted I read without delay. He was a man of great personal warmth with a deeper love for poetry than I have ever met in anybody else. The love was behind his increasingly strict conception of what a poem should and should not be. It would have seemed to him an insult to the poem that it could be used as a gymnasium for the ego. Poetry was an instrument for exploring the truth of things, as far as human beings can explore it, and it can do so with a greater verbal exactitude than prose can manage. Large generalised feelings (as in Whitman) were out, and rhetoric was the beginning of falsification. However, taken as I was with the charm and authority of the man and with the power of his persuasiveness, it already seemed to me that his conception of a poem was too rigid, excluding in practice much of what I could not but consider good poetry, let us say "Tom o' Bedlam" and "The force that through the green fuse drives the flower." The rigidity seemed to be the result of what I can only call an increasing distaste for the particulars of existence.

The Sense of Movement, then, was a much more sophisticated book than my first collection had been, but a much less independent one. There is a lot of Winters in it, a fair amount of Yeats, and a great deal of raw Sartre (strange bedfellows!). It was really a second work of apprenticeship. The poems make much use of the word "will". It was a favorite word of Sartre's, and one that Winters appreciated, but they each meant something very different by it, and would have understood but not admitted the other's use of it. What *I* meant by it was, ultimately, a mere Yeatsian wilfulness. I was at my usual game of stealing what could be of use to me.

It is still a very European book in its subject matter. I was much taken by the American myth of the motorcyclist, then in its infancy, of the wild man part free spirit and part hoodlum, but even that I started to anglicise: when I thought of doing a series of motorcyclist poems I had Marvell's mower poems in my mind as model.

At the end of the year I went, for the second time, to Texas by rail, but this time stopped off for a few days in Los Angeles. It was mid-1955, and Los Angeles was a place of wonder to me: it was already the city of *Rebel Without a Cause,* a movie that had not yet been made. The place was as foreign and exotic to me as ever Venice or Rome had been—the huge lines of palms beside the wide fast streets, the confident shoddiness of Hollywood Boulevard, and the dirty glamor of a leather bar called the Cinema, which was on Santa Monica Boulevard, almost a part of a closed gas station and right across from a vast cemetery.

I had been given an introduction to Christopher Isherwood. He asked me over to the set of a movie for which he had written the script, *Diane,* starring

Lana Turner as Diane de Poitiers. He was all warmth and kindness to the rather pushy English boy who had turned up out of the blue, and ended up by asking me to a dinner he had already been invited to, at Gerald Heard's. I had my own ideas about Heard, and argued brashly with him for much of the evening.

I can hardly say that meeting Isherwood was the start of the influence he has had on me, but it strengthened it and made it personal. In his talk, as in his books, he is able to present complexity through the elegance of simplicity, but without ever reducing it *to* mere simplicity. And such a manner was just what I needed to learn from.

I joined Mike in San Antonio, Texas, where I taught for a year. English friends thought it sounded an amusing place to be: we found it distinctly boring, starting with the hot and humid climate. However, the sand storms were of interest to one who had never seen them. Also, I got a motorcycle which I rode for about one month, and it was in San Antonio that I heard Elvis Presley's songs first and that I saw James Dean's films. I wrote only three poems during the whole year.

Then, full of nostalgia for the smell of eucalyptus in the dry sunshine of the San Francisco Peninsula, I dragged Mike back with me to do graduate work at Stanford, where I had got a teaching assistantship. On the way, while he stayed with his parents, I spent a few weeks in New York, beginning a life-long romance with it. If England is my parent and San Francisco is my lover, then New York is my own dear old whore, all flash and vitality and history.

Back at Stanford, Winters encouraged me to attend his workshops regularly, but I went to them less and less, from something of an instinct for self-preservation. The man was too strong; and for all my gratitude to him I knew I had, if necessary, to write my own bad poetry and explore its implications for myself. And I never did get a PhD.—most of the graduate work began to seem pointless after a while, and I had already decided not to go on with it when I was lucky enough to get an offer to teach English at the University of California at Berkeley, in 1958.

I lived for a couple of years in Oakland, a drab town next to Berkeley, then in 1960 spent several months on leave in Berlin, where I wrote the last poems to be included in my next book. When I returned, it was to San Francisco, across the Bay, and I still live there. San Francisco is a provincial town that goes in and out of fashion, but it is never boring and has much of the feel of the big city without trying to master you as the big city does. It leaves you alone: sitting in my yard, now, I could be a hundred miles away from San Francisco.

In the late fifties and early sixties I wrote a series of omnibus poetry reviews for the *Yale Review*. It is always good to make yourself read poetry with close attention, but I became more and more dissatisfied with the business of making comparatively fast judgments on contemporary poets. Specifically, there were books that I simply changed my mind about later on. For example, when it first came out, I sneered at Williams' final book to *Paterson,* and it wasn't until a few years later that I came to revere it as the great epilogue to a great work. And I am haunted by a remark I made about Howard Nemerov, based on a magnificent but unique poem: a piece of praise so high that it is still reprinted on his dust-jackets.

I stopped regular reviewing because I felt more and more that I had to live with a book for some time before I could really find out its value for me. And I was less ready to say unkind things about those who were practising the same art as I was, however differently. I have certainly done reviews and essays since 1954, but only about poets I liked.

In 1961 I published *My Sad Captains,* the name of the title poem having been suggested by Mike. The collection is divided into two parts. The first is the culmination of my old style—metrical and rational but maybe starting to get a little more humane. The second half consists of a taking up of that humane impulse in a series of poems in syllabics. Writing in a new form almost necessarily invited new subject matter, and in such a poem as "Adolescence" I was writing a completely different kind of poem from any I had done before. But after this book I couldn't go much further with syllabics, even though I did write other poems in the form during the next few years. It was really, it turned out, a way of teaching myself about unpatterned rhythms—that is, about free verse. But I have not abandoned meter, and in trying to write in both free verse and meter I think I am different from a lot of my contemporaries. Poets who started writing in the early fifties began with meter and rhyme, but most of them—especially the Americans— who switched to free verse at the end of the decade rounded on their earlier work with all the savagery of the freshly converted. I haven't done so: there are things I can do in the one form that I can't do in the other, and I wouldn't gladly relinquish either.

Rhythmic form and subject matter are locked in a permanent embrace: that should be an axiom nowadays. So, in metrical verse, it is the nature of the control being exercised that becomes part of the life being spoken about. It is poetry making great use of the conscious intelligence, but its danger is bombast—the controlling music drowning out everything else. Free verse invited a different style of experience, improvisation. *Its* danger lies in being too relaxed, too lacking in controlling energy. For me, at any rate, but I think my generalisations extend somewhat beyond my own practice.

In the first half of the sixties, though, little of the poetry I wrote satisfied me. Much of it was simply lacking in intensity. I was having difficulty in shaping the new "humane impulse" into anything worth reading; I was having difficulty, too, in understanding what *I* could do with free verse.

There was one poem I was working on with which I had a different kind of problem, though it turned out, simply, to be a matter of scale. The poem was about a man who supposes he is the last survivor of a massive global war, and about his surprise on seeing from the hill where he sits a group of refugees approaching on the plain beneath. My trouble with it, I began to realise, was that there was too much exposition for me to cram into a single short poem. Then somewhat later, while making a lengthy recovery from hepatitis, I fell on the notion that perhaps I could extend it into a long poem, or rather a series of linked poems in different forms that would add up to a narrative. This is how "Misanthropos" came about. Many of the themes and ideas in the poem originated in, or were at least helped along by, the wide-ranging discussions between my friends Don Doody and Tony Tanner, some of them across the bed of my recuperation. I conceived of the work at times as science fiction and at times as pastoral: there is something from William Golding's *The Inheritors* in it and there is also an Elizabethan echo song. The hill to which the last man has retreated shares characteristics with both Ladd's Hill in North Kent and Land's End in San Francisco.

I spent about two years over the whole poem, starting it in San Francisco and finishing it in London, where I spent a year of great happiness from mid-1964 to 1965. I was living on Talbot Road, a few blocks from my friend Tony White, in a large room on the second floor of a handsome Victorian house that has since been torn down. He was translating books from French into English at that time; we would work all morning in our respective rooms and then at midday emerge on our balconies where we would signal to each other (through binoculars) if we wanted to go for a beer and lunch together. London had never seemed more fertile: I think of that twelve months as moving to the tunes of the Beatles, for it started with their movie *A Hard Day's Night* and was punctuated by the rebellious joy of their singles. They stood for a great optimism, barriers seemed to be coming down all over, it was as if World War II had finally drawn to its close, there was an openness and high-spiritedness and relaxation of mood I did not remember from the London of earlier years. The last week I was there, an old woman across the street had what I took to be her grandson from the country staying with her. In the long summer evenings the boy would sit at a window gazing at what went on below him on Talbot Road. He sticks in my mind as an emblem of the potential and excitement and sense of wonder that I found all about me in the London of that year.

It was during this time I made a recording for the British Council which later got issued as part of a record, *The Poet Speaks*, shared with Ted Hughes, Sylvia Plath, and Peter Porter (though we were all four taped on separate occasions). I have made other records at different times: all are terrible, either because I was not reading at my best or because of the conditions of recording. *The Poet Speaks* is the only one that I like.

And I saw a lot of my brother and his family, who were living in Teddington. Looking through some of Ander's photographs I found interesting possibilities in a collaboration. I had always wanted to work with pictures, and he was taking just the kind that made a good starting point for my imagination. That was the beginning of the book called *Positives* (the title being Tony White's suggestion, as was much else in it). I was never very sure whether what I was writing opposite the photographs were poems or captions—they were somewhere between the two, I suspect—but that didn't matter, because what I was looking for was a form of fragmentary inclusiveness that could embody the detail and history of that good year. At the same time I was consciously borrowing what I could from William Carlos Williams, trying as it were to anglicize him, to help make his openness of form and feeling available to English writers. I enjoyed working on the book, the only collaboration I have yet tried, and it contains a London I found hard to recognize only eight years after.

So when I returned to San Francisco it was with half thoughts of ultimately moving back to London. But San Francisco in mid-1965 was only a little behind London in the optimism department and was prepared to go much further. It was the time, after all, not only of the Beatles but of LSD as well. Raying out from the private there was a public excitement at the new territories that were being opened up in the mind. Golden Gate Park, the scene of so many mass trips and rock concerts, seemed like

> The first field of a glistening continent
> Each found by trusting Eden in the human.

We tripped also at home, on rooftops, at beaches and ranches, some went to the opera loaded on acid, others tried it as passengers on gliders, every experience was illuminated by the drug. (The best account of these years in San Francisco is to be found in issue no. 207 of the *Rolling Stone*, a brilliant history put together ten years later.) These were the fullest years of my life, crowded with discovery both inner and outer, as we moved between ecstasy and understanding. It is no longer fashionable to praise LSD, but I have no doubt at all that it has been of the utmost importance to me, both as a man and as a poet. I learned from it, for example, a lot of information about myself that I had somehow blocked from my own view. And almost all of the poems that were to be in my next book, *Moly*, written between 1965 and 1970, have in some way however indirect to do with it.

The acid experience was essentially non-verbal. Yet it was clearly important, and I have always believed that it should be possible to write poetry about any subject that was of importance to you. Eventually a friend, Belle Randall, and I decided that it was time to stop generalizing the origin of the acid poem. (Her book that resulted from this decision was *101 Different Ways of Playing Solitaire*, not published until 1973.) By 1968 taking the drug was no longer an unusual experience, probably hundreds of thousands had had at least one experience with it, and many more knew about it without having taken it, so to write about its effect was not any more to be obscure or to make pretentious claims to experience closed to most readers.

Meter seemed to be the proper form for the LSD-related poems, though at first I didn't understand why. Later I rationalised about it thus. The acid trip is unstructured, it opens you up to countless possibilities, you hanker after the infinite. The only way I could give myself any control over the presentation of these experiences, and so could be true to them, was by trying to render the infinite through the finite, the unstructured through the structured. Otherwise there was the danger of the experience's becoming so distended that it would simply unravel like fog before wind in the unpremeditated movement of free verse. Thomas Mann, speaking about how he wrote *Doctor Faustus*, tells of "filtering" the character of the genius-composer through the more limited but thus more precise consciousness of the bourgeois narrator. I was perhaps doing something like Mann.

I had meanwhile left Berkeley, in 1966, a year after I had been given tenure. After that I taught intermittently at other institutions but now in the late 1970s I am teaching at Berkeley again, though for only one quarter a year and without tenure.

Around 1968 I finally began to learn how to give a poetry reading. Before that I had been petrified with fright at standing in front of an audience reading my own work (strange, since I was not nervous at teaching classes). But in this year I gave a series of readings on the California poetry circuit. Doing so many of them made me lose my nervousness and I was enabled to study the pacing and presentation of a public reading. I realised that I am so far from being an actor and am gifted with so monotonous and limited a voice that I can afford to dramatise my work as much as I want and still will not seem over-dramatic. And I learned that I should treat a poetry reading not as a recital for a bunch of devotees, which my audiences were clearly not, but more as an entertainment—an advertisement for poetry as a whole.

It was toward the end of the sixties that I began to see something of Robert Duncan, though I had first met him quite a few years before. If a certain amount of mutual influence has taken place, it may sound rather as if Fulke Greville and Shelley had been contemporaries capable of learning from each other. Would that they had been.

What Duncan has stressed is the importance of the *act* of writing. It is a reach into the unknown, an adventuring into places you cannot have predicted, where you may find yourself using limbs and organs you didn't know you possessed. Of course, all poets have always known that such adventuring is a normal part of the exercise and procedure of the imagination, but in the last few decades its importance had been minimised in favor of the end result, 'the poem on the page'. Duncan sees the adventure as on-

going, unfinished and unfinishable, and the poem on the page as marking
only one stage in it.

Because of a job at Princeton I was able to live in New York for the first
half of 1970, something I had always wanted to do for a while. It started
unpromisingly enough at the Albert, a hotel for 'transients and residents',
most of them under twenty or over sixty. My room was twice broken into
during the weeks I was there. But then I was lucky enough to sublease a loft
on Prince Street for the rest of my time in New York. It was about 125 feet
in length and still rather bare though fitted up with a bathroom and kitchen:
it was the best place I have ever lived in. I didn't even mind the large numbers
of mice or the smells from the bakery that filled the place in the early hours of
the morning. As I had caught Talbot Road at the moment of change, so I
caught SoHo just as it stopped being an Italian neighborhood: the first art
gallery appeared round the corner while I lived there. I enjoyed living by
myself for six months among the iron architecture, working only two days a
week at Princeton, writing a little but reading a lot, and running loose in the
West Village every night.

But the mood was changing everywhere. It was the time of numerous
bombings—I saw a rather famous town house go up in smoke—and of the
invasion of Cambodia. The feeling of the country was changing, and one
didn't know into what. I went back to England for a few months of the
summer, and when I returned to San Francisco I felt something strange
there too: there was a certain strain in attempting to preserve the euphoria
of the sixties, one's anxieties seemed obstructive. I had a couple of rather bad
trips on LSD that taught me no end of unpalatable facts about myself, to
my great edification.

But my life insists on continuities—between America and England,
between free verse and meter, between vision and everyday consciousness.
So, in the sixties, at the height of my belief in the possibilities of change, I
knew that we all continue to carry the same baggage: in my world, Christian
does not shed his burden, only his attitude to it alters. And now that the
great sweep of the acid years is over, I cannot unlearn the things that I
learned during them, I cannot deny the vision of what the world might be
like. Everything that we glimpsed—the trust, the brotherhood, the re-
possession of innocence, the nakedness of spirit—is still a possibility and
will continue to be so.

In the early seventies I went a few times with friends to the area in Sonoma
County, north of San Francisco, known as the Geysers. Some hundred or
more people camped there at weekends, fewer stayed through the week. We
camped anywhere, on the flanks of the hills, which were warm even at night,
or in the woodland, or beside the cool and the warm streams. Everyone
walked around naked, swimming in the cool stream by day and at night
staying in the hot baths until early in the morning. Heterosexual and homo-

sexual orgies sometimes overlapped: there was an attitude of benevolence and understanding on all sides that could be extended, I thought, into the rest of the world. When I remember that small, changing society of holidays and weekends, I picture a great communal embrace. For what is the point of a holiday if we cannot carry it back into working days? There is no good reason why that hedonistic and communal love of the Geysers could not be extended to the working life of the towns. Unless it is that human beings contain in their emotions some homeostatic device by which they must defeat themselves just as they are learning their freedom.

I wrote a group of poems about this place. Around the same time I was working on another, very loose group of short poems, to do with nightmare, which I called "Jack Straw's Castle". The poems were fragmentary, barely connected, and grotesque. Then what had happened with "Misanthropos" ten years before happened again—"Jack Straw" developed into a narrative. The result was the obverse of the Geyser poems in that, while in them I had been writing largely about escapes from the confinement of the individual consciousness, I was here dealing with just that confinement and with the terrors of self-destructiveness you may face when you are aware of being trapped in your own skull.

The myth behind the narrative had emerged in the following way. After living for ten years on Filbert Street, I had made the down-payment for a house on Cole Street on the other side of San Francisco, in a district which at that time had become very unfashionable. There were now three of us, but the process of moving our things and remodelling some of the house took us about a month in all. It thereupon became for me the theme of several months of anxiety-dreams. In them I was constantly finding that something had gone wrong with the moving: I had moved into the wrong house, for example, or it was an unrecognizable house, or I was sharing it with strangers (once Nixon turned up in my room), or—and this was the most common dream of all—I had moved into the right house but in it I found *new rooms* that I had known nothing about. It is a strange fact that almost everything that figures importantly in my life, an event, an idea, even a seies of dreams, finds its way sooner or later into poetry.

Writing poetry has in fact become a certain stage in my coping with the world, or in the way I try to understand what happens to me and inside me. Perhaps I could say that my poetry is an attempt to *grasp*, with grasp meaning both to *take hold of* in a first bid at possession, and also to *understand*. I certainly do not pretend that I ever do completely possess or understand, I can only say that I attempt to. Often it will be a long time before I can write of something. It took me years before I could begin writing about my father (and maybe I can one day write about my mother—if Duncan has not already written the ultimate mother-poem with his "My Mother Would Be a Falconress"). But sometimes I can write about something more quickly.

When Pretty Jim stole from his friends, and when I heard about the odd definition of trust he had made a few days before, "an intimate conspiracy", I puzzled and puzzled until out of my puzzlement I wrote "The Idea of Trust". I like this poem because in it I ended up with more sympathy for him than I started with, and consequently writing it minutely altered me, advanced my understanding in one small area. So, for all my many dry periods, I must count my writing as an essential part of the way in which I deal with my life.

I am however a rather derivative poet. I learn what I can from whom I can, mostly consciously. I borrow heavily from my reading because I take my reading seriously: it is part of my total experience and I base most of my poetry on my experience. I do not apologise for being derivative because I think a lot of other poets work in this way. I wonder if the real difference between the "plagiarist" and the Ben Jonson who "rearranges" Philostratus into "Drink to me only with thine eyes" is more between degrees of talent than between degrees of borrowing. Specifically, I have found usable modes in the work of other poets, and I have tried to invent some myself. Moreover, it has not been of primary interest to develop a unique poetic personality, and I rejoice in Eliot's lovely remark that art is the escape from personality. This lack in me has troubled some readers.

What more do I have to say about my life? I still live in San Francisco, and expect to go on living there. I visit England every three or four years, to see what has been happening to my friends and relatives. My income averages about half of that of a local bus driver or street sweeper, but it is of my own choosing, since I prefer leisure to working at a full-time job. I do not either like or dislike myself inordinately. I have just had *Jack Straw's Castle and Other Poems* published. I cannot guess what my next book will be like.

POSTSCRIPT

I have written the foregoing because the authors of this bibliography asked me to and they are nice men whom I would like to please. Another reason is that if I don't do it, someone else will, sooner or later, and he is likely to get it wrong. And another is that true history, like true gossip, is always of some interest. All this even though I have been reticent in the past, perhaps rather self-importantly exaggerating the desirability of my privacy. But there was another reason, a good one, for reticence, and I should like to conclude by explaining it.

The danger of biography, and equally of autobiography, is that it can muddy poetry by confusing it with its sources. James' word for the source of a work, its "germ", is wonderfully suggestive because the source bears the same relation to the finished work as the seed does to the tree—nothing is the same, all has developed, the historical truth of the germ is superseded by the derived but completely different artistic truth of the fiction.

Isherwood recently published a volume of autobiography, *Christopher and His Kind*. It is a book that I wouldn't wish unwritten for anything. But it is sure to confuse his novels and stories for the many people who prefer speculation to reading what is in front of them. They can say that Sally Bowles, for example, isn't *really* doing whatever she is clearly doing in the story, because in his autobiography Isherwood himself may have told us something additional or even contrary about Jean Ross, the original of Sally.

Here's an example of the kind of misunderstanding I'm talking about: what does it do if I say of a poem called "From an Asian Tent" that in it I am finally able to write about my father? My admission confuses matters, I think, being misleading both about the poem and about my relationship with my father. I would like the poem read as being about what it proclaims as its subject: Alexander the Great remembering Philip of Macedon. What is autobiographical about the poem, what I am drawing upon, is a secret source of feeling that might really be half-imagined, some Oedipal jealously for my father combined with a barely remembered but equally strong incestuous desire for him. And I am drawing upon the autobiographical without scruple, freed by the myth from any attempt to be fair or honest about my father. The poem's truth is in its faithfulness to a possibly imagined feeling, not to my history.

Another example. In my early twenties I wrote a poem called "Carnal Knowledge", addressed to a girl, with a refrain making variations on the phrase "I know you know". Now anyone aware that I am homosexual is likely to misread the whole poem, inferring that the thing "known" is that the speaker would prefer to be in bed with a man. But that would be a serious misreading, or at least a serious misplacement of emphasis. The poem, actually addressed to a fusion of two completely different girls, is not saying anything as clear-cut as that. A reader knowing nothing about the author has a much better chance of understanding it.

January, 1977

ABBREVIATIONS

Abbreviations for Thom Gunn's principal works, subsequently used in this bibliography, are listed alphabetically below.

AG	A GEOGRAPHY
FT	FIGHTING TERMS
JSC	JACK STRAW'S CASTLE
JSCx	JACK STRAW'S CASTLE (expanded editions)
Ma	MANDRAKES
Mo	MOLY
M & MSC	MOLY and MY SAD CAPTAINS
MSC	MY SAD CAPTAINS
P	POSITIVES
P 50–66	POEMS 1950–1966 A Selection
So	SONGBOOK
Su	SUNLIGHT
SP	SELECTED POEMS by Thom Gunn and Ted Hughes
T	TOUCH
TE	THE EXPLORERS
TG	THOM GUNN (The Fantasy Poets, Number Sixteen)
TMB	THE MISSED BEAT
TSOM	THE SENSE OF MOVEMENT
TTA	TO THE AIR

A

BOOKS, PAMPHLETS AND
BROADSIDES BY
THOM GUNN

In this section all books, pamphlets, and broadsides by Thom Gunn are listed chronologically. Data on reprints and new editions are also included. No attempt is made to denote textual differences in a poem when it is reprinted in a subsequent volume.

a. *First edition:*

[Cover title] [in brown orange (54)] THE FANTASY POETS | [long rule of 101 mm.] | [in brown orange (54)] THOM | [in brown orange (54)] GUNN | in brown orange (54)] NUMBER SIXTEEN

Collation: [1]⁴ = 4 leaves; 204 × 126 mm.

Binding: Stapled pamphlet; white wove paper; all edges trimmed.

Publication date: spring 1953

Price: 9d

Number of copies: "just under 300" [From a letter dated October 27, 1976 to the compilers, from Oscar Mellor, the publisher of Fantasy Press.]

Pagination: [1] title page; [2–7] text; [8] author biography and information about the Fantasy Press, with at the foot of the page: Printed by Fantasy Press at Swinford, Eynsham, Oxon. | PRICE NINEPENCE

Contents: Incident on a Journey—Wind in the Street—The Wound—The Beach Head—The Right Possessor—A Village Edmund.

A2   FIGHTING TERMS   1954

a. *First edition, first state:*

FIGHTING TERMS | [in strong yellow (84)] [short rule of 22 mm.] | [in strong yellow (84)] [three circles] | [in strong yellow (84)] [short rule of 22 mm.] | POEMS | BY | THOM GUNN | FANTASY PRESS

Collation: [1–4]⁶ = 24 leaves; 195–197 × 127–128 mm.

Note: In fourteen copies examined the trim size varied between the sizes listed above.

Binding: Bound in strong yellow (84) cloth and lettered on upper cover in deep reddish orange (36): FIGHTING TERMS | [long rule of 82 mm.] | [row of eighteen circles] | [long rule of 82 mm.] | POEMS | BY | THOM GUNN; white or cream laid paper; all edges trimmed; white or cream laid endpapers; issued without a dust wrapper.

Publication date: July 1, 1954

Price: 8s 6d

Number of copies: unknown (Combined total of first and second state is 305 copies.) [see note at end of this entry]

A. BOOKS, PAMPHLETS AND BROADSIDES

Pagination: [i–ii] blank; [1–2] blank; [3] title page; [4] Printed and published by | the Fantasy Press at | Swinford, Eynsham, Oxford | 1954 | [star] | All rights reserved; 5–6, CONTENTS; [7] eight lines of acknowledgements; [8] TO MIKE KITAY; 9–44, text; [45–46] blank.

Contents: Carnal Knowledge—The Wound—Here Come the Saints—To his Cynical Mistress—Wind in the Street—Lazarus Not Raised—A Village Edmund—Lofty in the Palais de Danse—Round and Round—Helen's Rape—The Secret Sharer—La Prisonnière—The Court Revolt—The Right Possessor—Looking Glass—Lerici—A Mirror for Poets—The Beach Head —Contemplative and Active—A King of Ethics—Tamer and Hawk— Captain in Time of Peace—Without Counterpart—For a Birthday— Incident on a Journey.

Note: The first state is distinguished by the error on page 38, in the first line of "Tamer and Hawk" where the final "t" of "thought" is omitted. At some point during the printing run this error was discovered and corrected. There is no record of how many copies contain the error. Copies both with and without the error have been examined, printed on both white and cream laid paper. Copies both with and without the error have been examined, sewn in three places as well as in four places. The copies were bound in two batches at two different binderies, 200 copies originally and the remaining 105 copies on November 11, 1954. Presumably, this accounts for the variation in trim size noted above as well as the variation in sewing. For many years the belief persisted that the distinguishing point on this book was a variant in the color of the binding cloth. After examination of 14 copies of this book in all the variations noted here, no variant in the color of the binding cloth has been found. Since records do not exist, and the memories of the persons involved with publication of this book have grown hazy on exact details, it seems safe to assume that sheets both with and without the printing error were bound in the initial 200 copies as well as in the subsequent 105 copies. Therefore, the printing error must be regarded as the only means of distinguishing the first from the second state of this book. A second printing error appears in the poem "Contemplative and Active", page 36, line 9, in which one word was omitted. The line should read: "In the waste of sand through which I charge". The word "which" was omitted. However, this error was not corrected and appears in all copies.

b. *First edition, second state:* 1954

Identical with the first state, except for the correction of the error on page 38. See *Note* at end of A2a entry.

c. *First American edition:* 1958

FIGHTING TERMS | BY | THOM GUNN | [publisher's logo] | Hawk's Well Press * New York * 1958

Collation: [1–6]⁴ = 24 leaves; 170 × 103 mm.

Binding: Glued into stiff white wove paper wrappers and printed in moderate violet (211) and dark gray brown (62); lettered down the spine in white: THOM GUNN FIGHTING TERMS HAWK'S WELL PRESS; on the upper wrapper in white: THOM GUNN | *fighting terms* | HAWK'S WELL PRESS; on the rear wrapper in white: [publisher's logo]; white wove paper; all edges trimmed.

Note: At some date after publication, a white label, 62 × 97 mm., lettered in strong brown (55), was pasted onto the lower portion of the upper wrapper, printing a six-line statement by Alfred Alvarez from a review in *Partisan Review.*

Publication date: November 1, 1958

Price: 75¢

Number of copies: 1,500

Pagination: [1] half-title; [2] blank; [3] title page; [4] COVER DESIGN BY EUCLIDES THEOHARIDES | Copyright 1958 by Thom Gunn | [thirteen lines of acknowledgements] | *Published by Hawk's Well Press, 50 Broad-* | *way, New York City 4, and printed in a first* | *edition of 1500 copies by Talleres Graficos,* | *Hija J. Ferrer, Barcelona, Spain.*; [5] CONTENTS; [6] blank; [7] TO MIKE KITAY; [8] blank; 9–46, text; [47–48] blank.

Contents: Same as A2a except for the omission of two poems from that edition: "A Village Edmund" and "Contemplative and Active".

Note: Gunn extensively revised the text of the poems for this American edition.

d. *Second English edition:*   1962

Fighting Terms | [decorative bulging rule] | THOM GUNN | FABER AND FABER | 24 Russell Square | London

Collation: [1]⁴ + [2–3]⁸ = 20 leaves; 218 × 140 mm.

Binding: Bound in deep blue (179) cloth and lettered down the spine in gold: FIGHTING TERMS · THOM GUNN FABER; white wove paper; all edges trimmed; white wove endpapers; dust wrapper strong pink (2) laid paper, printed in black and deep purplish blue (197).

Publication date: February 23, 1962

Price: 12s 6d

Number of copies: 1,600; second printing, January 20, 1966, 1,000 copies.

Pagination: [1] half-title; [2] *by the same author* | [star] | THE SENSE OF MOVEMENT | MY SAD CAPTAINS; [3] title page; [4] *First published*

in 1954 | *by the Fantasy Press* | *This edition with revisions* | *first published in* 1962 | *by Faber and Faber Limited* | 24 *Russell Square WC* 1 | *Printed by* | *The Bowering Press Plymouth* | © *This edition Thom Gunn* 1962; [5] TO MIKE KITAY; [6] blank; [7] CONTENTS; [8] blank; 9–38, text; 39. NOTE ON THE TEXT; [40] blank.

Contents: Same as A2a except for the omission of two poems from that edition; "A Village Edmund" and "Contemplative and Active"; the addition of the author's "Note on the Text"; and the moving of "Carnal Knowledge" to a new place in the order of the contents.

Note: Gunn further revised the text of these poems for this edition from the revisions he had made for the Hawk's Well Press edition (A2c).

Note: There were an unknown number of advance proof copies issued in pale blue (185) wove paper wrappers with the same information as appears on the title page printed on the upper wrapper with the additional imprint of: "Uncorrected Proof Copy".

e. *First English paperback edition:* 1970

Fighting Terms | [decorative bulging rule] | THOM GUNN | FABER AND FABER | London

Collection: [1]⁸ + [2]⁴ + [3]⁸ = 20 leaves; 183 × 123 mm.

Binding: Bound in white paper wrappers, the exterior of which is shiny, and printed in black and moderate blue (182); lettered down the spine: [in black] *FIGHTING TERMS* [in moderate blue (182)] [large dot] [in black] *THOM GUNN* [in white on a moderate blue (182) panel] FABER; on the upper wrapper: [in black] *FIGHTING* | [in black] *TERMS* | [in moderate blue (182)] *THOM* | [in moderate blue (182)] *GUNN* | [in white running down on a moderate blue (182) panel on the right side] FABER paper covered EDITIONS; on the rear wrapper is a moderate blue panel (182) which is identical to the one on the upper wrapper except that the lettering on the rear wrapper runs up, and the panel is on the left side of the rear wrapper; also on the rear wrapper, in black, is the continuation of a list of "Some Faber Paper Covered Editions" begun on the inner rear wrapper; the inner upper wrapper prints the price and a publisher's statement regarding the book; white wove paper; all edges trimmed.

Publication date: June 15, 1970

Price: 6s, £0.30; later a sticker was pasted over this printed price, raising it to £0.35; still later another sticker was pasted over the first sticker, raising the price to £0.50.

Number of copies: 6,000

A. BOOKS, PAMPHLETS AND BROADSIDES

Pagination: [1] half-title; [2] *by Thom Gunn* | [star] | THE SENSE OF MOVEMENT | MY SAD CAPTAINS | TOUCH | POEMS 1950–1966 | SELECTED POEMS | (with Ted Hughes); [3] title page; [4] *First published in* 1954 | *by the Fantasy Press* | *Second edition with revisions* | *first published in* 1962 | *by Faber and Faber Limited* | 24 *Russell Square London WC* 1 | *First published in Faber Paper Covered Edition* 1970 | *Printed in Great Britain by* | *Latimer Trend & Co Ltd Whitstable* | *All rights reserved* | *SBN (paper edition)* 571 09390 6 | *SBN (cloth edition)* 571 04503 0 | © *This edition Thom Gunn* 1962 | [at foot of page]: CONDITIONS OF SALE | [followed by five lines of conditions of sale, printed in italics]; [5] TO MIKE KITAY; [6] blank; [7] CONTENTS; [8] blank; 9–38, text; 39, NOTE ON THE TEXT; [40] blank.

Contents: Same as A2d.

A3   THE SENSE OF MOVEMENT   1957

a. *First edition:*

THOM GUNN | *THE SENSE OF MOVEMENT* | 'Je le suis, je veux l'être.' | *Auguste* in CINNA | FABER AND FABER LIMITED | 24 Russell Square | London

Collation: [1–4]⁸ = 32 leaves; 219 × 139 mm.

Binding: Bound in dark purplish red (259) cloth and lettered down the spine in white: THOM GUNN *THE SENSE OF MOVEMENT* FABER; off-white wove paper; all edges trimmed; off-white wove end-papers; dust wrapper very light yellowish green (134) laid paper printed in black and gray reddish orange (39).

Note: A wrap-around band, 43 × 485 mm., of brilliant greenish yellow (98) laid paper, printed in black, was issued with copies of the first printing; lettered across the upper panel: *Recommended by the* | *POETRY BOOK SOCIETY*; lettered down the spine panel in two lines: *Poetry Book Society* | *Recommendation*; and lettered across the rear panel: *The* | *SENSE OF MOVEMENT* | by *Thom Gunn*

Publication date: June 7, 1957

Price: 10s 6d

Number of copies: 1,000; second printing, April 9, 1959, 1,000 copies; third printing, November 14, 1961, 1,250 copies; fourth printing, February 3, 1969, 1,500 copies.

Pagination: [1–2] blank; [3] half-title; [4] blank; [5] title page; [6] *First published in mcmlvii* | *by Faber and Faber Limited* | 24 *Russell Square London*

35

A. BOOKS, PAMPHLETS AND BROADSIDES

*W.C.*1 | *Printed in Great Britain* | *at the Bowering Press Plymouth* | *All rights reserved*; [7] seven lines of acknowledgements; [8] blank; 9–10, CONTENTS; 11–62, text; [63–64] blank.

Contents: On the Move—The Nature of an Action—At the Back of the North Wind—Before the Carnival—Human Condition—A Plan of Self Subjection—Birthday Poem—First Meeting with a Possible Mother-in-law —Autumn Chapter in a Novel—The Wheel of Fortune—The Silver Age— The Unsettled Motorcyclists's Vision of His Death—Lines for a Book— Elvis Presley—Market at Turk—In Praise of Cities—The Allegory of the Wolf Boy—The Beaters—Julian the Apostate—Jesus and His Mother—St Martin and the Begger—To Yvor Winters, 1955—The Inheritated Estate— During an Absence—The Separation—High Fidelity—Legal Reform— Puss in Boots to the Giant—Thoughts on Unpacking—Merlin in the Cave: He Speculates Without a Book—The Corridor—Vox Humana.

Note: There were an unknown number of advance proof copies issued in light blue (181) wove paper wrappers with the same information as appears on the title page printed on the upper wrapper.

b. *First American edition:*   1959

THOM GUNN | *The* | *Sense* | *of* | *Movement* | [publisher's logo] | THE UNIVERSITY OF CHICAGO PRESS

Collation: [1–4]⁸ = 32 leaves; 215 × 138 mm.

Binding: Bound in vital red (11) cloth and lettered down the spine in gold: *THE SENSE OF MOVEMENT · GUNN* CHICAGO; white wove paper with a watermark: WARREN'S | OLDE STYLE; all edges trimmed, top edges stained brilliant yellow (83); white wove endpapers of a heavy, smooth stock; dust wrapper shiny white paper printed in strong reddish orange (35) and strong blue (178) with a drawing of a bird in flight.

Publication date: April 13, 1959

Price: $2.75

Number of copies: 1,018

Pagination: [1–2] blank; [3] half-title; [4] '*Je le suis, je veux l'être.*' | —*Auguste in* CINNA; [5] title page; [6] *Library of Congress Catalog Number: 59–8734* | THE UNIVERSITY OF CHICAGO PRESS, CHICAGO 37 | First published in England by Faber and Faber Limited | London, W.C. I, 1957 | *Copyright 1957 by Thomson William Gunn. All rights* | *reserved. Printed by* THE UNIVERSITY OF CHICAGO PRESS, | *Chicago, Illinois, U.S.A.*; [7] seven lines of acknowledgements; [8] blank; 9, CONTENTS; [10] blank; 11–62, text; [63–64] blank.

Contents: Same as A3a.

36

c. *First English paperback edition:* 1968

THOM GUNN | *THE SENSE OF MOVEMENT* | 'Je le suis, je
veus l'être.' | *Auguste* in Cinna | FABER AND FABER LIMITED | 24
Russell Square | London

Collation: [1–4]⁸ = 32 leaves; 184 × 121 mm.

Binding: Glued into stiff white wove paper wrappers, the exterior of which
is shiny, and printed in black and pale blue (185); lettered down the spine:
[in black] *THE SENSE OF MOVEMENT* [in pale blue (185)]
[large dot] [in black] *THOM GUNN* [in white on a black panel] FABER;
on the upper wrapper in black: [horizontal design in pale blue (185)] | *The
Sense | of | Movement* | [horizontal design in pale blue (185)] | *Thom Gunn* |
[horizontal design in pale blue (185) | [in white running down on a black
panel on the right side] FABER paper covered EDITIONS; on the rear
wrapper is a black panel which is identical to the one on the upper wrapper
except that the lettering on the rear wrapper runs up, and the panel is on the
left side of the rear wrapper; also on the rear wrapper, in black, is the con-
tinuation of a list of "Some Faber Paper Covered Editions" begun on the
inner rear wrapper; the inner upper wrapper prints the price and a publisher's
statement regarding the book; off-white wove paper; all edges trimmed.

Publication date: July 15, 1968

Price: 7s 6d

Number of copies: 7,000; second printing, August 3, 1972, 8,000 copies.

Pagination: [1–2] blank; [3] half-title; [4] blank; [5] title page; [6] *First
published in mcmlvii | by Faber and Faber Limited | 24 Russell Square London
W.C.* 1 | *Second impression mcmlix | First published in this edition mcmlxviii |
Printed in Great Britain | by Lowe and Brydone (Printers) Limited | London
N.W.* 10 | All right reserved | CONDITIONS OF SALE [followed by
five lines of conditions, printed in italics]; [7] seven lines of acknowledgements; [8] blank; 9–10, CONTENTS; 11–62, text; [63–64] blank.

Contents: Same as A3a.

A4   MY SAD CAPTAINS   1961

a. *First edition:*

My Sad Captains | *and other poems | by* | THOM GUNN | [bulging rule] |
FABER AND FABER | 24 Russell Square | London

Collation: [1–2]⁸ + [3]¹⁰ = 26 leaves; 217 × 140 mm.

Binding: Bound in dark reddish purple (242) cloth and lettered down the spine in gold: MY SAD CAPTAINS—Thom Gunn Faber; white wove paper; all edges trimmed; cream wove endpapers; dust wrapper very pale blue (184) laid paper, printed in dark blue gray (192) and deep reddish orange (36).

Publication date: September 1, 1961

Price: 12s 6d

Number of copies: 2,000

Pagination: [1–2] blank; [3] half-title; [4] by the same author | [star] | THE SENSE OF MOVEMENT; [5] title page; [6] *First published in mcmlxi* | *by Faber and Faber Limited* | *24 Russell Square London WC1* | *Printed in Great Britain* | *at the Bowering Press Plymouth* | *All rights reserved* | © *1961 by Thom Gunn*; [7] *Acknowledgements*; [8] blank; 9–10, *Contents*; [11] section title; [12] blank; 13–33, text; [34] blank; [35] section title; [36] blank; 37–51, text; [52] blank.

Contents: In Santa Maria del Popolo—The Annihilation of Nothing—The Monster—The Middle of the Night—Readings in French—From the Highest Camp—Innocence—Modes of Pleasure—Modes of Pleasure—A Map of the City—The Book of the Dead—The Byrnies—Black Jackets—Baudelaire among the Heroes—The Value of Gold—Claus von Stauffenberg —Waking in a Newly-Built House—Flying above California—Considering the Snail—"Blackie, the Electric Rembrandt"—Hotblood on Friday—The Feel of Hands—L'Epreuve—Rastignac at 45—Lights Among Redwood—Adolescence—A Trucker—Loot—My Sad Captains.

Note: There were an unknown number of advance proof copies issued in green gray (155) wove paper wrappers with the same information as appears on the title page printed on the upper wrapper with the additional imprint of: "Uncorrected Proof Copy".

b. *First American edition, hardcover issue:* 1961

my | sad | captains | *and* | *other* | *poems* | *by* | *thom* | *gunn* | THE | UNIVERSITY [publisher's logo] OF CHICAGO | PRESS

Collation: [1–3]⁸ = 24 leaves; 202 × 133 mm.

Binding: Bound in light gray (264), medium gray (265) and moderate pink (5) striped wove paper covered boards; on the upper cover is a 51 × 46 mm. white wove paper label printed in black: my | sad | *captains* | *thom gunn*; white wove paper; all edges trimmed; white wove endpapers; issued without a dust wrapper.

Publication date: September 19, 1961

Price: $2.50

A. BOOKS, PAMPHLETS AND BROADSIDES

Number of copies: 528; second printing, February 1967, 473 copies.

Pagination: [1–2] blank; [3] half-title; [4] blank; [5] title page; [6] [eleven lines of acknowledgements] | *Library of Congress Catalog Card Number: 61–15933* | THE UNIVERSITY OF CHICAGO PRESS, CHICAGO 37 | Faber and Faber Limited, London W.C. 1, England | © 1961 by Thom Gunn. Published 1961 | Composed and printed by The University of Chicago Press | Chicago, Illinois, U.S.A.; [7–8] CONTENTS; [9] section title; [10] blank; 11–30, text; [31] section title; [32] blank; 33–47, text; [48] blank.

Contents: Same as A4a.

c. *First American edition, paperback issue:*   1961

[The transcription of the title page is identical with that of the first American edition, hardcover issue.]

Collation: [1–3]⁸ = 24 leaves; 202 × 134 mm.

Binding: Glued into stiff white wove paper wrappers, the exterior of which is shiny, and printed in black, moderate yellowish brown (77), gray reddish purple (245), medium gray (265) and light gray (264); upper wrapper contains a drawing of five men on the right, and on the left, lettered: [in white] my | [in white] sad | [in white] captains | [in medium gray (265)] and other | [in medium gray (265)] poems | [in medium gray (265)] by [in light gray (264)] thom | [in light gray (264)] gunn | [in white] P74 $1.50; rear wrapper contains, in black and white, a photograph of Thom Gunn, and in black, a short biographical sketch of Gunn, and two excerpts from book reviews, and at the bottom: [in gray reddish purple (245)] *A* PHOENIX BOOK *published by the University of Chicago Press*; inner wrappers list other Phoenix Books, P1 through P35 on the inner upper wrapper and P36 through P76 on the inner rear wrapper; white wove paper; all edges trimmed.

Publication date: September 19, 1961

Price: $1.50

Number of copies: 2,505; second printing, October 1965, 1,518 copies; third printing, March 1967, 1,632 copies.

Pagination: Same as A4b.

Contents: Same as A4a.

d. *Second American edition, hardcover issue:*   1973

MOLY | *AND* | *My Sad Captains* | [design depicting a moly] | THOM GUNN | FARRAR, STRAUS AND GIROUX NEW YORK

Collation: [1]¹⁶ + [2]²⁰ + [3]¹⁶ = 52 leaves; 202 × 138 mm.

A. BOOKS, PAMPHLETS AND BROADSIDES

Binding: Bound in moderate green (145) paper covered boards and lettered down the spine in gold: MOLY *AND My Sad Captains* | GUNN | [publisher's logo] [in three lines] Farrar | Straus | Giroux; the upper cover is blind stamped with the moly design; white wove paper; all edges trimmed; top edges stained moderate orange (53); strong greenish yellow (99) textured wove endpapers; dust wrapper white wove paper with shiny exterior surface printed in black, deep bluish green (165) and vital orange (48), repeating the moly design on the front panel and with a photograph of Thom Gunn by Ander Gunn on the rear panel.

Publication date: April 23, 1973

Price: $7.50

Number of copies: Publisher prefers not to reveal the number of copies printed.

Pagination: [i] half-title; [ii] blank; [iii] title page; [iv] Copyright © 1961, 1971, 1973 by Thom Gunn | All rights reserved | Library of Congress catalog card number: 72–96312 | First American edition of *Moly*, 1973 | Printed in the United States of America | Designed by Pat de Groot; [v] ACKNOWLEDGEMENTS; [vi] blank; [vii-ix] CONTENTS; [x] blank; [1] MOLY | *for Mike and Bill,* | *with love*; [2] blank; [3] ten line note by author on origin of moly; [4] blank; 5–45, text; [46] blank; [47] *My Sad Captains*; [48] blank; [49] section title; [50] three line note by author; 51–73, text; [74] blank; [75] section title; [76] blank; 77–91, text; [92–94] blank.

Contents: Same as A4a plus A16a.

Note: There were an unknown number of advance uncorrected proof copies issued in moderate bluish green (164) wove paper wrappers with the same information as appears on the title page printed on the upper wrapper with the additional imprint of: UNCORRECTED PROOF, printed diagonally across the top of the wrapper. These are actually bound galleys, rather than page proofs.

e. *Second American edition, paperback issue:*   1973

[The transcription of the title page is identical with that of the second American edition, hardcover issue.]

Collation: [1–2]⁸ + [3–4]¹⁰ + [5–6]⁸ = 52 leaves; 200 × 134 mm.

Binding: Glued into a stiff white paper wrapper, the exterior of which is shiny, and printed in black, deep bluish green (165) and vital orange (48); and lettered down the spine in black: MOLY *AND My Sad Captains* | GUNN / [publisher's logo] | [across the spine] N449; the upper wrapper is lettered in black: MOLY | *AND* | *My Sad Captains* | [identical moly design as appears on dust wrapper of A4d] | NOONDAY 449 $2.95; the

rear wrapper is lettered in black: [in upper left corner] N 449—POETRY |
ISBN 0–374–51072–5 [and in upper right corner] $2.95 | THOM GUNN |
MOLY | *AND* | *My Sad Captains* | [seventeen lines of critical statement
and biographical notes] | *Cover design by Pat de Groot* | THE NOONDAY
PRESS | 19 UNION SQUARE WEST | NEW YORK 10003; white
wove paper; all edges trimmed.

Publication date: April 23, 1973

Price: $2.95; second printing, $4.95

Number of copies: Publisher prefers not to reveal number of copies printed;
second printing March 1977.

Pagination: Same as A4d.

Contents: Same as A4d.

f. *First English paperback edition:*   1974

My Sad Captains | *and other poems* | by | THOM GUNN | [bulging rule] |
FABER AND FABER | 3 Queen Square | London

Collation: [1–2]⁸ + [3]¹⁰ = 26 leaves; 196 × 128 mm.

Binding: Glued into stiff white wove paper wrappers with a dust wrapper
glued to it on the spine; white wove paper; all edges trimmed; dust wrapper
white wove paper printed in yellow gray (93), vital red (11), dark reddish
brown (44), and dark blue gray (192).

Publication date: January 28, 1974

Price: 95p

Number of copies: 2,500

Pagination: Same as A4a except for additional material on pages [4] and [6],
which here read: [4] by the same author | [star] | THE SENSE OF MOVE-
MENT | FIGHTING TERMS | SELECTED POEMS | (With Ted
Hughes); [6] *First published in 1961* | *by Faber and Faber Limited* | *3 Queen
Square London WC1* | *First published in this edition 1974* | *Printed in Great
Britain by* | *Whitstable Litho, Straker Brothers Ltd* | *All rights reserved* | *ISBN
0 571 10438 X (paper covers)* | CONDITIONS OF SALE | [followed by
six lines of conditions of sale, printed in italics] | © *1961 by Thom Gunn*

Contents: Same as A4a.

A5   SELECTED POEMS   1962

a. *First edition:*

SELECTED POEMS | by | THOM GUNN | and | TED HUGHES |
FABER AND FABER | 24 Russell Square | London

Collation: 32 single leaves; 184 × 120 mm.

A. BOOKS, PAMPHLETS AND BROADSIDES

Binding: A perfect binding glued into stiff white wove paper wrappers, the exterior of which is shiny, printed in black, very pale green (148), and strong red (12); lettered down the spine: [in black] THOM GUNN [in strong red (12)] [large dot] [in black] TED HUGHES [in strong red (12)] [large dot] SELECTED POEMS [large dot] [in white on a black panel] FABER; the upper wrapper [running up, on the left side] [in strong red (12)] SELEC-TED [across] [in strong red (12)] POEMS | [in black] Thom | [in black] Gunn | [in black] & | [in black] Ted | [in black] Hughes | [in white on a black panel] FABER [in white running down on a black panel on the right side] FABER paper covered EDITIONS; the rear wrapper has a black panel with white lettering identical to the one on the upper wrapper, except that the lettering on the rear wrapper runs up and the panel is on the left side of the rear wrapper, also on the rear wrapper, in black on very pale green (148) is the continuation of a list of "Some Faber Paper Covered Editions" begun on the inner rear wrapper; the inner upper wrapper prints the price and a publisher's statement regarding the book; white wove paper; all edges trimmed.

Publication date: May 18, 1962

Price: 5s

Number of copies: 7,500; second printing, July 10, 1963, 6,000 copies; third printing, November 19, 1964, 8,000 copies; fourth printing, December 12, 1966, 8,000 copies; fifth printing, March 18, 1968, 12,000 copies; sixth printing, July 14, 1972, 15,000 copies; seventh printing, October 29, 1973, 25,000 copies.

Pagination: [1] half-title; [2] by the same authors | [star] | THOM GUNN | *Fighting Terms* | *The Sense of Movement* | *My Sad Captains* | [star] | TED HUGHES | *The Hawk in the Rain* | *Lupercal* | (for children) | *Meet My Folks;* [3] title page; [4] *First published in this edition mcmlxii | by Faber and Faber Limited | 24 Russell Square London W.C.1 | Printed in Great Britain by | R. MacLehose and Company Limited | All rights reserved | For copyright reasons, this book | may not be issued to the public on | loan or otherwise except in its | original soft cover. | © This selection Faber and Faber Ltd., 1962;* [5–6] CONTENTS; 7–64 text.

Contents: The Wound—The Beach Head—Tamer and Hawk—For a Birthday—Incident on a Journey—On the Move—The Unsettled Motor-cyclist's Vision of his Death—In Praise of Cities—During an Absence—The Corridor—Vox Humana—In Santa Maria del Popolo—The Annihila-tion of Nothing—Innocence—The Byrnies—Claus von Stauffenberg—Considering the Snail—'Blackie, the Electric Rembrandt'—My Sad Captains.

Note: The poems by Gunn appear on pages 7–33. Pages 34–64 contain 24 poems by Ted Hughes.

A6 A GEOGRAPHY 1966

a. First edition:

THOM GUNN | [in deep reddish orange (38)] A GEOGRAPHY | The Stone Wall Press, 1966 | Iowa City

Collation: [1–3]⁶ = 18 leaves; 190 × 119 mm.

Binding: Glued into deep red (13) textured paper wrappers and lettered on the upper wrapper in black: THOM GUNN | A GEOGRAPHY; Rives white paper; edges untrimmed.

Publications date: April 21, 1966

Price: $2.25

Number of copies: 216

Note: Colophon states 220 copies, but information supplied by the publisher states that only 216 were published.

Pagination: [i-ii] blank; [1] half-title and author's holograph signature; [2] blank; [3] engraving by John Roy; [4] blank; [5] title page; [6] Copyright 1966 by Thom Gunn; [7] eight lines of acknowledgements; 8–31, text; [32] Two hundred twenty copies, signed | by the author, have been printed | on Rives paper from Romanee type.; [33–34] blank.

Contents: The Goddess—The Kiss at Bayreuth—Berlin in Ruins —Confessions of the Life Artist—Breakfast—A Geography—The Vigil of Corpus Christi.

A7 POSITIVES 1966

a. First edition:

VERSES BY | THOM GUNN | [in open face type] POSITIVES | PHOTOGRAPHS BY | ANDER GUNN | FABER AND FABER | 24 Russell Square | London

Collation: [1–5]⁸ = 40 leaves; 242 × 175 mm.

Binding: Bound in moderate red (15) cloth and lettered down the spine in gold: [within the frame of a single rule] POSITIVES Thom and Ander Gunn Faber; white wove matte finish paper; all edges trimmed; white wove endpapers; dust wrapper white wove paper with shiny exterior surface, printed in black with photographs from the book on the front and rear panels.

Publication date: September 24, 1966

Price: 32s 6d

Number of copies: 1,500

Pagination: [1] half-title; [2] *Also by Thom Gunn* | * | FIGHTING TERMS | THE SENSE OF MOVEMENT | MY SAD CAPTAINS | SELECTED POEMS of | Thom Gunn and Ted Hughes; [3] title page; [4] *First published in mcmlxvi | by Faber and Faber Limited | 24 Russell Square London WC1 | Printed in Great Britain | by Balding and Mansell Ltd | All rights reserved | Verses* © *by Thom Gunn 1966 | Photographs* © *by Ander Gunn 1966*; [5, 7, 9, 11, 13, 15, 17, 19, 21, 23, 25, 27, 29, 31, 33, 35, 37, 39, 41, 43, 45, 47, 49, 51, 53, 55, 57, 59, 61, 63, 65, 67, 69, 71, 73, 75, 77, 79, 80] photographs; 6, 8, 10, 12, 14, 16, 18, 20, 22, 24, 26, 28, 30, 32, 34, 36, 38, 40, 42, 44, 46, 48, 50, 52, 54, 56, 58, 60, 62, 64, 66, 68, 70, 72, 74, 76, 78, text.

Contents: She has been a germ, a fish—The body blunders forward—But childhood takes a long time.—'Drink Me'—In watchful community—He rides up and down, and around:—and they start to cross the road,—Youth is power. He knows it,—She rests on and in—♪ The music starts ‖ tentative — PETE—two mirrors—It is a lament, and then—an impetus: its roar, its music—She can't help it, can't—She trembles slightly: her flesh—The responsibilities—In a family, there is—No music in this booser.—SYON HOUSE—LEBENSRAUM—Like a cliff, Marble—We didn't do up this pub,—He raises the pick, point against—Money is a form of dirt—The rubble rises in smoke.—At times, on the edge of smoke—The liver and onions is off,—I have closed my brief-case, dropped my—You have no idea what a —The pigeon lifts, a few feet—The memoirs of the body—He feels a breeze rise from—It is stone: and if ripples—The mould from baked beans that—Poking around the rubbish,—Something approaches, about.

Note: Except for three of the poems in this sequence, the poems are untitled. The three with titles are listed above in all capitals, as they appear in the book. All other poems are listed by first line in the above contents listing.

Note: The photographs on pages [25] and [27] are reversed. This error was corrected in A7c.

b. *First American edition:*   1967

VERSES BY | THOM GUNN | [in open face type] POSITIVES | PHOTOGRAPHS BY | ANDER GUNN | THE UNIVERSITY OF CHICAGO PRESS

Collation: [1–5]^8 = 40 leaves; 242 × 175 mm.

Binding: Bound in moderate red (15) cloth and lettered down the spine in gold: [within the frame of a single rule] POSITIVES Thom and Ander Gunn [in two lines] THE UNIVERSITY | OF CHICAGO PRESS; white wove matte finish paper; all edges trimmed; white wove endpapers; dust wrapper white wove paper with shiny exterior surface, printed in black with photographs from the book on the front and rear panels.

A. BOOKS, PAMPHLETS AND BROADSIDES

Publication date: March 28, 1967

Price: $5.50

Number of copies: 1,038

Pagination: Same as A7a except for information on pages [3] and [4], which here read: [3] title page (as transcribed above); [4] *The University of Chicago Press, Chicago 37 | Faber and Faber Limited, London, W.C.1, England | Verses © by Thom Gunn 1966 | Photographs © by Ander Gunn 1966 | Composed and printed in England*

Contents: Same as A7a.

c. *First English paperback edition:*   1973

VERSES BY | THOM GUNN | [in open face type] POSITIVES | PHOTOGRAPHS BY | ANDER GUNN | FABER AND FABER

Collation: [1–5]⁸ = 40 leaves; 236 × 174 mm.

Binding: Glued into stiff white wove paper wrappers, the exterior of which is shiny, and printed in black and strong purplish red (255); lettered down the spine: [in strong purplish red (255)] POSITIVES [in black] *Verses by Thom Gunn   Photographs by Ander Gunn* [in white on a black panel] FABER; on the upper wrapper [in strong purplish red (255)] Positives | [in strong purplish red (255)] VERSES BY THOM GUNN | [in strong purplish red (255)] PHOTOGRAPHS BY ANDER GUNN | [in strong, purplish red (255)] [photograph from book], [black vertical rule 56 mm.], [in black running down on a white panel on the right side] Faber paper covered editions; on the rear wrapper, in strong purplish red (255) is a photograph from the book and a white panel which is identical to the one on the upper wrapper except that the lettering on the rear wrapper runs up and the panel is on the left side of the rear wrapper; inner upper wrapper prints the price and a publisher's statement regarding the book; inner rear wrapper lists seven other books also by Thom Gunn.

Publication date: October 1, 1973

Price: £1.20

Number of copies: 6,000

Pagination: Same as A7a except for pages [2], [3] and [4], which here read: [2] [same as A7a, but with the addition of two titles at the end of the list which appears in A7a]: TOUCH | MOLY; [3] title page (as transcribed above); [4] *First published in 1966 | First published in this edition 1973 | by Faber and Faber Limited | 3 Queen Square London WC1 | Printed in Great Britain | by Balding and Mansell Ltd | All rights reserved | [on a label pasted*

over a misprint] ISBN 0 571 10391 X | *Verses © by Thom Gunn 1966* |
Photographs © by Ander Gunn 1966

Contents: Same as A7a.

Note: The photographs on pages [25] and [27] appear correctly here. In A7a
and A7b they were incorrectly transposed.

A8   TOUCH   1967

a. *First edition:*

TOUCH | Thom Gunn | FABER & FABER | 24 Russell Square London
Collation: [1]⁶ + [2–3]⁸ + [4]⁶ = 28 leaves; 217 × 140 mm.

Binding: Bound in black cloth and lettered down the spine in gold: TOUCH
| Thom Gunn   *Faber*; white wove paper; all edges trimmed; white wove
endpapers; dust wrapper yellow white (92) wove paper printed in black and
moderate reddish brown (43).

Publication date: September 28, 1967

Price: 15s

Number of copies: 4,000

Pagination: [There are no pages 1–4]; [5] half-title; [6] also by Thom Gunn |
Fighting Terms | The Sense of Movement | My Sad Captains | Positive *with
photographs by Ander Gunn* | with Ted Hughes | Selected Poems; [7] title
page; [8] *First published in mcmlxvii* | *by Faber and Faber Limited* | *24 Russell
Square London WC1* | *Printed in Great Britain by* | *Latimer Trend & Co Ltd
Plymouth* | *All rights reserved* | *© Thom Gunn 1967*; [9] ten lines of
acknowledgements; [10] blank; 11, Contents; [12] blank; 13–58, text; [59–60]
blank.

Contents: The Goddess—The Kiss at Bayreuth—Berlin in Ruins —Bravery
—Confessions of the Life Artist—No Speech from the Scaffold—Breakfast
—Taylor Street—Touch—The Vigil of Corpus Christi—Misanthropos:
The Last Man; Memoirs of the World; Elegy on the Dust; The First Man—
Snowfall—The Girl of Live Marble—In the Tank—Pierce Street—The
Produce District—Back to Life.

Note: There were an unknown number of advance proof copies issued in
gray yellow green (122) wove paper wrappers with the same information as
appears on the title page printed on the upper wrapper with the additional
imprint of: UNCORRECTED | PROOF COPY | Not for Sale | Nor
for review or serialization | without the publisher's permission | Publication
date not yet settled

A. BOOKS, PAMPHLETS AND BROADSIDES

b. *First American edition:*   1968

TOUCH | Thom Gunn | THE UNIVERSITY OF CHICAGO PRESS

Collation: [1–4]⁸ = 32 leaves; 215 × 140 mm.

Binding: Bound in mottled light gray (264) wove paper covered boards; on the upper cover is a 57 × 54 mm. white wove paper label printed in black: TOUCH | Thom Gunn; white wove paper; all edges trimmed; white wove endpapers; issued without a dust wrapper.

Publication date: January 30, 1968

Price: $3.95

Number of copies: 947

Pagination: [1–4] blank; [5] half-title; [6] blank; [7] title page; [8] The University of Chicago Press, Chicago 60637 | Faber and Faber Limited, London WC1 | *Library of Congress Catalog Card Number 67–24300* | © *1967 by Thom Gunn. All rights reserved* | *Published 1968* | *Composed and printed in England*; [9] ten lines of acknowledgements; [10] blank; 11, Contents; [12] blank; 13–58, text; [59–64] blank.

Contents: Same as A8a.

c. *First American paperback edition:*   1968

TOUCH | Thom Gunn | THE UNIVERSITY OF CHICAGO PRESS

Collation: [1–4]⁸ = 32 leaves; 204 × 134 mm.

Binding: Glued into stiff white wove paper wrappers, the exterior of which is shiny, and printed in black and dark pink (6); lettered down the spine in black on a background of dark pink (6): gunn touch [across the spine] PP | 11 [down the spine] chicago; on the upper wrapper in black on a background of dark pink (6): [in the upper right corner] PP $1.45 | [lettered diagonally from upper left to lower right, across a photograph of two hands touching] touch | new poems by thom gunn; on the rear wrapper in black on a background of dark pink (6) is an excerpt from Gunn's poem "Confessions of the Life Artist" and a critical statement by Julian Symonds and at the bottom: Phoenix Poets published by The University of Chicago Press; white wove paper; all edges trimmed.

Publication date: September 15, 1968

Price: $1.45

Number of copies: 3,004

Pagination: Same as A8b.

Contents: Same as A8a.

d. *First English paperback edition:* 1974

TOUCH | Thom Gunn | FABER & FABER | 3 Queen Square London

Collation: [1–4]⁸ = 32 leaves; 197 × 139 mm.

Binding: Glued into stiff white wove paper wrappers with a dust wrapper glued to it on the spine; white wove paper; all edges trimmed; dust wrapper yellow white (92) wove paper printed in black and moderate reddish brown (43).

Publication date: January 28, 1974

Price: £1.00

Number of copies: 3,000

Pagination: Same as A8a except for pages [6], [7], and [8], which here read: [6] also by Thom Gunn | Fighting Terms | The Sense of Movement | My Sad Captains | Positives *with photographs by Ander Gunn* | Poems 1950–1966: A Selection | Moly | with Ted Hughes | Selected Poems; [7] title page (as transcribed above); [8] *First published in 1967 | by Faber and Faber Limited | 3 Queen Square London WC1 | First published in this edition 1974 | Printed in Great Britain by | Whitstable Litho, Straker Brothers Ltd | All rights reserved | ISBN 0 571 10544 0 (paper covers) | ISBN 0 571 08201 7 (Hard bound edition)* | CONDITIONS OF SALE | [followed by six lines of conditions of sale, printed in italics] | © *Thom Gunn 1967*

Contents: Same as A8a.

A9   THE GARDEN OF THE GODS   1968

a. *First edition, surpressed issue:*

THE GARDEN | OF THE GODS | Thom Gunn | PYM-RANDALL PRESS | *361 Harvard Street | Cambridge, Mass. 02138*

Collation: [1]² = 2 leaves; 226 × 156 mm.

Binding: Sewn into vital reddish purple (236) wallet-edged textured paper wrappers; on upper wrapper, lettered in black: THE GARDEN | OF THE GODS | Thom Gunn; white laid paper; all edges trimmed.

Publication date: Surpressed

Price: Never offered for sale

Number of copies: 230 printed; 220 destroyed; 10 retained.

Note: These figures were supplied to the compilers by William Ferguson, the printer, in a letter dated February 18, 1978.

Pagination: [1] title page; [2] © 1968 by Thom Gunn; [3] text; [4] *This is one of a series | of broadsides and pamphlets | designed and printed by William Ferguson for the Pym-Randall Press. | This edition consists of two hundred | numbered and twenty-six lettered | copies. Each copy has been | signed by the author. | February 1968 | Copy*

Contents: The Garden of the Gods.

Note: This issue was surpressed because both the text and cover papers were considered too thin to make a presentable pamphlet. None of the ten copies retained by the publisher were ever signed or numbered, and not all copies retained were sewn. A sewn copy was sent to Thom Gunn.

b. *First edition, published issue:* 1968

[The transcription of the title page is identical with that of the first edition, suppressed issue.]

Collation: [1]² ᶠʳᵉⁿᶜʰ ᶠᵒˡᵈ = 2 French fold leaves; 228 × 152 mm.

Binding: Sewn into vital reddish purple (236) wallet-edged stiff textured paper wrappers with deckel fore-edge on upper wrapper; on upper wrapper, lettered in black: THE GARDEN | OF THE GODS | Thom Gunn; white textured paper, French fold; untrimmed and uncut.

Published: February 26, 1968

Price: $3.00

Number of copies: 230: 200 numbered, 26 lettered and 4 over-run copies.

Note: Only the 200 numbered copies were for sale; the 26 lettered copies and 4 over-run copies were not offered for sale but were for the use of the author and publisher.

Pagination: Same as A9a, except on page [4] after the word *Copy* [holograph number in black ink] | [holograph signature in black ink] Thom Gunn

Note: On page [4] of the lettered copies, the letter is press-printed.

Contents: Same as A9a.

A10   THE EXPLORERS   1969

a. *First edition, "holograph issue":*

[Not seen]

THE | EXPLORERS | by | THOM GUNN

Collation: [1]²⁶ = 26 leaves; [dimensions unknown].

Binding: Bound in dark olive green (126) Niger goat leather; lettered up the spine in gold, between two raised ribs across the spine: THE

EXPLORERS; white laid paper; all edges trimmed and gilt; white laid endpapers; issued without a dust wrapper.

Note: Copies were bound to order. The publisher reports that as recently as 1976 he sold the last copy of this issue in an unbound state. It is probable that other copies were sold unbound, especially since Stanley Bray of Sangorski & Sutcliffe reported, in a conversation with the compilers in October 1976, that their records show that they bound only one copy in the binding described above. The above binding description is based on information provided by Sangorski & Sutcliffe.

Publication date: January 1969

Note: The publisher states that he received and distributed the first copies of this book in January 1969, and therefore we are using this as publication date. We have found no copy, in any issue, dated earlier than February 20, 1969, and most copies are dated later.

Price: £60.00

Number of copies: 6 (numbered 1–6)

Pagination: [i–vi] blank; [vii] title page; [viii] blank; [unpaged leaf on which appears "The Wound" in the author's holograph]; 1–2, text; [unpaged leaf on which appears "Jesus and His Mother" and "Adolescence" in the author's holograph]; 3–4, text; [unpaged leaf on which appears "The Corridor" and "On the Move" in the author's holograph]; 5–6, text; [unpaged leaf on which appears "The Book of the Dead" and "The Byrnies" in the author's holograph]; 7–8, text; [two unpaged leaves on which appears "In Santa Maria del Popolo" and "Vox Humana" in the author's holograph]; 9–10, text; [unpaged leaf on which appears "Touch" in the author's holograph]; 11–12, text; [unpaged leaf on which appears five short poems from *Positives,* "On the Motorcycle", "The Laugh", "Two Old Men", "The Left-Handed Irishman" and "The Old Woman" in the author's holograph]; 13–14, text; [unpaged leaf on which appears "My Sad Captains" and "Epitaph for Anton Schmidt" in the author's holograph]; 15–16, text; [unpaged leaf on which appear "From the Wave" and "The Sand Man" in the author's holograph]; 17, text; [18] Published by | RICHARD GILBERTSON | BOW, CREDITON, DEVON | in a limited edition of one hundred copies. | 1–6. Interleaved throughout with blank paper, on which the | poet has written out each of the nineteen poems in full, to face the | printed text. Bound in full dark green levant morocco gilt, by | Sangorski & Sutcliffe. | 7–16. Interleaved with three manuscript poems. Bound in half [*sic.*] | morocco gilt by Sangorski & Sutcliffe. | 17–36. Contains one poem in manuscript— these vary and include | *Touch, The Sand Man, My Sad Captains, The Wound, From the* | *Wave.* Bound in decorative wrappers. | 37–100. Copies signed and numbered by the author. Bound as | above. | [holograph number in black ink] | [holograph signature, date and place in black ink] Thom Gunn | [various dates used] | San Francisco | Suttons, Paigntion—18363; [19–24] blank.

Note: This description of the pagination is based on an unbound copy inasmuch as no bound copy of this issue could be located.

Note: All copies bear a holograph number and author's signature in black ink; in some copies these are followed by a date and place, but not in all copies; the date used varies from copy to copy. A check of sixteen copies from this edition found that no copies in the ordinary issue bear the date and place; some copies from the other three issues bear the date and place and some do not.

Contents: The Wound—Jesus and His Mother—Adolescence—The Corridor—On the Move—The Book of the Dead—The Byrnies—In Santa Maria del Popolo—Vox Humana—Touch—Positives: On the Motorcycle; The Laugh; Two Old Men; The Left-Handed Irishman; The Old Woman—My Sad Captains—Epitaph for Anton Schmidt—From the Wave—The Sand Man.

b. *First edition, "deluxe issue":*   1969

[The transcription of the title page is identical with that of the first edition, "holograph issue".]

Collation: [1]^{26} = 26 leaves; 258 × 190 mm.

Binding: Quarter bound in dark olive green (126) Niger goat leather with dark green (125) buckram covered boards; lettered up the spine in gold, between two raised ribs across the spine THE EXPLORERS; white laid paper; all edges trimmed; white laid endpapers; issued without dust-wrapper.

Publication date: January 1969 [see note after *Publication date* in A10a entry]

Price: £16.16.0

Number of copies: 10 (numbered 7–16)

Pagination: The pagination is identical with that of the first edition, "holograph issue", A10a, except that poems in the author's holograph appear on only three of the ten unpaged leaves and those leaves on which poems do not appear remain blank. The three poems in author's holograph vary from copy to copy, and therefore appear on different leaves in different copies.

Contents: Same as A10a.

c. *First edition, "special issue":*   1969

[The transcription of the title page is identical with that of the first edition, "holograph issue".]

Collation: [1]^{14} = 14 leaves; 255 × 190 mm.

Binding: Sewn into gray olive green (122) stiff wove paper wrappers blind stamped with a design of simulated pony-hide on the exterior surface; lettered on upper wrapper in black: THE | EXPLORERS | by | THOM GUNN; white wove paper; all edges trimmed.

Publication date: January 1969 [see note after *Publication date* in A10a entry]

Price: £5.5.0

Number of copies: 20 (numbered 17–36)

Pagination: [i–ii] blank; [iii] title page; [iv] blank; 1–8, text; [two unpaged leaves on which a poem appears in the author's holograph], 9–17, text; [18] colophon with holograph additions as in A10a [see after *Pagination* in A10a entry]; [19–20] blank.

Contents: Same as A10a.

d. *First edition, "ordinary issue":*   1969

[The transcription of the title page is identical with that of the first edition, "holograph issue."]

Collation: [1]^{12} = 12 leaves; 255 × 190 mm.

Binding: The binding is identical with that of the first edition, "special issue", A10c.

Publication date: January 1969 [see note after *Publication date* in A10a entry]

Price: £2.2.0

Number of copies: 64 (numbered 37–100)

Pagination: [i–ii] blank; [iii] title page; [iv] blank; 1–17, text; [18] colophon with holograph additions as in A10a [see note after *Pagination* in A10a entry]; [19–20] blank.

Contents: Same as A10a.

A11   THE FAIR IN THE WOODS   1969

a. *First edition:*

[cover title] [in moderate reddish brown (43)] THOM GUNN | [in moderate reddish brown (43)] The Fair in the Woods | [in moderate reddish brown (43)] Sycamore Broadside 6

Collation: Broadside: single sheet, printed on both sides, folded vertically twice to make six unnumbered panels; 204 × 330 mm. [size of fully open sheet]

Binding: White wove paper, printed in black and moderate reddish brown (43); all edges trimmed.

Publication date: February 13, 1969

Price: 6d

Number of copies: 500

Pagination: [upper panel, when closed] title page; [when sheet is fully open]: [left panel] blank; [center and right panels] text; [verso of right panel] blank; [verso of center panel] [in moderate reddish brown (43)] [five lines of biographical statement] | [long rule of 93 mm.] | *Sycamore Press, 4 Benson Place, Oxford. Winter 1969*

Contents: The Fair in the Woods.

Note: Two experimental copies were printed on deep yellow (85) Glastonbury wove paper, 202 × 222 mm. [size of fully open sheet], printed in black and moderate reddish brown (43). These two copies have a single vertical fold to make four unnumbered panels with the following pagination: [1] [in moderate reddish brown (43)] title page; [2–3] text; [4] [in moderate reddish brown (43)] [same transcription as appears on the verso of the center panel of the first edition].

A12   POEMS 1950–1966: A SELECTION   1969

a. *First edition:*

POEMS 1950–1966 | *A Selection* | *by* | THOM GUNN | FABER AND FABER | 24 Russell Square | London

Collation: 24 single leaves; 184 × 120 mm.

Binding: A perfect binding glued into stiff white wove paper wrappers, the exterior of which is shiny, printed in black, light bluish green (163) and deep red (13); lettered down the spine in black: [on a light bluish green (163) panel] THOM GUNN POEMS [on a white panel] 1950–1966 a selection [on a deep red (13) panel] [in white] FABER; on the upper wrapper in black: [on a light bluish green (163) panel] THOM | GUNN | [on a deep red (13) panel] poems | 1950–1966 | [on a light bluish green (163) panel] a selection | [in white running down on a black panel on the right side] FABER paper covered EDITIONS; the rear wrapper has a black panel with white lettering identical to the one on the upper wrapper, except that the lettering on the rear wrapper runs up and the panel is on the left side of the rear wrapper; also on the rear wrapper, in black, is the continuation of a list of "Some Faber Paper Covered Editions" begun on the inner rear wrapper; the inner upper wrapper prints the price and a publisher's statement regarding the book; white wove paper; all edges trimmed.

Publication date: March 24, 1969

Price: 7s £0.35

Number of copies: 8,000

Pagination: [1] half-title; [2] *by Thom Gunn* | [star] | THE SENSE OF MOVEMENT | MY SAD CAPTAINS | TOUCH | FIGHTING TERMS | SELECTED POEMS | (with Ted Hughes); [3] title page; [4] *First published in this edition in 1969* | *by Faber and Faber Limited* | *24 Russell Square London WC1* | *Printed in Great Britain by* | *R. MacLehose & Co Ltd* | *The University Press Glasgow* | *All rights reserved* | SBN 571 08845 7 | © Thom Gunn 1954, 1957, 1961, 1966, 1967 | © this selection by Thom Gunn | 1969 | CONDITIONS OF SALE | [followed by five lines of conditions of sale, printed in italics]; 5–6, *Contents*; 7–47, text; [48] blank.

Contents: The Wound—Here Come the Saints—To His Cynical Mistress—Lazarus Not Raised—A Mirror for Poets—The Beach Head—A Kind of Ethics—For a Birthday—Incident on a Journey—On the Move—Autumn Chapter in a Novel—The Silver Age—The Unsettled Motorcyclist's Vision of his Death—The Allegory of the Wolf Boy—Jesus and His Mother—To Yvor Winters, 1955—During an Absence—The Corridor—Vox Humana—In Santa Maria Del Popolo—The Annihilation of Nothing—From the Highest Camp—Innocence—Modes of Pleasure—The Byrnies—Flying Above California—Considering the Snail—'Blackie, the Electric Rembrandt'—Adolescence—My Sad Captains—Canning Town—The Left-handed Irishman—The Conversation of Old Men—The Old Woman—The Goddess—Touch —The Vigil of Corpus Christi—A Geography—Memoirs of the World—A Snow Vision—Epitaph for Anton Schmidt—Elegy on the Dust—Pierce Street.

Note: There were an unknown number of advance proof copies issued in light blue (181) wove paper wrappers with the same information as appears on the title page printed on the upper wrapper with the additional imprint of: UNCORRECTED | PROOF COPY | Not for Sale | Nor for review or serialization | without the publisher's permission | Publication date not yet settled

Note: Although the published book is perfect bound these advance proof copies are in three signatures of eight leaves each.

A13   SUNLIGHT   1969

a. *First edition:*

[in vital orange (48)] [single vertical rule on the left side running the height of the page] | [in vital orange (48)] Sunlight | [in vital orange (48)] by | [in vital orange (48)] Thom Gunn | ALBONDOCANI PRESS | NEW YORK 1969

Collation: [1]¹⁰ = 10 leaves; 210 × 152 mm.

Binding: Sewn into stiff black wove paper wrappers with a marble paper dust wrapper of moderate orange yellow (71), moderate reddish orange (37) and moderate brown (58) sewn over the wrappers; on the upper panel of the dust wrapper is a 25 × 152 mm. white wove paper label which extends onto the rear panel of the dust wrapper, and is printed on the front, in black: *Sunlight by Thom Gunn;* (very) light gray (264) laid paper with two watermarks: 1) an extended hand with a four-leaf clover at the tip of the hand; 2) a head with a halo, enclosed in the outline of a banner, with the date 1399 beneath; top and bottom edges trimmed, fore-edges untrimmed.

Publication date: December 22, 1969

Price: $15.00

Number of copies: 180: 150 numbered, 26 lettered and 4 over-run copies.

Note: Only the 150 numbered copies were for sale; the 26 lettered copies and 4 over-run copies were not offered for sale but were for the use of the author and publisher.

Pagination: [1–2] blank; [3] title page; [4] [five lines of acknowledgements] | *Copyright 1969 by Thom Gunn;* [5] CONTENTS; [6] blank; 7–15, text; [16] blank; [17] *This first edition of* | SUNLIGHT | *published in December 1969* | *is limited to* | *one hundred and seventy-six copies.* | *The type is Palatino,* | *the paper Charter Oak,* | *and the hand-sewn wrappers are* | *a French marble paper.* | *One hundred and fifty copies* | *numbered 1–150 are for sale.* | *Twenty-six copies* | *lettered A–Z for the use* | *of the author and publisher* | *are not for sale.* | *All copies are signed* | *by the author.* | *This is number* | [holograph number in red ink] | [holograph signature in brown ink] Thom Gunn; [18] Printed by William Ferguson | Cambridge, Massachusetts | Albondocani Press Publication No. 8; [19–20] blank.

Contents: Rites of Passage—Three—Street Song—The Color Machine—At the Center—Listening to Jefferson Airplane—Sunlight.

A14   MY SAD CAPTAINS   1970

a. *First separate edition:*

[Not seen]

[My Sad Captains]

Collation: Broadside: single sheet; 915 × 610 mm.

Binding: "Urryu Cha" straw texture brown and ochre papers, printed in black; top and bottom edges deckle.

Publication date: Summer 1970

Price: Not offered for sale

Number of copies: "not more than 20" [This and all descriptive information in this entry was provided to the compilers by Edward Phelps, the artist and printer, in two letters, one undated from May 1977 and one dated 6 March 1978.]

Pagination: Printed by silk screen on one side only: [across top] [three portraits, reading from left to right: William Blake, Abraham Lincoln and John Keats] | [text of poem printed without title] | [left side] [holograph with black felt-tip pen] My Sad Captains by Thom Gunn [right side] [holograph with black felt-tip pen] print by Edward Phelps

Contents: My Sad Captains.

Note: This broadside was designed and printed for the Library at St. John's College, York, England.

Note: "The graphic element consists of heads of Lincoln, Blake, and Keats who were my own sad captains at the time." [From the undated letter (May 1977) cited above.]

b. *Second separate edition:*   1977

[My Sad Captains]

Collation: Broadside: single sheet; 948 × 637 mm.

Binding: Gray yellow (90) laid paper, printed in black; bottom edge trimmed, other edges deckle.

Publication date: spring 1977

Price: Not offered for sale

Number of copies: 3

Pagination: Printed by silk screen on one side only: [across top] [three portraits, reading from left to right: William Blake, Abraham Lincoln and John Keats] | [text of poem printed without title] | [left side] [holograph, in black ink] POEM "MY SAD CAPTAINS" by THOM GUNN [right side] [holograph signature and date in black ink] Edward Phelps '77

Contents: Same as A14a.

A15   MOLY   1971

a. *First edition:*

MOLY | Thom Gunn | FABER AND FABER | 3 Queen Square London

Collation: [1–2]⁸ + [3]⁴ + [4]⁸ = 28 leaves; 217 × 137 mm.

Binding: Bound in vital yellow (82) cloth and lettered down the spine in gold: MOLY Thom Gunn Faber; white wove paper; all edges trimmed; white wove endpapers; dust wrapper white wove paper printed in black, vital yellow (82) and gray olive (110).

Publication date: March 23, 1971

Price: £1.00

Number of copies: 4,000

Pagination: [1–2] blank; [3] half-title; [4] also by Thom Gunn | Fighting Terms | The Sense of Movement | My Sad Captains | Touch | Poems 1950–1966: A Selection | with Ted Hughes | Selected Poems; [5] title page; [6] *First published in 1971 | by Faber and Faber Limited | 3 Queen Square London WC1 | Printed in Great Britain by | Latimer Trend & Co Ltd Plymouth | All rights reserved | ISBN 0 571 09650 6 | © Thom Gunn 1971;* [7] for Mike and Bill, | with love; [8] blank; [9] Contents; [10] blank; 11, twelve line note by author on origin of moly; [12] blank; 13–54, text; 55, Acknowledgements; [56] blank.

Contents: Rites of Passage—Moly—For Signs—Justin—Phaedra in the Farm House—The Sand Man—Apartment Cats—Three—Words—From the Wave—Tom-Dobbin—The Rooftop—The Colour Machine—Street Song—The Fair in the Woods—Listening to Jefferson Airplane—To Natty Bumppo—The Garden of the Gods—Flooded Meadows—Grasses—The Messenger—Being Born—At the Centre—The Discovery of the Pacific—Sunlight.

Note: There were an unknown number of advance proof copies issued in pale green (149) wove paper wrappers; lettered down the spine in black: MOLY; and with same information as appears on the title page printed in black on the upper wrapper with the additional imprint of: UNCOR-RECTED | PROOF COPY | Not for sale | Nor for review or serialization | without the publisher's permission | Publication date not yet settled

b. *First American edition, hardcover issue:*   1973

MOLY | *AND* | *My Sad Captains* | [design depicting a moly] | THOM GUNN | FARRAR, STRAUS AND GIROUX NEW YORK

Collation: [1]¹⁶ + [2]²⁰ + [3]¹⁶ = 52 leaves; 202 × 138 mm.

Binding: Bound in moderate green (145) paper covered boards and lettered down the spine in gold: MOLY *AND My Sad Captains* | GUNN | [publisher's logo] [in three lines] Farrar | Straus | Giroux; the upper cover is blind stamped with the moly design; white wove paper; all edges trimmed; top edges stained moderate orange (53); strong greenish yellow (99) textured wove endpapers; dust wrapper white wove paper with shiny exterior surface printed in black, deep bluish green (165) and vital orange (48), repeating the moly design on the front panel and with a photograph of Thom Gunn by Ander Gunn on the rear panel.

Publication date: April 23, 1973

Price: $7.50

Number of copies: Publisher prefers not to reveal the number of copies printed.

Pagination: [i] half-title; [ii] blank; [iii] title page; [iv] Copyright © 1961, 1971, 1973 by Thom Gunn | All rights reserved | Library of Congress catalog card number: 72–96312 | First American edition of *Moly*, 1973 | Printed in the United States of America | Designed by Pat de Groot; [v] ACKNOWLEDGEMENTS; [vi] blank; [vii–ix] CONTENTS; [x] blank; [1] MOLY | *for Mike and Bill,* | *with love*; [2] blank; [3] ten line note by author on origin of moly; [4] blank; 5–45, text; [46] blank; [47] *My Sad Captains*; [48] blank; [49] section title; [50] three line note by author; 51–73, text; [74] blank; [75] section title; [76] blank; 77–91, text; [92–94] blank.

Contents: Same as A15a plus A4a.

Note: There were an unknown number of advance uncorrected proof copies issued in moderate bluish green (164) wove paper wrappers with the same information as appears on the title page printed on the upper wrapper with the additional imprint of: UNCORRECTED PROOF, printed diagonally across the top of the wrapper. These are actually bound galleys, rather than page proofs.

c. *First American edition, paperback issue:*   1973

[The transcription of the title page is identical with that of the second American edition, hardcover issue.]

Collation: [1–2]^8 + [3–4]^{10} + [5–6]^8 = 52 leaves; 200 × 134 mm.

Binding: Glued into a stiff white paper wrapper, the exterior of which is shiny, and printed in black, deep bluish green (165) and vital orange (48); and lettered down the spine in black: MOLY *AND My Sad Captains* | GUNN / [publisher's logo] | [across the spine] N 449; the upper wrapper is lettered in black: MOLY | *AND* | *My Sad Captains* | [identical moly design as appears on dust wrapper of A15b] | NOONDAY 449 $2.95; the rear wrapper is lettered in black: [in upper left corner] N 449—POETRY | ISBN 0–374–51072–5 [and in upper right corner] $2.95 | THOM GUNN | MOLY | *AND* | *My Sad Captains* | [seventeen lines of critical statement and biographical notes] | *Cover design by Pat de Groot* | THE NOONDAY PRESS | 19 UNION SQUARE WEST | NEW YORK 10003; white wove paper; all edges trimmed.

Publication date: April 23, 1973

Price: $2.95; second printing, $4.95

Number of copies: Publisher prefers not to reveal number of copies printed; second printing, March 1977.

Pagination: Same as A15b.

Contents: Same as A15b.

A16   LAST DAYS AT TEDDINGTON   1971

a. *First edition:*

LAST | DAYS AT | TEDDINGTON

Collation: Broadside: single sheet; 390 × 282 mm.

Binding: Yellow white (92) laid paper, watermarked with a crown above old-English lettering: Abbey Mills | Greenfield; all edges trimmed.

Publication date: October 19, 1971

Price: Sold only by subscription for second folio (twelve broadsides) £7.35

Number of copies: 1,000

Pagination: Printed on one side only: LAST | [short rule] DAYS AT [long rule, which together with the short rule form the top of a four-sided rule border] | TEDDINGTON [and the first line of the poem] | [text of the poem] | [holograph signature in black ink] Thom Gunn | [the word TEDDINGTON, the text of the poem, and the holograph signature are surrounded left, right and below by a single rule which forms the three remaining sides of the four-sided rule border] | Last Days at Teddington by Thom Gunn published by Poem-of-the-Month Club Ltd, 27 Brynmaer Road, S.W.11. | Printed by John Roberts Press Ltd. Copyright (1971) Poem-of-the-Month Club Ltd.

Contents: Last Days at Teddington.

A17   POEM AFTER CHAUCER   1971

a. *First edition:*

[cover title] POEM AFTER CHAUCER | BY THOM GUNN | [in vital yellow green (115)] [circular drawing of crocus] | *And smale foweles maken melodye,* | *That slepen al the nyght with open ye* | —*Chaucer*

Collation: [1]² = 2 leaves; 168 × 117 mm.

Binding: Stapled into light yellow (86) heavy laid paper wrappers with a deckle fore-edge on upper wrapper, printed in black and vital yellow green (115); white laid paper; all edges trimmed; issued in white wove paper envelope with a 184 × 133 mm. piece of stiff textured wove paper as a backing.

Note: When this poem was later collected the title was changed to "All Legs Pointed East". (A24)

Publication date: December 14, 1971

Price: Not for sale

Number of copies: 320

Pagination: [1] HOLIDAY GREETINGS | AND | BEST WISHES | FOR THE | COMING YEAR | FROM | ALBONDOCANI PRESS | AND | AMPERSAND BOOKS [see note below]; [2] *Copyright* © *1971 by Thom Gunn*; [3] text; [4] *This first printing of* | POEM AFTER CHAUCER | *published in December 1971* | *is limited to* | *three hundred copies* | *to be used* | *as a holiday greeting* | *by the author and publisher.* | *None are for sale.* | Cover drawing by Robert Dunn | *Printed by* | *William Ferguson* | *for Albondocani Press*

Contents: Poem After Chaucer.

Note: 160 copies contain the greeting on page [1] as given above; on the other 160 copies the greeting consists of only the first five lines, the last four lines being omitted. These copies were for the use of the author and artist. There is no other difference between the two issues, and no priority.

A18   THE SPELL   1973

a. *First edition:*

The Spell

Collation: Broadside: single sheet; 454 × 372 mm.

Binding: White wove paper printed in moderate violet (211) and strong red (12) (with many lighter gradations), with black overprinting and touches of gold added by hand; all edges trimmed.

Publication date: March 1973

Price: 20p

Number of copies: 500

Pagination: Printed on one side only: an overall design, bled to the edges of the sheet, of spheres, moons with faces and wavy lines: [on a small strong red (12) sphere in upper left corner] [in moderate violet (211)] ALL IN 18 |

design Nina Carroll | 31 Headlands Kettering | Northants | [on a large strong red (12) sphere approximately center] [in black, applied by silkscreen] [text of the poem] | [to the right of poem] [on a white sphere] [in black applied by silkscreen with touches of gold added by hand] [a moon with a face] | [in black applied by silkscreen] Thom Gunn

Contents: The Spell.

A19   SONGBOOK   1973

a. *First edition:*

[in moderate olive green (125)] [single vertical rule on the left side running the height of the page] | [in moderate olive green (125)] *Songbook* | [in moderate olive green (125)] *by* | [in moderate olive green (125)] *Thom Gunn* | [in moderate olive green (125)] *with drawings by Bill S.* | ALBONDOCANI PRESS | NEW YORK 1973

Collation: [1]¹² = 12 leaves; 209 × 151 mm.

Binding: Sewn into stiff moderate olive (107) wove paper wrappers with a marble-paper dust wrapper of gray brown (61), light orange yellow (70), dark green (146) and gold sewn over the wrappers; on the upper panel of the dust wrapper is a 26 × 158 mm. white wove paper label which extends onto the rear panel of the dust wrapper, and printed on the front, in black: *Songbook by Thom Gunn*; white laid and wove papers; top and bottom edges trimmed, fore-edges untrimmed.

Publication date: December 1, 1973

Price: $17.50

Number of copies: 230: 200 numbered, 26 lettered and 4 over-run copies.

Note: Only the 200 numbered copies were for sale; the 26 lettered copies and 4 over-run copies were not offered for sale but were for the use of the author and publisher.

Pagination: [1–2] blank; [3] title page; [4] [five lines of acknowledgements] | © Copyright 1973 by Thom Gunn; [5] CONTENTS; [6] blank; 7–8, text; [9–10] drawings; 11–14, text; [15–16] drawings; 17–18, text; [19–20] blank; [21] *This first edition of* | SONGBOOK | *published in December 1973* | *is limited to* | *two hundred and twenty-six copies.* | *The type is Palatino,* | *the paper is WSH & Co. Cream Wove,* | *and the hand-sewn wrappers are* | *a French marble paper.* | *The drawings are printed* | *on Fabriano Text.* | *Two hundred copies* | *numbered 1–200 are for sale.* | *Twenty-six copies* | *lettered A–Z for the use* | *of the author, artist and publisher* | *are not for sale.* | *All copies are signed* | *by the author* | *and the artist.* | *This is number* | [holograph number in red ink] | [holograph signature in black ink] Thom Gunn | [holograph signature in red ink] Bill S; [22] Printed by William & Raquel Ferguson | Cambridge, Massachusetts | Albondocani Press Publication No. 18; [23–24] blank.

Contents: The Night-Piece—Baby Song—Hitching into Frisco—The Spell—New York Billy—Encolpius—Rita—Sparrow.

A20   TO THE AIR   1974

a. *First edition:*

Thom Gunn | [within a vertical rectangle formed by a single rule] TO THE AIR | David R. Godine

Collation: [1–2]⁸ = 16 leaves; 216 × 142 mm.

Binding: Bound in white wove paper covered boards printed with an overall leaf design in strong greenish blue (169); lettered down the spine in black: [on a white panel with a surrounding rectangular single black rule] THOM GUNN; on the upper cover, at the top, on a white panel, 34 × 58 mm., in black, bordered by a double rule (outer rule wider than inner rule): *Thom Gunn* | TO THE AIR, and at the bottom of the upper cover on a white panel, 33 × 28 mm., in black, bordered by a double rule (outer rule wider than inner rule): [in white on a black panel surrounded by a single black rule] [publisher's logo] | GODINE; white wove paper; all edges trimmed; white wove endpapers; issued without a dust wrapper.

Publication date: May 1974

Price: $2.50

Number of copies: 2,000

Pagination: [i–ii] blank; [1] title page; [2] David R. Godine Publisher | Boston, Massachusetts | Copyright © 1974 by Thom Gunn | LCC 73–89045 | ISBN 0–87923–086–x | [three lines of acknowledgements] | *Designed by Carol Shloss* | *Number 6 in the* | FIRST GODINE POETRY | CHAPBOOK SERIES | Jan Schreiber, General Editor; [3] half-title; [4] blank; 5–24, text; [25–30] blank.

Contents: The Bed—Diagrams—Iron Landscapes (and the Statue of Liberty) —Fever—The Corporal—The Geysers: Sleep by the Hot Stream; The Cool Stream; The Geyser; Discourse from the Deck; The Bath House.

A21   MANDRAKES   1974

a. *First edition, first binding:*

THOM GUNN | [panel and surrounding rule in moderate reddish brown

A. BOOKS, PAMPHLETS AND BROADSIDES

(43)] [lettered in white script within panel] Mandrakes | Illustrated by Leonard Baskin | THE RAINBOW PRESS

Collation: [1]² + [2–5]⁴ + [6]² = 20 leaves; 285–290 × 192–195 mm.

Binding: Quarter bound in white goat vellum and gray reddish brown (46) textured Japanese paper covered boards and stamped with a vertical gold rule on the front and rear covers where the vellum and paper meet; lettered down the spine in gold: MANDRAKES [an open star] THOM GUNN; heavy white wove paper; top edges trimmed, other edges untrimmed; top edges gilt; heavy white wove endpapers; issued in a dark red (16) buckram covered slipcase lined with white flannel.

Note: 150 copies were numbered and signed and copies 1–75 were bound as described above. There were also four copies bound in this first binding which were unnumbered and unsigned and not for sale. Copies 76–150 were bound in the second binding [see A21b]. [In a letter from Olwyn Hughes, the publisher, dated September 23, 1976, it was stated that "I have them bound in batches of 30 or so at a time".]

Publication date: November 28, 1974

Price: £40 (affecting copies 1–95); raised in 1977 to £50 (affecting copies 96–150)

Number of copies: 79 [see note above]

Pagination: [i–ii] blank; [1] half-title; [2] drawing; [3] title page; [4] Text © Thom Gunn 1973 | Drawings © Leonard Baskin 1973 | Printed in Great Britain; [5] CONTENTS; 6–7, text; [8] drawing; 9–12, text; [13] drawing; 14–17, text; [18] drawing; 19–28, text; [29] drawing; 30–33, text; [34] blank; [35] publisher's logo; [36] This edition of one hundred and fifty | numbered copies, signed by the author | and illustrated by Leonard Baskin | was designed and printed by Will Carter | at the Rampart Lions Press, Cambridge | on Barcham Green paper, set in Ehrhardt. | Bound in quarter white goat vellum | by Sangorski and Sutcliffe, London | the work was finished in the | autumn of 1973. | This is copy number | [holograph number in black ink] | [holograph signature in black ink] Thom Gunn | [37–38] blank.

Contents: The Plunge—Wrestling with Angels—Santurnalia—An Amorous Debate—Faustus Triumphant—Solus Ipse—The Idea of Trust—Mandrakes—Thomas Bewick—Breaking Ground.

Note: The title of the poem "Faustus Triumphant", while spelled correctly on the contents page, is misspelled as "Faustus Truimphant" on page 19.

b. *First edition, second binding:*   1974

These copies are the same in every respect as A21a except that dark red (16) buckram (the same as is used to cover the slipcase) has been substituted for the Japanese paper on the upper and rear covers. [see note after *Binding* in A21a]

Number of copies: 75 (numbered 75–150)

A22   JACK STRAW'S CASTLE   1975

a. *First edition, paperback issue:*

THOM GUNN | [in strong reddish brown (40)] *Jack* | [in strong reddish brown (40)] *Straw's* | [in strong reddish brown (40)] *Castle* | FRANK HALLMAN | 1975

Collation: [1]^{16} = 16 leaves; 189 × 126 mm.

Binding: Stapled into stiff white laid paper wrappers; white laid paper; all edges trimmed; dust wrapper strong red (12) laid paper, printed in black on the upper panel: THOM GUNN | *Jack* | *Straw's* | *Castle*

Publication date: November 14, 1975

Price: $3.50

Number of copies: 352: 300 issued with dust wrapper as described above; 52 over-run copies without dust wrapper, unissued.

Pagination: [1–2] blank; [3] title page; [4] *First published in 1975 by:* | Frank Hallman | Box 246, Cooper Station | New York, N.Y. 10003 | *Copyright* © *1975 by Thom Gunn. All* | *rights reserved. Parts of this poem have* | *appeared in* Manroot. *Part 8 first ap-* | *peared in* MANDRAKES [*Rainbow Press:* | *London 1974*]. *Library of Congress Cat-* | *alog Card Number: 75–18065. Design:* | *R. Schaubeck.*; [5] half-title; [6] blank; [7–9] text; [10] blank; [11–13] text; [14] blank; [15–17] text; [18] blank; [19] text; [20] blank; [21–25] text; [26] blank; [27–28] text; [29] JACK STRAW'S CASTLE | *is published in an edition of four hundred* | *copies, of which one hundred are hard-* | *bound and signed by the author.*; [30] M. BIXLER, PRINTER: BOSTON; [31–32] blank.

Contents: Jack Straw's Castle [an eleven-part poem].

b. *First edition, limited hardcover issue:*   1976

[The transcription of the title page is identical with that of the first edition, paperback issue.]

Collation: [1]^{16} = 16 leaves; 185 × 122 mm.

Binding: Bound in natural linen cloth and lettered on the upper cover in dark gray brown (62): JACK STRAW'S | CASTLE | [66 mm. double rule] | THOM GUNN; white laid paper; all edges trimmed; white wove endpapers; dust wrapper strong red (12) laid paper printed in black. [same as A22a]

Publication date: July 12, 1976

Price: $15.00

Number of copies: 120

Note: There were 20 over-run copies bound; these were lettered after the colophon on page [29]: [holograph in red ink] Author's copie | [holograph number in red ink] [i–xx] | [holograph signature in blue ink] Thom Gunn

Pagination: Same as A22a, except after the colophon on page [29] appears: [holograph number in red ink] | [holograph signature in blue ink] Thom Gunn

Contents: Same as A22a.

A23   THE MISSED BEAT   1976

a. *First edition:*

THOM GUNN The Missed Beat WITH | A WOOD ENGRAVING BY SIMON BRETT | [engraving of aqueduct in moderate yellow (87)] | THE JANUS PRESS NEWARK VERMONT | 1976

Collation: [1]⁸ ᶠʳᵉⁿᶜʰ ᶠᵒˡᵈ = 8 French fold leaves; 228–231 × 158 mm.

Binding: Quarter bound in dark gray (266) cloth and vertically striped moderate greenish yellow (102) and light olive (106) Fabriano Ingres paper covered boards; lettered down the spine in black on a 6 × 71 mm. moderate greenish yellow (102) laid paper label: THOM GUNN THE MISSED BEAT; toned Okawara handmade paper, French fold; top edges uncut, fore-edges untrimmed, bottom edges trimmed and untrimmed; dark greenish yellow (103) laid endpapers; issued in a slipcase, the sides of which are covered with vertically striped moderate greenish yellow (102) and light olive (106) Fabriano Ingres paper (as on the boards of the book), and the spine, top and bottom edges of the slipcase are covered with dark gray (266) cloth; lettered down the spine of the slipcase in black on a 7.5 × 88 mm. moderate greenish yellow (102) laid paper label: THOM GUNN: THE MISSED BEAT

Note: The paper used on the endpapers, boards and sides of the slipcase is variously watermarked with: INGRES COVER FABRIANO; however, this watermark does not appear on all copies, nor necessarily in all three places on the same copy.

Publication date: May 1, 1976

Price: $35.00

c

A. BOOKS PAMPHLETS AND BROADSIDES

Number of copies: 50

Note: There were about 20 copies of the complete sheets with The Janus Press imprint, with the signature of both the author and the artist on the colophon page, which were sewn into dark greenish yellow (103) laid paper wrappers and were divided between the publisher of The Janus Press and the publisher of The Gruffyground Press. These copies were not offered for sale.

Also, five incomplete copies, sewn into dark greenish yellow (103) laid paper wrappers, were sent to Thom Gunn at the time that the edition was published. These copies lack the title page, copyright page, "The Missed Beat" and the colophon page. On the next to last page, which is blank in these copies, Gunn has written out in holograph in black ink "The Missed Beat" poem and added in holograph, in red ink, his own colophon, number and signature at the bottom of the same page.

Pagination: [1] half-title; [2] blank; [3] title page; [4] [in moderate yellow (87)] eight lines of acknowledgements, including the copyright notice; [5–10] text; [11] engraving of aqueduct (same as on title page) printed in black; [12–13] text; [14] [in moderate yellow (87)] The wood engraving was printed from Simon Brett's | original block; the text is handset Times New Roman | printed on Okawara at The Janus Press in Newark, West | Burke, Vermont in the United States of America by Claire | van Vliet for Anthony Baker at The Gruffyground Press, | Ladram, Sidcot, Winscombe, Somerset in England. The | cover is Fabriano Ingres. | The edition is limited to two hundred & twenty copies | of which fifty are for The Janus Press and one hundred | and seventy are for The Gruffyground Press. | [holograph signature in pencil] Thom Gunn | [15–16] blank.

Contents: The Soldier—Light Sleeping—Excursion—From an Asian Tent —The Clock—Aqueduct—The Missed Beat.

---

b. *First English edition, first state:* 1976

THOM GUNN The Missed Beat WITH | A WOOD ENGRAVING BY SIMON BRETT | [engraving of aqueduct in moderate yellow (87)] | SIDCOT · THE GRUFFYGROUND PRESS | 1976

Collation: [1]⁶ French fold = 6 French fold leaves; 230–233 × 159 mm.

Binding: Sewn into wallet-edged French fold dark greenish yellow (103) Fabriano Ingres laid paper wrappers and printed on the upper wrapper in black: THOM GUNN: THE MISSED BEAT; toned Okawara hand-made paper, French fold; top edges uncut; fore-edges untrimmed, bottom edges trimmed and untrimmed.

Publication date: May 24, 1976

Price: £6.00

Number of copies: "about 70"

Note: In "about 70" copies the space between the first and second lines on the title page is 16 mm. Thereafter, the title page was "tightened" and in all remaining copies, including those with The Janus Press imprint, the space between the first and second lines of the title page is 11 mm.

Pagination: [1] title page; [2] [in moderate yellow (87)] eight lines of acknowledgements, including the copyright notice; [3–8] text; [9] engraving of aqueduct (same as on title page) printed in black; [10–11] text; [12] [colophon in moderate yellow (87), same as in first edition, A24a, but with the addition below the author's holograph signature of:] [holograph signature in pencil] Simon Brett. | [holograph rule]

Contents: Same as A24a.

Note: There was a press over-run of about ten additional copies. In addition, one copy with The Gruffyground Press imprint was bound into a cloth and paper covered board binding similar to The Janus Press edition, but without a slipcase, and this copy bears only Thom Gunn's signature on the colophon.

c. *First English edition, second state:*　　　　　　　　　　　　1976

These copies are the same in every respect as A24b except for the spacing on the title page. In these copies the space between the first and second lines on the title page is 11 mm. [see note after *Number of copies* in A24a]

Number of copies: "about 100"

A24　　　　　　　JACK STRAW'S CASTLE　　　　1976
　　　　　　　　　　[and other poems]

a. *First edition, hardcover issue:*

THOM GUNN | Jack Straw's Castle | FABER AND FABER | 3 Queen Square, London

Collation: [1–5]⁸ = 40 leaves; 217 × 137 mm.

Binding: Bound in vital reddish orange (34) cloth and lettered down the spine in gold: JACK STRAW'S CASTLE [solid square] THOM GUNN [solid square] FABER; white wove paper; all edges trimmed; white wove endpapers; dust wrapper pale yellow (89) wove paper printed in black, vital ornage (48) and strong blue (178).

Publication date: September 20, 1976

Price: £3.25

Number of copies: 750; second printing, May 24, 1977, 350 copies.

A. BOOKS, PAMPHLETS AND BROADSIDES

Pagination: [1-2] blank; [3] half-title; [4] by the same author | MOLY | POEMS 1950–1966: A SELECTION | TOUCH | POSITIVES | SELECTED POEMS (with Ted Hughes) | FIGHTING TERMS | MY SAD CAPTAINS | THE SENSE OF MOVEMENT; [5] title page; [6] *First published in 1976* | *by Faber and Faber Limited* | *3 Queen Square London WC1* | *Printed in Great Britain by* | *Latimer Trend & Company Ltd Plymouth* | *All rights reserved* | *ISBN 0 571 10974 8 (hardbound edition)* | *ISBN 0 571 11010 x (Faber Paperbacks)* | © *Thom Gunn, 1976*; [7] To the memory of | Tony White; [8] blank; 9–10, Contents; [11] section title; [12] blank; 13–30, text; [31] section title; [32] blank; 33–58, text; [59] section title; [60] blank; 61–77, text; 78, Acknowledgements; [79–80] blank.

Contents: The Bed—Diagrams—Iron Landscapes—The Corporal—Fever—The Night Piece—Last Days at Teddington—All Night, Legs Pointed East—The Geysers: Sleep by the Hot Stream; The Cool Stream; The Geyser; The Bath House—Three Songs: Baby Song; Hitching into Frisco; Sparrow—The Plunge—Bringing to Light—Thomas Bewick—Wrestling—The Outdoor Concert—Saturnalia—Faustus Triumphant—Dolly—Jack Straw's Castle 1–11—An Amorous Debate—Autobiography—Hampstead: the Horse Chestnut Trees—The Roadmap—The Idea of Trust—Courage, a Tale—Behind the Mirror—The Cherry Tree—Mandrakes—Yoko—The Release—Breaking Ground.

Note: There were an unknown number of advance proof copies issued in gray reddish orange (39) wove paper wrappers; lettered down the spine in black: JACK STRAW'S CASTLE; and with the same information as appears on the title page printed in black on the upper wrapper with the additional imprint of: UNCORRECTED | PROOF COPY | Not for sale | Nor for review or serialization | without the publisher's permission | Publication date not yet settled

b. *First edition, paperback issue:*   1976

[The transcription of the title page is identical with that of the first edition, hardcover issue.]

Collation: [1–5]⁸ = 40 leaves; 217 × 135 mm.

Binding: Glued into stiff white wove paper wrappers, the exterior of which is shiny, and printed in black, pale yellow (89), vital orange (48) and strong blue (178); lettered down the spine in black: JACK STRAW'S CASTLE [solid strong blue (178) square] THOM GUNN [solid strong blue (178) square] [in pale yellow (89) on a vital orange (48) panel] FABER; on the upper wrapper: [in pale yellow (89) and strong blue (178) on a black panel] THOM | GUNN | [in black on vital orange (48) and pale yellow (89) panels] JACK | STRAW'S | CASTLE; on the rear wrapper, in black on pale yellow (89), is the price and the publisher's statement regarding the book; the inner upper wrapper lists other books by Thom Gunn; the inner rear wrapper lists other poets published by Faber and Faber; white wove paper; all edges trimmed.

Publication date: September 20, 1976

Price: £1.95

Number of copies: 4,000; second printing, April 15, 1977, 2,500 copies.

Pagination: Same as A24a, except for page [6], where lines seven and eight are reversed, and with the addition between line eight and the final line of: CONDITIONS OF SALE | [followed by six lines of conditions of sale, printed in italics].

Contents: Same as A24a.

c. *First American edition:*   1976

THOM GUNN | Jack Straw's Castle | *and Other Poems* | [publisher's logo] | FARRAR, STRAUS AND GIROUX NEW YORK

Collation: [1]¹⁶+[2]⁸+[3]¹⁶ = 40 leaves; 208 × 136 mm.

Binding: Bound in moderate reddish purple (241) cloth; lettered down the spine in silver; Thom Gunn JACK STRAW'S CASTLE *Farrar Straus Giroux*; yellow white (92) laid paper; all edges trimmed; light gray (264) wove textured endpapers; dust wrapper white wove paper printed in black, gray purplish red (256) and brilliant greenish blue (168).

Publication date: October 29, 1976

Price: $7.95

Number of copies: Publisher prefers not to reveal the number of copies printed.

Pagination: [1] half-title; [2] blank; [3] By Thom Gunn | *Fighting Terms* | *The Sense of Movement* | *Selected Poems* (with Ted Hughes) | *Positives* (with Ander Gunn) | *Touch* | *Poems 1950–1966: A Selection* | *Moly and My Sad Captains* | *Jack Straw's Castle and Other Poems*; [4] blank; [5] title page; [6] Copyright © 1971, 1973, 1974, 1975, 1976 by Thom Gunn | All rights reserved | First published in 1976 by Faber & Faber Limited | First American printing, 1976 | Printed in the United States of America | Library of Congress Cataloging in Publication Data | Gunn, Thom. | Jack Straw's castle and other poems. | I. Title. | PR6013.U65J34 1976 821'.9'14 76–40937; [7] To the memory of | Tony White; [8] blank; 9–10, Contents; [11] section title; [12] blank; 13–30, text; [31] section title; [32] blank; 33–58, text; [59] section title; [60] blank; 61–77, text; [78] Acknowledgements; [79–80] blank.

A. BOOKS, PAMPHLETS AND BROADSIDES

Contents: Same as A24a.

Note: There were an unknown number of advance proof copies issued in strong greenish yellow (99) wove paper wrappers with the same information as appears on the title page printed on the upper wrapper with the additional imprint of: UNCORRECTED PAGE PROOF

d. *First American paperback edition:*   1977

[The transcription of the title page is identical with that of the first American edition.]

Collation: 40 single leaves; 209 × 136 mm.

Binding: A perfect binding glued into stiff white wove paper wrappers, the exterior of which is shiny, printed in black, gray purplish red (256) and brilliant greenish blue (168); lettered down the spine: [in gray purplish red (256)] Thom Gunn [in black] JACK STRAW'S CASTLE [publisher's logo] N 568; on the upper wrapper in black: [surrounded by a frame of panels in gray purplish red (256) and brilliant greenish blue (168)] Jack | Straw's | Castle | and | Other | Poems | [single rule of 62 mm.] | Thom Gunn; on the rear wrapper in black [in the upper left] N 568 | ISBN 0–374–51417–8 | [in the upper right] $3.45 | [in gray purplish red (256)] THOM GUNN | [five line quotation from a review by Raymond Oliver] | [in gray purplish red (256)] Jack Straw's Castle | [eleven line publisher's statement] | *Cover design by Charles Skaggs* | THE NOONDAY PRESS | A division of Farrar, Straus and Giroux | 19 Union Square West | New York 10003; white wove and white laid paper; all edges trimmed.

Publication date: September 9, 1977

Price: $3.45

Number of copies: Publisher prefers not to reveal the number of copies printed.

Pagination: Same as A24c.

Contents: Same as A24a.

A25   A CRAB   1978

a. *First edition:*

[in deep red (13)] A Crab | Thom Gunn

Collation: [1]² = 2 leaves; 242 × 190 mm.

Binding: Leaflet; white laid paper; all edges trimmed; issued in white wove paper envelope.

A. BOOKS, PAMPHLETS AND BROADSIDES

Publication date: May 1978

Price: Not for sale

Number of copies: 30

Pagination: [1] title page; [2] blank; [3] text; [4] Number [holograph number in red ink] of 30 copies handset & handprinted, May 1978 [publisher's logo: skull and crossbones]

Note: Only 26 copies were numbered; four were unnumbered.

Contents: A crab.

Note: Laid into copies, a photocopied letter on white wove paper, 172 × 127 mm. the text of which is as follows: Dear [ribbon typed name of recipient and comma] | Enclosed is a piracy of an | uncollected Thom Gunn poem. | We hope you like it. It's a | gift, but it's also a small | reminder that we still live | in a country where secret | underground presses aren't | usually necessary. We'd like | to keep it that way. | If you believe in press | freedom, maybe you'd consider | sending the equivalent of | what this poem would cost in | a bookshop (about $10—or | more if you can afford it) | for 'The Body Politic Free | the Press Fund' in Canada to: | Lynn King in Trust for The Body Politic, | 111 Richmond St. W., | Suite 320, | Toronto, | CANADA M5H 3N6. | Thanks, | THE PIRATES.

B

BOOKS AND PAMPHLETS EDITED,
OR WITH CONTRIBUTIONS BY
THOM GUNN

In this section, books and pamphlets in which a contribution by Thom Gunn appears either for the first time in a book or for the first time in print are listed chronologically. Any material which was previously unpublished is identified.

POETRY | FROM | CAMBRIDGE | 1951–1952 | A selection of verse by members of the University. | *Edited by* | THOM GUNN | THE FORTUNE PRESS | LONDON, S.W. 1.

Collation: [1–3]⁸ = 24 leaves; 188–190 × 124–128 mm.

Binding: Quarter bound in black cloth with imitation snake-skin grained black paper covered boards and lettered up the spine in gold: *POETRY FROM CAMBRIDGE* 1951–52; white wove paper; top edges trimmed, other edges untrimmed; white wove endpapers; dust wrapper medium gray (265) printed in deep red (13).

Publication date: 1952, sometime after June during 1952.

Price: 6s

Number of copies: unknown

Contents: "Introduction", p. 5; "To his cynical mistress", p. 27, collected in *FT*; "Helen's rape", pp. 27–28, collected in *FT*; "A mirror for poets", pp. 28–29, collected in *FT*; "Lazarus not raised", pp. 29–30, collected in *FT, P 50–66*.

Note: The prose introduction appears here for the first time in print.

B2   SPRINGTIME   1953

SPRINGTIME | *An Anthology of Young Poets* | *and Writers edited by* | *G. S. Fraser and* | *Iain* [*sic.*] *Fletcher* | PETER OWEN LIMITED | *London*

Collation: [1]⁴ + [2–9]⁸ = 68 leaves; 210 × 135 mm.

Binding: Bound in dark purplish red (259) cloth and lettered down the spine in gold: *Springtime Peter Owen;* white wove paper; all edges trimmed; white wove endpapers; dust wrapper white wove paper printed in dark purplish red (259) and deep blue (179).

Note: Ian Fletcher's name is consistently misspelled on the title page and on the upper dust wrapper.

Note: An unrecorded number of the total edition were bound in black cloth. The publisher's records do not record which binding takes precedence. In a conversation with the publisher, he stated that the dark purplish red (259) was probably first.

Publication date: March 30, 1953

Price: 12s 6d

Number of copies: 1,500

Contents: "Carnal knowledge", pp. 48–49, collected in *FT*.

Note: The contents also include "A mirror for poets" and "Helen's rape" which were previously collected.

B3   POETRY FROM CAMBRIDGE 1952–4   1955

Poetry from Cambridge | 1952–4 | [rule with an open triangular space in the center] | Edited by Karl Miller | Fantasy Press

Collation: [1]²² = 22 leaves; 191 × 117 mm.

Binding: Stapled into a moderate blue (182) wove paper wrapper lettered across the upper wrapper in black: POETRY | FROM | CAMBRIDGE | 1952–4 | [three solid dots 3 mm. in diameter in moderate reddish brown (43)] | EDITED BY KARL MILLER | FANTASY PRESS; white wove paper; all edges trimmed; dust wrapper moderate blue (182) wove paper printed in black and moderate reddish brown (43).

Publication date: May 10, 1955

Price: 5s

Number of copies: 100

Note: Another 199 copies were published on May 26, 1955, and are indistinguishable from the first 100.

Contents: "Matter and spirit", pp. 22–23; "Earthborn", p. 24; and "Cameleon", p. 26.

Note: The poem "Cameleon" appears here for the first time in print.

Note: The contents also include "The beachhead", "Tamer and hawk", and "For a birthday", all of which were previously collected.

B4   NEW POEMS 1955   1955

New Poems | [interrupted rule with decorative circle in center] [within decorative circle] 1955 | *Edited by* | PATRIC DICKINSON | J. C. HALL | ERICA MARX | *with an introduction* | [publisher's logo] | *London* | MICHAEL JOSEPH

Collation: [1–7]⁸ + [8]⁶ = 62 leaves; 202 × 130 mm.

Binding: Quarter bound in dark reddish brown (44) cloth with white and moderate reddish brown (43) decorative paper covered boards and lettered across the spine in gold: *New* | *Poems* | [rule interrupted with dot in center] | *1955* | [rule interrupted with dot in center] | *a* | *P.E N.* | *Anthology* | [publisher's logo] | MICHAEL | JOSEPH; white wove paper; all edges trimmed; top edges stained dark reddish brown (44); white wove endpapers; dust wrapper moderate reddish orange (37) wove paper printed in dark purplish blue (201).

Publication date: October 17, 1955

Price: 12s 6d

Number of copies: 2,500

Contents: "Jesus and His mother", pp. 16–17, collected in *TSOM, TE* and *P 50–66*.

Note: The contents also contain "Earthborn" which was previously collected.

B5   NEW LINES   1956

NEW LINES | [decorative rule] | *An Anthology* | *edited by* | ROBERT CONQUEST | LONDON | MACMILLAN & CO LTD | NEW YORK · ST MARTIN'S PRESS | 1956

Collation: [1–7]⁸ = 56 leaves; 227× 137 mm.

Binding: Bound in moderate green (145) cloth and lettered across the spine in gold: NEW | LINES | [decorative rule] | *An* | *Anthology* | *Macmillan*; white wove paper; all edges trimmed; white wove endpapers; dust wrapper white wove paper printed in moderate bluish green (164).

Publication date: June 28, 1956

Price: 12s 6d

Number of copies: 1,500; second printing, September 24, 1956, 750 copies; third printing, April 23, 1957, 1,000 copies; fourth printing, October 25, 1961, 1,000 copies; fifth printing, January 26, 1967, 500 copies in cloth and 3,000 copies in paper wrappers.

Contents: "On the move", pp. 31–33, collected in *TSOM, SP, TE, P 50–66*; "Human condition", pp. 33–34, collected in *TSOM*; "Merlin in the cave: he speculates without a book", pp. 34–37, collected in *TSOM*; "Autumn chapter in a novel", pp. 37–38, collected in *TSOM, P 50–66*; "A plan of self-subjection", pp. 38–39, collected in *TSOM*; "Puss in boots to the giant", pp. 39–40, collected in *TSOM*; "The inherited estate", pp. 40–42, collected in *TSOM*.

Note: The poems "Puss in boots to the giant" and "The inherited estate" appear here for the first time in print.

B. BOOKS AND PAMPHLETS

Note: The contents also include "Lerici" which was previously collected.

B6   NEW POEMS 1956   1956

New Poems | [rule interrupted with decorative circle in center] [within decorative circle] 1956 | *Edited by* | STEPHEN SPENDER | ELIZA-BETH JENNINGS | DANNIE ABSE | [publisher's logo] | *London* | MICHAEL JOSEPH

Collation: [1–7]⁸ + [8]¹⁰ = 66 leaves; 202 × 130 mm.

Binding: Quarter bound in dark yellowish pink (30) cloth with white, light yellowish pink (28), light olive gray (112) and deep purple (219) decorative paper covered boards and lettered across the spine in white: *New* | *Poems* | [rule interrupted with dot in center] | *1956* | [rule interrupted with dot in center] | *a* | *P. E N.* | *Anthology* | [publisher's logo] | MICHAEL JOSEPH; white wove paper; all edges trimmed; top edges stained dark yellowish pink (30); white wove endpapers; dust wrapper moderate greenish blue (173) wove paper printed in dark blue (183).

Publication date: July 2, 1956

Price: 12s 6d

Number of copies: 2,500; second printing, September 7, 1956, 500 copies.

Contents: "The silver age", p. 113; and "The corridor", pp. 113–114, collected in *TSOM*.

B7   POETRY NOW   1956

POETRY NOW | *an anthology* | *edited by* | G. S. FRASER | FABER AND FABER | 24 Russell Square | London
Collation: [1–12]⁸ + [13]⁴ = 100 leaves; 202 × 132 mm.

Binding: Bound in dark yellowish pink (30) cloth and lettered across the spine in gold: *POETRY* | *NOW* | an | anthology | edited | by | G. S. FRASER | Faber | and | Faber; white wove paper; all edges trimmed; white wove endpapers; dust wrapper light blue gray (190) wove paper printed in black and vital red (11).

Publication date: October 12, 1956

Price: 15s

Number of copies: 3,390

Contents: "Light sleeping", pp. 81–82, collected in *TMB*.

Note: Contents also contain "Helen's rape" which was previously collected.

New Poems | [rule interrupted with decorative circle in center] [within decorative circle] 1957 | *Edited by* | KATHLEEN NOTT | C. DAY LEWIS | THOMAS BLACKBURN | [publisher's logo] | *London* | MICHAEL JOSEPH

Collection: $[1–8]^8 + [9]^6 = 70$ leaves; 202×132 mm.

Binding: Quarter bound in brilliant greenish yellow (98) cloth with black and white decorative paper covered boards and lettered across the spine in black: *New* | *Poems* | [rule interrupted with a dot in center] | 1957 | [rule interrupted with a dot in center] | *a* | *P. E N.* | *Anthology* | [publisher's logo] | MICHAEL JOSEPH; white wove paper; all edges trimmed; white wove endpapers; dust wrapper pale green (149) wove paper printed in dark purplish blue (201).

Publication date: October 21, 1957

Price: 15s

Number of copies: 2,600

Contents: "Canzon: the flagellants", pp. 59–60 which is an earlier version of "The beaters" which was published in *TSOM* prior to the appearance of the earlier version in this book.

Note: The contents also contain "Vox humana" which was previously collected.

New Poems | [rule interrupted with decorative circle in center] [within decorative circle] 1958 | *Edited by* | BONAMY DOBRÉE | LOUIS MacNEICE | PHILIP LARKIN | [publisher's logo] | *London* | MICHAEL JOSEPH

Collation: $[1–7]^8 + [8]^6 = 62$ leaves; 200×132 mm.

Binding: Quarter bound in vital red (11) cloth with white, strong red (12), dark gray (266) and light olive (106) decorative paper covered boards and lettered across the spine in white: *New* | *Poems* | [rule interrupted with dot in center] | *1958* | [rule interrupted with dot in center] | *a* | *P. E N.* | *Anthology* | [publisher's logo] | MICHAEL | JOSEPH; white wove paper; all edges trimmed; white wove endpapers; dust wrapper light gray (264) wove paper printed in dark reddish orange (38).

Publication date: November 10, 1958

Price: 13s 6d

Number of copies: 2,600

Contents: "The byrnies", pp. 44–45, collected in *MSC, SP, TE, P 50–66, M & MSC.*

B10   THE GUINNESS BOOK OF POETRY   1959
1957/58

THE GUINNESS | BOOK OF POETRY | 1957/58 | [publisher's logo] | PUTNAM | 42 GREAT RUSSELL STREET | LONDON MCMLIX

Collation: [1–9]^8 = 72 leaves; 215 × 140 mm.

Binding: Bound in moderate blue (182) cloth and lettered across the spine in gold: [block of five rules] | *The* | *Guinness* | *Book of* | *Poetry* | [block of five rules] | *2* | [block of three rules] | *PUTNAM* | [block of three rules]; white wove paper; all edges trimmed; top edges stained pale blue (185); white wove endpapers; dust wrapper white wove paper printed in black and light blue (181).

Publication date: May 4, 1959

Price: 10s 6d

Number of copies: 3,000

Contents: "Interrogated to interrogator", p. 69.

B11   THE GUINNESS BOOK OF POETRY   1960
1958/59

THE GUINNESS | BOOK OF POETRY | 1958/59 | [publisher's logo] | PUTNAM | 42 GREAT RUSSELL STREET | LONDON

Collation: [1–7]^8 + [8]^{10} + [9]^8 = 74 leaves; 215 × 139 mm.

Binding: Bound in moderate blue (182) cloth and lettered across the spine in gold: [block of five rules] | *The* | *Guinness* | *Book of* | *Poetry* | [block of five rules] | *3* | [block of three rules] | *PUTNAM* | [block of three rules]; white wove paper; all edges trimmed; top edges stained pale blue (185); white wove endpapers; dust wrapper white wove paper printed in black and brilliant orange yellow (67).

Publication date: April 11, 1960

Price: 10s 6d

Number of copies: 3,000

Contents: "All-night burlesque", p. 65.

B12 45–60 AN ANTHOLOGY OF ENGLISH 1960
POETRY 1945–60

45–60 | AN ANTHOLOGY OF | ENGLISH POETRY | 1945–60 |
Chosen by | THOMAS BLACKBURN | [publisher's logo] | PUTNAM
| 42 GREAT RUSSELL STREET | LONDON

Collation: [1–11]⁸ = 88 leaves; 185 × 110 mm.

Binding: Bound in strong red (12) cloth and lettered on the spine in gold:
[across] BLACKBURN | [down] 45–60 AN ANTHOLOGY OF
ENGLISH POETRY | [across] PUTNAM; white wove paper; all
edges trimmed; top edges stained strong red (12); dark red (16) wove endpapers; dust wrapper white wove paper printed in black, light gray (264),
strong red (12) and brilliant greenish yellow (98).

Publication date: November 14, 1960

Price: 18s

Number of copies: 3,500

Contents: "The book of the dead", p. 87, collected in *MSC, TE,* and *M &
MSC;* "The monster", pp. 89–90, collected in *MSC* and *M & MSC.*

Note: The contents also include "The corridor" which was previously
collected.

B13 THE GUINNESS BOOK OF POETRY 1961
1959/60

*THE GUINNESS | BOOK OF POETRY | 1959/60 | [publisher's
logo] | PUTNAM | 42 GREAT RUSSELL STREET | LONDON*

Collation: [1–7]⁸ + [8]⁶ + [9]⁸ = 70 leaves; 216 × 138 mm.

Binding: Bound in moderate blue (182) cloth and lettered across the spine in
gold: [block of five rules] | *The* | *Guinness* | *Book of* | *Poetry* | [block of five
rules] | 4 | [block of three rules] | *PUTNAM* | [block of three rules];
white wove paper; all edges trimmed; top edges stained pale blue (185); white
wove endpapers; dust wrapper white wove paper printed in black and strong
purplish red (255).

Publication date: May 8, 1961

Price: 10s 6d

Number of copies: 3,000

Contents: "Map of the city", p. 69, collected in *MSC* and *M & MSC* as
"A map of the city".

B14 COMMISSIONED POEMS 1962 1962

The Poetry Festival was held at the San Francisco | Museum of Art from June 21 through June 24, 1962. | The Festival was dedicated to the memory of Dag | Hammarskjold and the Cause of World Peace. | [in simulated open face type] COMMISSIONED POEMS | 1962 | POETRY FESTIVAL | the POETRY CENTER, San Francisco State College

Collation: One gathering of 17 leaves; 276 × 210 mm.

Binding: Stapled into a heavy white wove paper wrapper printed on the upper wrapper in black and vital orange (48) and on the spine in vital orange (48); the rear wrapper remains white. Lettered across the upper wrapper, as part of a block print of a man holding a poster: POETRY | FESTIVAL. Beneath the lettering is a 15 × 83 mm. portion of the upper wrapper that has been cut out and COMMISSIONED POEMS | 1962 from the title page shows through; white wove paper; all edges trimmed.

Publication date: "late spring 1962"

Price: distributed free

Number of copies: "two hundred and fifty to five hundred copies, no more"

Note: Publication details were provided by James Schevill who edited the publication.

Contents: "In the tank", p. 12, collected in *T*.

Note: The poem "In the tank" appears here for the first time in print.

B15 POET'S CHOICE 1962

a. *First edition:*

POET'S CHOICE | [rule with a simple knot in its center] | EDITED BY | Paul Engle and Joseph Langland | [publisher's logo] | THE DIAL PRESS NEW YORK 1962

Collation: [1–8]¹⁶ + [9]⁴ + [10–11]¹⁶ = 164 leaves; 230–232 × 154–156 mm.

Binding: Bound in strong reddish brown (40) cloth and lettered across the spine in gold: [decorative device] | [down] POET'S CHOICE | [across] [decorative device] | EDITED BY | ENGLE | AND | LANGLAND | [publisher's logo] | DIAL; white wove paper, top edges trimmed, other edges untrimmed; deep reddish orange (38) wove endpapers; dust wrapper shiny pale orange yellow (73) wove paper printed in black, gold, and deep reddish orange (38).

Publication date: October 29, 1962

Price: $6.00 until December 31, 1962, and after that $6.95.

B. BOOKS AND PAMPHLETS

Number of copies: Data unavailable from the publisher.

Contents: Prose statement with reproduction of Thom Gunn's signature explaining why he chose "My sad captains" as his choice for inclusion in this book, p. 279.

Note: The prose statement appears here in print for the first time.

b. *First paperback edition:*

POET'S | CHOICE | [rule with a single knot in its center] | EDITED BY | Paul Engle and Joseph Langland | [publisher's logo] A DELTA BOOK · 1966

Collation: 160 single leaves; 202 × 134 mm.

Binding: A perfect binding glued into a white heavy wove paper wrapper printed in shiny black, medium gray (265) and vital green (139) and lettered on the spine: [across] [in vital green (139)] 6982 [down] [in black] POET'S CHOICE edited by Engle and Langland [across] [in vital green (139)] [publisher's logo]; the upper wrapper is lettered across [in medium gray (265)] $1.95 $2.25 IN CANADA | [surrounded by a vital green (139) border connecting with the lower panel] [in black] POET'S | CHOICE | [on a vital green (139) panel] [in white] edited by Paul Engle and Joseph Langland | [in black] over one hundred great poets choose their | favorite poem from their own work | and give the reasons for their choices. | [in white] Robert Frost / William Carlos Williams | Marianne Moore / Conrad Aiken | E. E. Cummings / Archibald MacLeish | Robert Graves / Langston Hughes | Ogden Nash / Robert Penn Warren | John Betjeman / Theodore Roethke | Stephen Spender / Karl Shapiro | Randall Jarrell / John Ciardi / Allen Tate | Robert Lowell / Howard Nemerov | Allen Ginsberg / Alistair Reed | con't on back cover | [in dark gray (266)] [publisher's logo] | DELTA; on the rear wrapper [on a vital green (139) panel] [in dark gray (266)] [publisher's logo] | [in white] E. J. Pratt / Edmund Blunden / Louise Bogan | Leonine Adams / Oscar Williams / Robert Francis | Brewster Ghiselin / Earle Birney / Richard Eberhart | John Holmes / Patrick Kavanagh / Stanley Kunitz | E. L. Mayo / Phyllis McGinley / William Empson | Richmond Lattimore / Vernon Watkins / Elizabeth Bishop | J. V. Cunningham / Josephine Miles / Kenneth Patchen | Roy Fuller / Irving Layton / George Barker | John Frederick Nims / Delmore Schwartz / John Berryman | Barbara Howes / William Stafford / Henry Rago | John Malcolm Brinnin / Peter Viereck / Gwendolyn Brooks | Charles Causely / Joseph Langland / John Heath-Stubbs | William Jay Smith / Lawrence Ferlinghetti | William Meredith / Reed Whittemore / James Schevill | Richard Wilbur / Kingsley Amis / Donald Davie | Anthony Hecht / Philip Larkin / Howard Moss | Daniel G. Hoffman / Denise Levertov / William H. Matchett | Louis Simpson / Edgar Bowers / Michael Hamburger | Vassar

B. BOOKS AND PAMPHLETS

Miller / Donald Justice / John Wain | Elizabeth Jennings / James Merrill / W. D. Snodgrass | David Wagoner / Henri Coulette / Galway Kinnell | W. S. Merwin / Charles Tomlinson / Phyllis Webb | William Dickey / Donald Hall / Thomas Kinsella | Philip Levine / Anne Sexton / Thom Gunn / John Hollander | X. J. Kennedy / Ted Hughes / Jay McPherson | Leonard Cohen / John Hall Wheelock / John Crowe Ransom | Mark VanDoren / C. Day Lewis / Paul Engle | Robinson Jeffers | [in dark gray (266)] Dell Publishing Co., Inc. Printed in U S A; white wove paper; all edges trimmed.

Publication date: January 1966

Price: $1.95

Number of copies: Data unavailable from publisher.

Contents: Same as B15a.

c. *Second paperback edition:*

POET'S CHOICE | *EDITED BY* | *Paul Engle and Joseph Langland* | *with a new introduction by Paul Engle* | [publisher's logo] | TIME Reading Program Special Edition | TIME INCORPORATED · NEW YORK

Collation: 168 single leaves; 202 × 130 mm.

Binding: A perfect binding glued into a card cover that has a wavy pattern in multiple shades of blue, green, tan, and gray with the title always in white, across the spine: POET'S | CHOICE | edited | by | Engle | and | Langland; on the upper wrapper: POET'S | CHOICE | edited by Paul Engle | and Joseph Langland; on the rear wrapper in the upper right corner there is the signature of "Frank Bozzo" and a publisher's logo in the lower left corner; white wove paper; all edges trimmed; inner front and inner rear wrappers moderate greenish yellow (102).

Publication date: August 9, 1966

Price: $1.25 to subscribers

Number of copies: 80,000

Contents: Same as B15a.

B16   FIVE AMERICAN POETS   1963

Five | *American Poets* | [rule] | EDGAR BOWERS | HOWARD NEMEROV | HYAM PLUTZIK | LOUIS SIMPSON | WILLIAM STAFFORD | *edited by* | *Thom Gunn and Ted Hughes* | FABER AND FABER | 24 Russell Square | London

Collation: [1–7]⁸ = 56 leaves; 216 × 137 mm.

Binding: Bound in gray purplish blue (204) cloth and lettered down the spine in gold: [enclosed in a ruled box] FIVE AMERICAN POETS *Faber and Faber*; white wove paper; all edges trimmed; white wove endpapers; dust wrapper pale yellow green (121) wove paper printed in black, deep purplish blue (197) and deep reddish orange (36).

Publication date: May 31, 1963

Price: 21s

Number of copies: 2,500

Contents: "Foreword", (signed "T.G. T.H.") p. 7; "Edgar Bowers", p. 13; "Howard Nemerov", p. 33; "Hyam Plutzik", p. [55]; "Louis Simpson", p. [71]; and "William Stafford", p. [95].

Note: The "Foreword" and all the introductory biographical notes were collaborative efforts of Thom Gunn and Ted Hughes and appear here in print for the first time.

B17   EROTIC POETRY   1963

[left-hand title page] [in black] Erotic Poetry | [in strong blue (178)] DECORATION BY WARREN CHAPPELL
[right-hand title page] [in black and strong blue (178)] [line drawing] | [in black] *The Lyrics, Ballads, Idyls | and Epics of Love—* | *Classical to Contemporary* | *Edited by WILLIAM COLE* | Forward by Stephen Spender | [in strong blue (178)] [publisher's logo] | [in strong blue (178)] [rule] | [in black] RANDOM HOUSE | [in strong blue (178)] 1963

Collation: [1–13]¹⁶+[14]⁸+[15–18]¹⁶ = 280 leaves; 238 × 157–160 mm.

Binding: Bound in moderate green (145) cloth and lettered across the spine in gold: [in deep red (13)] [three rules] | [in deep red (13)] [a band of scallop shell design] | Erotic | Poetry | [dot] | WILLIAM | COLE | [in deep red (13)] [a band of scallop shell design] | [publisher's logo] | RANDOM HOUSE | [in deep red (13)] [three rules]; on the upper cover in gold: EROTIC POETRY | [in deep red (13)] [line drawing]; white wove paper; top and bottom edges trimmed, fore-edges untrimmed; top edges stained deep pink (3); light gray brown (60) wove endpapers; dust wrapper white wove paper printed in black, brilliant yellow (83), strong yellow (84), deep red (13), deep green (142), strong yellowish green (131), brilliant greenish blue (168), pale orange yellow (73), moderate yellowish brown (77) and dark brown (59).

Publication date: September 1963

Price: $8.95

Number of copies: Publisher prefers not to reveal the number of copies printed.

Contents: "Das liebesleben", pp. 402–403.

Note: The contents also contain "Loot" previously collected.

B18   THE CONCISE ENCYCLOPEDIA OF   1963
ENGLISH AND AMERICAN POETS AND
POETRY

a. *First edition:*

The Concise Encyclopedia of | ENGLISH AND AMERICAN | Poets and Poetry | Edited by | STEPHEN SPENDER and | DONALD HALL | [publisher's logo] Hutchinson of London

Collation: [1–26]⁸ = 208 leaves; 246 × 185 mm.

Binding: Bound in moderate orange yellow (71) cloth and lettered across the spine in gold: [rule] | [title on dark red (16) panel] THE CONCISE | Encyclopedia of | English | and American | Poets & Poetry | [rule] | Edited by | STEPHEN SPENDER | & DONALD HALL | [publisher's logo] | HUTCHINSON; in the lower right hand corner of the upper cover blind stamped [publisher's series logo]; white wove paper and white shiny paper; all edges trimmed; top edges stained moderate orange (53); white wove endpapers with shiny composite photograph of books of poetry displayed on bookshelves; dust wrapper heavy white wove paper printed with the same photograph as used on endpapers with additional printing in black and brilliant greenish yellow (98).

Note: Of this edition the title page of all copies examined is tipped in.

Publication date: October 28, 1963

Price: £5.00

Number of copies: Publisher prefers not to reveal the number of copies printed.

Contents: "Thomas Chatterton", pp. 72–73; "Hart Crane", pp. 101–102; "Sir Walter Raleigh", pp. 270–271; "Theodore Roethke", pp. 277–278; "[Arthur] Yvor Winters", p. 359; and "Thomas Wyatt", pp. 362–363.

Note: The six prose statements appear here in print for the first time.

b. *First American edition:*

The Concise Encyclopedia of | ENGLISH AND AMERICAN | Poets and Poetry | Edited by | STEPHEN SPENDER and | DONALD HALL | HAWTHORN BOOKS INC · *Publishers* · NEW YORK

B. BOOKS AND PAMPHLETS

Collation: [1–26]⁸ = 208 leaves; 247 × 187 mm.

Binding: Bound in moderate blue (182) cloth and lettered across the spine in gold: [title and editors within a gold rule border] THE CONCISE | ENCYCLOPEDIA OF | ENGLISH AND | AMERICAN | POETS & POETRY | EDITED BY | STEPHEN SPENDER | AND DONALD HALL | HAWTHORN; white wove paper and white shiny paper; all edges trimmed; top edges stained dark blue gray (192); endpapers the same as in the first edition; dust wrapper the same as for the first edition with the substitution of: [in white] HAWTHORN [instead of HUTCHINSON] at the foot of the spine panel of the dust wrapper.

Publication date: 1963

Note: The publisher does not have more precise information on the date of publication of the first printing or subsequent reprints.

Price: $17.95

Note: $17.95 was the price supplied by the publisher, however the one copy of the dust wrapper found for examination was printed with the price $12.95/ $15.00 on the front inner flap.

Number of copies: The publisher does not have data on the number of copies printed in the first printing or subsequent reprints.

Note: On the verso of the title page of the first printing of the American edition there is a statement "Printed in England" which is not present in the second printing.

Contents: Same as B18a.

B19   NEW POEMS 1963   1963

a. *First edition:*

[abstract floral design] | NEW POEMS | 1963 | A P.E.N. Anthology of | Contemporary Poetry | [abstract floral design] | *Edited by* | LAWRENCE DURRELL | HUTCHINSON OF LONDON

Collation: [1–10]⁸ = 80 leaves; 200 × 133 mm.

Binding: Quarter bound in black imitation-cloth paper with white paper covered boards printed in dark gray (266) and vital red (11) and lettered across the spine: [in gold] New | Poems | [in white] [bulging rule] | [in gold] 1963 | [in white] [publisher's logo] | [in white] HUTCHINSON; white wove paper; all edges trimmed; white wove endpapers; dust wrapper white wove paper printed in black and vital red (11).

Publication date: November 18, 1963

Price: 21s

Number of copies: Publisher prefers not to reveal the number of copies printed.

Contents: "A crab", p. 57; "The goddess", p. 58, collected in *AG, T, P 50–66.*

b. *First American edition:*

[abstract floral design] | NEW POEMS | 1963 | A British | P.E.N. Anthology | [abstract floral design] | *Edited by* | LAWRENCE DURRELL | HARCOURT, BRACE & WORLD, INC. | NEW YORK

Collation: [1–10]⁸ = 80 leaves; 198 × 132 mm.

Binding: Quarter bound in black imitation-cloth paper with white paper covered boards printed in dark gray (266) and vital red (11) and lettered across the spine: [in gold] New | [in gold] Poems | [in white] [bulging rule] | [in gold] 1963 | [in white] HARCOURT | [in white] BRACE; white wove paper; all edges trimmed; white wove endpapers; dust wrapper shiny white wove paper printed in black and moderate blue (182).

Publication date: April 8, 1964

Price: $3.95

Number of copies: 1,030

Contents: Same as B19a.

B20   15 POEMS FOR WILLIAM   1964
                       SHAKESPEARE

a. *First trade edition:*

[entire text of title page is enclosed within a double rule border] 15 *Poems* | *for William* | *Shakespeare* | [rule] | *edited by* Eric W. White | *with an introduction by* | Patrick Garland | John Lehmann & | William Plomer | [rule] | 1964: *Stratford-upon-Avon* | The Trustees & Guardians | of Shakespeare's Birthplace

Collation: [1]¹² = 12 leaves; 249 × 148 mm.

Binding: Sewn into a lighter shade of light yellowish brown (76) wallet-edge wove paper wrapper; on the upper wrapper: [ornamental floral border printed in very dark green (147) serving as a border surrounding the title] [in decorative type] 15 | [in decorative type] POEMS | *for William* | *Shakespeare* | Edmund Blunden Dom Moraes | Charles Causley Peter Porter | Roy Fuller   W. J. Snodgrass | Thom Gunn   Stephen Spender | Randall Jarrell   Derek Walcott | Thomas Kinsella   Vernon Watkins | Laurie Lee

David Wright | Hugh MacDiarmid | [thick ornamental floral rule in very dark green (147)]; white wove paper; all edges trimmed.

Publication date: June 1964

Price: 3s 6d

Number of copies: 1,000

Contents: "The kiss", p. [15], later collected and retitled "The kiss at Bayreuth" in *AG* and *T.*

Note: The poem "The kiss" appears here for the first time in print.

b. *First limited edition:*

[The transcription of the title page is identical to that of the first trade edition.]

Collation: [1]^{12} = 12 leaves; 247 × 149 mm.

Binding: Bound in paper vellum covered boards stamped in gold on the upper cover: [portrait of William Shakespeare surrounded by a rule and then surrounded by] ∧ WILLIAM SHAKESPEARE ∧ STRATFORD UPON AVON | 1564 ∧ 1964 | 15 POEMS | *for William* | *Shakespeare*; white wove paper; all edges trimmed; white wove endpapers; the verso of the title page carries a statement of limitation and the copy number.

Publication date: June 1964

Price: 10s 6d

Number of copies: 100

Contents: Same as B20a.

B21   NEW POETRY 1964   1964

[cover title] [top left side of the upper wrapper] [in black] Sylvia Plath | Philip Larkin | R. S. Thomas | Thom Gunn | Ted Hughes | Karen Gershon | Jon Stallworthy | William Stafford | Louis Simpson | Theodore Roethke | Adrienne Rich | Robert Bly | James Wright | Anne Sexton | [top right side of the upper wrapper] [in white] New | Poetry | 1964 | [in black] PRICE ONE SHILLING | CRITICAL QUARTERLY POETRY SUPPLEMENT NUMBER 5 | [graphic design lower half of upper wrapper]

Collation: [1]^{12} = 12 leaves; 219 × 132 mm.

Binding: Stapled into a white card wrapper printed in black and deep greenish yellow (100); the rear wrapper gives information about The Critical Quarterly Society; white wove paper; all edges trimmed.

Publication date: autumn 1964

Price: 1s

Number of copies: 9,000

Contents: "Berlin in ruins", p. 10, collected in *AG* and *T.*

B22   THE OBSERVER REVISITED   1964

THE | OBSERVER | REVISITED | 1963–64 | *Compiled by* | CYRIL DUNN | [publisher's logo] HODDER AND STOUGHTON

Collation: [1–16]⁸ = 128 leaves; 216 × 135 mm.

Binding: Bound in dark purplish red (259) imitation-cloth paper covered boards and lettered across the spine in gold: *The | Observer | Revisited | ** |* compiled by | CYRIL | DUNN | [publisher's logo]; white wove paper; all edges trimmed; top edges stained moderate red (15); white wove endpapers; dust wrapper shiny white paper printed in black and vital green (139).

Publication date: October 26, 1964

Price: 21s

Number of copies: 4,000

Contents: "Driving to Florida", p. 256.

B23   MOMENTS OF TRUTH   1965

[decorative rule: hourglass alternating with abstract floral design] | Moments of Truth | Nineteen Short Poems | by Living Poets | [decorative rule: (as above)] | London | The Keepsake Press | 1965 | [decorative rule: (as above)]

Collation: [1]¹⁴ = 14 leaves; 171 × 108 mm.

Binding: Stapled into a lighter shade of light gray yellowish brown (79) card wrapper printed in dark yellowish brown (78) on the right side of the upper wrapper: MOMENTS | OF TRUTH | George Barker | Martin Bell | John Betjeman | Edwin Brock | Robert Conquest | Gavin Ewart | Roy Fuller | Thom Gunn | Bernard Gutteridge | Francis Hope | Ted Hughes | Edward Lowbury | Kathleen Nott | Peter Porter | Peter Redgrove | James Reeves | Peter Russell | David Wevill | Hugo Williams; the left side of the upper wrapper and the entire rear wrapper have an applied serigraph of a wavy pattern in multiple shades of gray and purplish blue; white wove paper; top edges untrimmed, other edges trimmed.

Publication date: autumn 1965

Price: 5s

Number of copies: 328

B. BOOKS AND PAMPHLETS

Note: The colophon states "Of this edition each contributor receives 12 copies as keepsakes; 100 are for sale."

Contents: "The night out", p. 7, collected in *P* (untitled) and in *P 50–66* (as "Canning town").

Note: The poem "The night out" appears here for the first time in print.

B24   WILLIAM CARLOS WILLIAMS   1966

a. *First edition, hardcover issue:*

WILLIAM CARLOS | WILLIAMS | A COLLECTION OF CRITICAL ESSAYS | Edited by | *J. Hillis Miller* | Prentice-Hall, Inc. [publisher's logo] *Englewood Cliffs, N.J.*

Collation: [1–6]¹⁶ = 96 leaves; 203 × 140 mm.

Binding: Bound in black cloth and lettered down the spine in gold: WILLIAM CARLOS WILLIAMS *Edited by* J. Hillis Miller Prentice-Hall; white wove paper; all edges trimmed; white wove endpapers; dust wrapper white wove paper printed in shiny black and very light bluish green (162).

Publication date: June 17, 1966

Price: $3.95

Number of copies: 5,000

Contents: "William Carlos Williams", pp. 171–173.

Note: This reprint contains only the final seven paragraphs of the original essay.

b. *First edition, paperback issue:*

[The transcription of the title page is identical with that of the first edition, hardcover issue.]

Collation: 96 single leaves; 202 × 137 mm.

Binding: A perfect binding glued in heavy white wove paper wrappers printed in shiny black and very light bluish green (162); lettered down the spine in light bluish green (162): [in two lines] TWENTIETH | CENTURY VIEWS | [in one line] WILLIAM CARLOS WILLIAMS | [in two lines] *Edited by* | J. Hillis MILLER | [across the spine] S-TC-61 | [publisher's series logo] | A SPECTRUM BOOK; on the upper wrapper printed in light bluish green (162): TWENTIETH CENTURY VIEWS | WILLIAM CARLOS | WILLIAMS | *A Collection of Critical Essays* | *Edited by* J. HILLIS MILLER | [abstract illustration] |

B. BOOKS AND PAMPHLETS

A SPECTRUM BOOK [publisher's series logo] S-TC-61 $1.95; on the rear wrapper [in black] there is a publisher's statement.

Publication date: June 17, 1966

Price: $1.95

Number of copies: 8,000

Note: The book was reprinted but the publisher does not have the date of reprinting or the number of copies of the reprint edition.

Contents: Same as B24a.

B25   NEW POEMS 1966   1966

[cover title] [in black] CRITICAL QUARTERLY POETRY SUPPLEMENT NUMBER 7 | [rule in white] | [in white] *New Poems 1966* | [rule in white] | [in black] Thom Gunn, Robert Lowell, R. S. Thomas, Gary Snyder, Ted Hughes | Randall Jarrell, Seamus Heaney, Donald Davie, Louis Simpson | Charles Tomlinson, Edward Braithwaite, Sylvia Plath | Iain Crichton Smith, David Holbrook, Elizabeth Jennings | [in white] [illustration of leaves] | [in black] PRICE | ONE SHILLING

Collation: [1]¹² = 12 leaves; 218 × 137 mm.

Binding: Stapled into a white card wrapper printed in black and vital purple (216); the rear wrapper gives information about The Critical Quarterly Society; white wove paper; all edges trimmed.

Publication date: autumn 1966

Price: 1s

Number of copies: 9,000

Contents: "Back to life", pp. 2–3, collected in *T*; "Pierce Street", pp. 3–4, collected in *T* and *P 50–66*.

B26   THE BEST OF GRANTA   1967

THE BEST OF | *Granta* | 1889–1966 | Edited by | JIM PHILIP | JOHN SIMPSON | NICHOLAS SNOWMAN | LONDON | SECKER & WARBURG

Collation: [1–7]¹⁶ = 112 leaves; 196 × 167 mm.

Binding: Bound in dark purplish red (259) imitation-cloth paper covered boards and lettered down the spine in gold: THE BEST OF *GRANTA* 1889–1966 SECKER & WARBURG; white wove paper; all edges trimmed; white wove endpapers; dust wrapper shiny white paper printed in black, vital red (11), and very light bluish green (162).

Publication date: June 5, 1967

Price: 25s

Number of copies: 4,000

Contents: "Elizabeth Barrett Barrett", pp. [127]–128.

B27   WORD IN THE DESERT   1968

WORD | IN THE DESERT | *The Critical Quarterly* | *Tenth Anniversary Number* | edited by | C. B. Cox and A. E. Dyson | *London* | OXFORD UNIVERSITY PRESS | NEW YORK TORONTO | 1968

Collation: [1–13]⁸ = 104 leaves; 216 × 137 mm.

Binding: Bound in deep reddish orange (36) cloth and lettered across the spine in gold: [double rule] | [title on a dark olive green (126) panel] Word | in the | Desert | [double rule] | OXFORD; white laid paper; all edges trimmed; white wove endpapers; dust wrapper white wove paper printed in shiny vital yellow (82), moderate olive brown (95) and vital reddish orange (34).

Publication date: July 25, 1968

Price: 35s

Number of copies: 1,978

Contents: "Aqueduct", p. 56, collected in *TMB*.

B28   SELECTED POEMS OF FULKE   1968
                        GREVILLE

a. *First edition:*

Selected Poems of | FULKE GREVILLE | Edited with an Introduction by | THOM GUNN | FABER AND FABER | 24 Russell Square | London

Collation: [1–10]⁸ = 80 leaves; 200 × 132 mm.

Binding: Bound in moderate blue (182) cloth and lettered across the spine in gold: [title on a black panel surrounded by a gold rule] *Selected* | *Poems* | *of* | *Fulke* | *Greville* | *Faber*; white wove paper; all edges trimmed; white wove endpapers; dust wrapper very light greenish blue (171) wove paper printed in black and strong reddish orange (35).

Publication date: September 30, 1968

Price: 21s

Number of copies: 4,000

Contents: "Note on text", p. 7; "Life and Works", pp. 9–12; "Introduction", pp. 13–41; footnotes throughout the book; all appear here for the first time in print.

b. *First American edition:*

Selected Poems of | FULKE GREVILLE | Edited with an Introduction by | THOM GUNN | [publisher's logo] | THE UNIVERSITY OF CHICAGO PRESS

Collation: [1–10]⁸ = 80 leaves; 200 × 132 mm.

Binding: Bound in moderate blue (182) cloth and lettered across the spine in gold: [title on a black panel surrounded by a gold rule] *Selected* | *Poems* | *of* | *Fulke* | *Greville* | CHICAGO; white wove paper; all edges trimmed; white wove endpapers; dust wrapper very light greenish blue (171) wove paper printed in black and strong reddish orange (35).

Publication date: April 29, 1969

Price: $4.75

Number of copies: 1,481

Contents: Same as B28a.

B29   RUTH PITTER: HOMAGE TO A POET   1969

a. *First edition:*

RUTH PITTER: | HOMAGE TO A POET | Edited by Arthur Russell | With an introduction | by | David Cecil | [initials within decorative oval] R P | rapp + whiting

Collation: [1–8]⁸ = 64 leaves; 215 × 137 mm.

Binding: Bound in white and dark greenish blue (174) linen-grained paper covered boards and lettered down the spine in gold: [across] [three rules] | Ruth Pitter: Homage to a poet [six-spoked decorative device] [across] [three rules]; on the upper cover in the lower left corner in gold: rapp + whiting; white laid paper; all edges trimmed; white wove endpapers; dust wrapper light blue gray (190) wove paper printed in black and strong blue (178).

Publication date: spring 1969

Price: 35s

Number of copies: 700

Contents: "Urania as poet", pp. 63–65.

Note: The prose statement "Urania as poet" appears here for the first time in print.

b. *First American edition:*

RUTH PITTER: | HOMAGE TO A POET | Edited by Arthur Russell | With an introduction | by | David Cecil | [initials within decorative oval] R P | Dufour Editions Inc.

Collation: [1–8]⁸ = 64 leaves; 215 × 137 mm.

Binding: Bound in white and dark greenish blue (174) linen-grained paper covered boards and lettered down the spine in gold: [across] [three rules] | Ruth Pitter: Homage to a Poet | [across] Dufour | [across] [three rules]; white laid paper; all edges trimmed; white wove endpapers; dust wrapper light blue gray (190) wove paper printed in black and strong blue (178).

Publication date: Data unavailable from publisher.

Price: $6.00

Number of copies: 300

Contents: Same as B29a

B30   CONTEMPORARY POETS OF THE   1970
            ENGLISH LANGUAGE

CONTEMPORARY POETS | OF THE | ENGLISH | LAN-GUAGE | WITH A PREFACE BY | C. DAY LEWIS | EDITOR | ROSALIE MURPHY | DEPUTY EDITOR | JAMES VINSON | ST JAMES PRESS | CHICAGO LONDON

Collation: [1]¹⁰ + [2–39]¹⁶ + [40]¹⁴ = 632 leaves; 245 × 173 mm.

Binding: Bound in brown black (65) cloth and lettered across the spine in gold: Contemporary | Poets | of the | English | Language | St. James Press; and across the upper cover in gold: Contemporary | Poets | of the | English | Language; white wove paper; all edges trimmed; white wove endpapers; dust wrapper of a linen finish gray yellowish brown (80) paper printed in gold.

Publication date: August 1970

Price: $25.00, £8.50

Number of copies: 3,000

Note: The book was retitled "CONTEMPORARY POETS" in the second printing, June 1, 1973, 1,000 copies; third printing, March 15, 1974, data on the number of copies of this reprint unavailable from the publisher. A second edition titled "CONTEMPORARY POETS" with different editors and design was published in June 1975 (St. James Press, London), August 1975 (St. Martin's Press, New York, N.Y.), total imprint 7,000 copies.

Contents: [autobiographical statement] p. 455; [biographical and critical statement about Gary Snyder] pp. 1026–1027.

Note: Both prose statements appear here for the first time in print.

Note: In the second edition (1975) the autobiographical statement by Thom Gunn was omitted.

B31   THE CAMBRIDGE MIND   1970

a. *First edition:*

THE | CAMBRIDGE | MIND | Ninety years of the *Cambridge Review* | 1879–1969 | [rule] | *edited by* ERIC HOMBERGER, | WILLIAM JANEWAY *and* SIMON SCHAMA | [publisher's logo] | JONATHAN CAPE | THIRTY BEDFORD SQUARE LONDON

Collation: [1–9]⁸ + [10]¹² + [11–18]⁸ + [19]⁶ + [20]⁸ = 162 leaves; 216 × 139 mm.

Binding: Bound in pink gray (10) imitation-cloth paper covered boards and lettered across the spine in gold: THE | CAMBRIDGE | MIND | [decorative loop] | EDITED BY | ERIC | HOMBERGER | WILLIAM | JANEWAY | AND | SIMON | SCHAMA | [publisher's logo]; white wove and shiny paper; all edges trimmed; white wove endpapers; dust wrapper white wove paper printed in strong pink (2) and black.

Publication date: October 29, 1970

Price: 80s

Number of copies: 3,000

Contents: [prose] "The energy of Dylan Thomas", pp. 285–287; [poem] "The death of a stranger", p. 288.

b. *First American edition:*

THE | CAMBRIDGE MIND | *Ninety Years of the Cambridge Review* | *1879–1969* | *edited by Eric Homberger,* | *William Janeway and Simon Schama* | *with illustrations* | [publisher's logo] *Little, Brown and Company* | *Boston Toronto*

Collation: [1–3]¹⁶ + [4]⁴ + [5–11]¹⁶ = 164 leaves; 208 × 138 mm.

Binding: Bound in strong purplish pink (255) imitation-cloth paper covered boards and lettered down the spine in deep purplish blue (197): [in two lines] THE *edited by Homberger, Janeway and Schama* | CAMBRIDGE MIND [across the spine] *Little, Brown;* on the upper cover, blind stamped publisher's logo in lower right corner; white wove paper; all edges trimmed; light gray purplish pink (261) wove endpapers; dust wrapper shiny white paper printed in deep purple (219), very deep purplish red (257) and moderate reddish brown (43).

Publication date: June 10, 1971

Price: $8.50

Number of copies: Publisher prefers not to reveal the number of copies printed.

Contents: Same as B31a

B32   A LISTENER ANTHOLOGY   1970

A Listener Anthology | August 1967–June 1970 | Edited by Karl Miller | British Broadcasting Corporation

Collation: [1–15]⁸ = 120 leaves; 228 × 151 mm.

Binding: Bound in gray reddish purple (245) imitation-cloth paper covered boards and lettered down the spine in gold: A Listener Anthology BBC; white wove paper; all edges trimmed; white wove endpapers; dust wrapper white wove paper printed in shiny black, pale yellow (89), and deep purple (219).

Publication date: November 26, 1970

Price: £2.25

Number of copies: 2,000

Contents: "Grasses", p. 162, collected in *M* and *M & MSC*.

B33   FOR BILL BUTLER   1971

For Bill Butler | Wallrich Books London | 1970

Collation: [1]⁴ + [2–8]⁸ + 1 loose leaf inserted = 61 leaves; 253 × 182 mm.

Note: A broadside poem folded twice and loosely inserted into the book is counted as one loose leaf since it is a part of the book and is listed in the contents.

Binding: Glued in a white card cover lettered down the spine in black: FOR BILL BUTLER Wallrich Books; on the upper wrapper, left of center, in black: FOR | BILL | BUTLER, plus a design of solid black trapezoidal blocks; on the rear wrapper is a similar design of interconnected trapezoidal blocks in black outline and printed left of center in black: FOR | BILL | BUTLER; white wove paper; all edges trimmed.

Publication date: "early 1971" (from the publisher)

Price: £2.25

Number of copies: 500

Contents: "The light", p. 49.

B34   NEW POEMS 1970–71   1971

[abstract floral design] | NEW POEMS | 1970–71 | A P.E.N. Anthology | of Contemporary Poetry | [abstract floral design] | *Edited by* | ALAN BROWNJOHN | SEAMUS HEANEY | JON STALLWORTHY | HUTCHINSON OF LONDON

Collation: [1–7]⁸ = 56 leaves; 195 × 127 mm.

Binding: Bound in black imitation-cloth paper covered boards and lettered down the spine in gold: NEW POEMS 1970/71 [across] [rule] A P.E.N. ANTHOLOGY HUTCHINSON; on the rear cover in the lower right corner in gold: ISBN 0 09 106770 7; white wove paper; all edges trimmed; light gray (264) wove endpapers; dust wrapper white wove paper printed in black, white, and brilliant yellowish green (130).

Publication date: April 19, 1971

Price: £1.50

Number of copies: Publisher prefers not to reveal the number of copies printed.

Contents: "The discovery of the Pacific", p. 41, collected in *M* and *M & MSC.*

B35   MARK IN TIME   1971

MARK IN TIME | PORTRAITS & POETRY / SAN FRAN-CISCO | PHOTOGRAPHER: CHRISTA FLEISHMANN CO-ORDINATOR: ROBERT E. JOHNSON | EDITOR: NICK HARVEY PUBLISHER: GLIDE PUBLICATIONS, SAN FRANCISCO

Collation: [1–12]⁸ = 96 leaves; 227 × 236 mm.

Binding: Bound in gray yellowish brown (80) cloth and lettered down the spine in pale yellow green (121); MARK IN TIME PORTRAITS & POETRY / SAN FRANCISCO; on the upper cover in pale yellow green (121): MARK IN TIME | PORTRAITS & POETRY / SAN FRANCISCO; white wove paper; all edges trimmed; deep purple (219) wove endpapers; dust wrapper shiny white paper printed in black and deep reddish purple (238).

Publication date: June 21, 1971

Price: $10.95

Number of copies: 2,500

Contents: [autobiographical statement] p. 177.

Note: This short autobiographical statement appears here for the first time in print.

Note: Contents also contain "The discovery of the Pacific" which was previously collected.

B36   50 MODERN AMERICAN & BRITISH   1973
POETS, 1920–1970

a. *First edition, hardcover issue:*

50 | MODERN | AMERICAN | & BRITISH | POETS, | 1920–1970 | [double rule] | *Edited, with a Biographical | and Critical Commentary, by* | LOUIS UNTERMEYER | DAVID McKAY COMPANY, INC. | *New York*

Collation: [1–12]¹⁶ = 192 leaves; 211 × 142 mm.

Binding: Bound in moderate blue (182) cloth and lettered down the spine: [in vital red (11)] UNTERMEYER [in gold] [in two lines] 50 MODERN AMERICAN | & BRITISH POETS, 1920–1970 [across] [in vital red (11)] [publisher's logo] | McKAY; white wove paper; all edges trimmed; white wove endpapers; dust wrapper white wove paper printed in shiny black, vital red (11) and vital blue (176).

Publication date: February 8, 1973

Price: $7.95

Number of copies: 7,250; second printing, August 1974, 1,500 copies at $11.95.

Contents: A short untitled, prose statement about syllabics and metrical verse, p. 333. The contents also contain two poems previously collected.

B. BOOKS AND PAMPHLETS

b. *First edition, paperback issue:*

[The transcription of the title page is identical with that of the first edition, hardcover issue.]

Collation: $[1-12]^{16}$ = 192 leaves; 212 × 142 mm.

Binding: Bound in heavy white wove paper and printed in shiny black, vital blue (176), and vital red (11) and lettered down the spine: [in three lines] [in black] 50 MODERN AMERICAN | & BRITISH POETS [in vital red (11)] 1920–1970 | [in vital red (11)] LOUIS UNTERMEYER [across] [in vital red (11)] McKAY [across] [in white on a vital blue (176) panel that extends across the entire lower quarter of the rear wrapper, the lower quarter of the spine and the lower quarter of the upper wrapper, the names of the poets included in the book] [beginning at the left on the rear wrapper and going across to the right of the upper wrapper] ROBERT FROST WALLACE STEVENS WILLIAM CARLOS WILLIAMS ANNA WICKHAM EZRA POUND MARIANNE MOORE T. S. ELIOT | CONRAD AIKEN ARCHIBALD MACLEISH E. E. CUMMINGS HART CRANE LANGSTON HUGHES RICHARD EBERHART STANLEY KUNITZ | A. D. HOPE W. H. AUDEN THEODORE ROETHKE STEPHEN SPENDER ELIZABETH BISHOP MURIEL RUKEYSER RANDALL JARRELL | JOHN BERRYMAN BARBARA HOWES DYLAN THOMAS JOHN MALCOLM BRINNIN GWENDOLYN BROOKS ROBERT LOWELL | WILLIAM JAY SMITH MAY SWENSON RICHARD WILBUR MONA VAN DUYN JAMES DICKEY LOUIS SIMPSON ANTHONY HECHT | W. D. SNODGRASS ALLEN GINSBERG W. S. MERWIN GALWAY KINNELL JOHN ASHBERY JAMES WRIGHT ANNE SEXTON THOM GUNN | ADRIENNE RICH DEREK WALCOTT TED HUGHES SYLVIA PLATH WENDELL BERRY LEROI JONES JIM HARRISON ERICA JONG; on the upper wrapper is printed in shiny black, vital red (11), and vital blue (176): 50 | [in black] MODERN | AMERICAN | & BRITISH | POETS [in vital red (11)] 1920–1970 | [in vital red (11)] LOUIS UNTERMEYER | [and then the vital blue (176) panel described above]; the rear wrapper is printed exactly the same as the upper wrapper; white wove paper; all edges trimmed.

Publication date: February 8, 1973

Price: $3.95

Number of copies: 2,600; second printing, August 1974, 3,500 copies at $4.95.

Contents: Same as B36a.

B. BOOKS AND PAMPHLETS

B37   CORGI MODERN POETS IN FOCUS: 5   1973

Corgi Modern Poets | in Focus: 5 | Edited by | DANNIE ABSE | CORGI
BOOKS | A DIVISION OF TRANSWORLD PUBLISHERS
LTD | A NATIONAL GENERAL COMPANY

Collation: 80 single leaves; 178 × 110 mm.

Binding: A perfect binding glued into a heavy white wove paper wrapper
stamped in very light gray, black and a spectrum of colors and lettered on
the spine in black: [across] 0 552 | 09187 | 1 | POETRY | [circle] | [down]
[in two lines] CORGI MODERN POETS IN FOCUS 5 | Edited
by Dannie Abse; on the upper wrapper printed in black: [upward in the
upper left corner] 0 552 09187 1 [across the upper right side] Ezra Pound |
Thom Gunn | Bernard Spencer | Sylvia Plath | Fleur Adcock | John Ormond
| Edited by Dannie Abse | [to the left of center] CORGI | MODERN
POETS | IN FOCUS | [on lower half] a multicolored and stylized 5; on
the rear wrapper is a listing of the contents of previous volumes in the series,
a publisher's statement, and a listing of prices.

Publication date: April 17, 1973

Price: 35p

Number of copies: 12,500

Contents: An untitled autobiographical prose statement on his own poetry,
pp. 37–39.

Note: The prose statement appears here in print for the first time. The
contents also contain eleven poems, all previously collected.

B38   LET THE POET CHOOSE   1973

a. *First edition, hardcover issue:*

[in gray yellow green (122)] *Let the* | *Poet Choose* | edited by JAMES
GIBSON | [publisher's logo] | HARRAP LONDON

Collation: [1–12]⁸ = 96 leaves; 216 × 138 mm.

Binding: Bound in vital orange (48) imitation-cloth paper covered boards
and lettered down the spine in gray olive green (127): LET THE POET
CHOOSE JAMES GIBSON HARRAP; white wove paper; all edges
trimmed; white wove endpapers; dust wrapper white wove paper printed in
shiny deep brown (56) and strong orange yellow (68).

Publication date: May 14, 1973

Price: £1.70

Number of copies: 2,000

Contents: Untitled prose statement explaining why he chose "The wound" and "Three" for inclusion in this book, p. 69.

Note: The prose statement appears here in print for the first time. The contents also contain the two poems (*vide supra*) which were previously collected.

b. *First edition, paperback issue:*

[The transcription of the title page is identical with that of the first edition, hardcover issue.]

Collation: [1–12]⁸ = 96 leaves; 215 × 138 mm.

Binding: Bound in heavy white paper with a simulated cloth texture and printed in gray brown (61) and vital orange yellow (66) and lettered down the spine in white: Gibson Let the Poet Choose [across] [publisher's logo]; on the upper wrapper is printed in white surrounded by concentric elliptical rules in white and vital orange yellow (66): edited by James Gibson; and in white surrounded by concentric white and vital orange yellow (66) circles: Let | the Poet | Choose; and below that in vital orange yellow (66), surrounded by a double interrupted rule of vital orange yellow (66) and white, facsimiles of the signatures of poets that contributed to the book; the rear wrapper has the same basic design with a publisher's statement inserted inside the concentric circles and across the bottom in white: HARRAP ISBN 0 245 519 343

Publication date: May 14, 1973

Price: 80p

Number of copies: 10,000; second printing, May 5, 1976, 5,000 copies at £1.25.

Contents: Same as B38a.

B39   BOTTEGHE OSCURE READER   1974

a. *First edition, hardcover issue:*

BOTTEGHE OSCURE | READER | Edited by GEORGE GARRETT | with the assistance of KATHERINE GARRISON BIDDLE | Introduction by GEORGE GARRETT | WESLEYAN UNIVERSITY PRESS | *Middletown, Connecticut*

Collation: [1–7]¹⁶ + [8–9]¹² + [10–16]¹⁶ = 248 leaves; 228 × 138 mm.

Binding: Bound in deep reddish orange (36) cloth and lettered up the spine in black: BOTTEGHE OSCURE | [across the foot of the spine] READER; white wove paper; all edges trimmed; white wove endpapers;

dust wrapper white wove paper printed in black and vital reddish orange (34).
Publication date: February 28, 1974

Price: $12.50

Number of copies: 750

Contents: "Apocryphal", pp. 179–180; "Excursion", pp. 180–181, collected in *TMB*.

b. *First edition, paperback issue:*

[The transcription of the title page is identical with that of the first edition, hardcover issue.]

Collation: [1–7]¹⁶ + [8–9]¹² + [10–16]¹⁶ = 248 leaves; 228 × 138 mm.

Binding: Glued into a heavy white paper wrapper printed in black and vital reddish orange (34) and lettered up the spine: in black BOTTEGHE OSCURE | [across the foot of the spine in vital reddish orange (34)] READER; the upper wrapper is lettered: [in black] BOTTEGHE | OSCURE | READER | [in white on a vital reddish orange (34) panel] [publisher's statement about the book]; the rear wrapper contains at the top, in the left corner, in black: 633 / Poetry & Short stories | [a list of contributors to this book] | [to the left in vital reddish orange (34)] WESLEYAN UNIVERSITY PRESS | [in vital reddish orange (34)] *Middletown, Connecticut 06457* | $2.95 | ISBN: 0–8195–6033–2 Printed in U.S.A.; white wove paper; all edges trimmed.

Publication date: February 28, 1974

Price: $2.95

Number of copies: 2,000

Contents: Same as B39a.

B40   BEN JONSON   1974

[left-hand title page] BEN JONSON [right-hand title page] Selected by | Thom Gunn | [publisher's logo] | Penguin Books

Collation: 104 single leaves; 182 × 110 mm.

Binding: A perfect binding glued into a heavy white paper cover and lettered down the spine: [in brilliant blue (177)] BEN JONSON [in strong purplish blue (196)] SELECTED BY THOM GUNN [across] [in white] D175 [down] [in two lines] [in white] ISBN 0 14 | 042.175 0 [across] [publisher's logo]; on the upper wrapper: [in white] POET TO POET [in upper right corner] [in white] [publisher's logo] | [in brilliant blue (177)] Ben Jonson | [in white] SELECTED BY | [in strong purplish blue (196)] Thom Gunn | [a portrait, surrounded by a white rule, of Ben Jonson in a multitude of colors with a superimposed insert black and white photograph of Thom Gunn surrounded by a white rule]; across the rear wrapper [in white] [upper left corner] POET TO POET [in upper right corner] [in white] [publisher's logo] | [in brilliant blue (177)] [publisher's statement] | [in lower left corner] [in white] United Kingdom 30p | Australia $1.00 (recommended) | New Zealand $1.00 | Canada $1.25 | U.S.A. $1.25 | [in lower right corner] [in white] Poetry | ISBN 014 | 042.175 0; white wove paper; all edges trimmed.

Publication date: June 27, 1974

Price: 30p

Number of copies: 10,000

Contents: "Introduction", pp. 9–22; "Notes", pp. 202–208; all appear here for the first time in print.

B41   WORLDS   1974

WORLDS | SEVEN MODERN POETS | CHARLES CAUSLEY | THOM GUNN | SEAMUS HEANEY | TED HUGHES | NORMAN MacCAIG | ADRIAN MITCHELL | EDWIN MORGAN | Photographs by | Fay Godwin, Larry Herman and Peter Abramowitsch | [rule] | Edited by Geoffrey Summerfield | Penquin Education

Collation: [1–9]^{16} = 144 leaves; 210 × 146 mm.

Binding: Glued into a heavy white wove cover with an imitation cloth texture on the exterior surfaces and printed in black, dark gray brown (62) and vital orange (48) and lettered down the spine: [in black] WORLDS [in two lines] seven | modern poets [in white] [in two lines] ISBN 0 14 | 08 0345 9 [across the foot of the spine] [publisher's logo]; on the upper wrapper in black: [upper left corner] WORLDS | seven modern poets | Charles Causley, Thom Gunn | Seamus Heaney, Ted Hughes | Norman MacCaig, Adrian Mitchell | Edwin Morgan | edited by Geoffrey Summerfield | [publisher's logo] [upper right corner] [a silhouette of a leafless tree] [across the bottom in vital orange (48) superimposed on dark gray brown (62)] [separate portraits of four of the seven poets included in the book]; the rear wrapper contains [in black] a similar silhouette of a leafless tree, [in vital orange (48) superimposed on dark gray brown (62)] a publisher's statement, [across the bottom] three additional separate portraits of poets included in the book, and: [in vital orange (48)] Published by | [in vital orange (48)] Penguin | [in vital orange (48)] Education | [in vital orange (48)] POETRY [in vital orange (48)] ISBN o 14 | [in vital orange (48)] 08 0345 9; white wove paper; all edges trimmed.

Publication date: September 26, 1974

Price: 80p

Number of copies: 20,000; second printing, June 29, 1976, 13,000 copies.

Contents: [prose] "My suburban muse", pp. 58–59, 61–62; [poem] "Autobiography", p. 62, collected in *JSCx.*

Note: The prose essay appears here for the first time in print.

Note: The contents also contain eighteen poems by Thom Gunn that were previously collected as well as two poems added by Thom Gunn "for purposes of comparison", "Second Take on *Rites of Passage*" by Robert Duncan and "Song" attributed to John Dowland.

B42   NEW POEMS 1975   1975

[abstract floral design] | NEW POEMS | 1975 | A P.E.N. Anthology | of Contemporary Poetry | [abstract floral design] | *Edited by* | PATRICIA BEER | HUTCHINSON OF LONDON

Collation: [1]¹⁴ + [2–6]¹⁶ = 94 leaves; 192 × 126 mm.

Binding: Bound in dark reddish orange (38) imitation-cloth paper covered boards and lettered down the spine in gold: [in two lines] NEW POEMS 1975 Edited by Patricia Beer | A P.E.N. Anthology of Contemporary Poetry [across the foot of the spine] [publisher's logo] | HUTCHINSON; white wove paper; all edges trimmed; white wove endpapers; dust wrapper strong yellowish green (131) wove paper printed in black.

Publication date: November 17, 1975

Price: £3.25

Number of copies: Publisher prefers not to reveal the number of copies printed.

Contents: "Bringing to light", pp. 111–113, collected in *JSCx.*

B43   MY CAMBRIDGE   1977

My Cambridge | MURIEL BRADBROOK   ELEANOR BRON LORD CARADON | DONALD DAVIE   SIMON GRAY | THOM GUNN   RAYMOND LEPPARD   NEVILL MOTT | PIERS PAUL READ ARIANNA STASSINOPOULOS | JOHN VAIZEY   RAYMOND WILLIAMS | Edited and introduced by | RONALD HAYMAN | [publisher's logo] Robson Books

Collation: [1–3]¹⁶ + [4]¹⁸ + [5–7]¹⁶ = 114 leaves; 215 × 135 mm.

Binding: Bound in very deep red (14) imitation-cloth paper covered boards and lettered down the spine in gold: *My Cambridge* [across the foot of the spine] [publisher's logo] | Robson | Books; white wove and shiny paper; all edges trimmed; white wove endpapers; the front endpapers have a reproduction of "Cambridge from the Ely Road" and the rear endpapers of "St John's College"; dust wrapper white wove paper printed in shiny moderate reddish brown (43) with six sepia tone reproductions of photographs.

Publication date: March 31, 1977

Price: £4.75

Number of copies: 3,500

Contents: [essay] pp. [135]–148.

Note: This autobiographical essay appears here for the first time in print.

B44   POETRY SUPPLEMENT   1977

Poetry Supplement | COMPILED BY | COLIN FALCK | FOR THE | POETRY BOOK | SOCIETY | *CHRISTMAS* | 1977

Collation: [1–3]⁸ + [4]⁴ = 28 leaves; 214 × 140 mm.

Binding: Glued in a strong yellow (84) paper wrapper printed across the upper wrapper in black: [enclosed in a ruled box] [in strong brown (55)] [publisher's logo] | POETRY | SUPPLEMENT | [in strong brown (55)] COMPILED BY | COLIN FALCK | [in strong brown (55)] for the POETRY | [in strong brown (55)] BOOK SOCIETY | CHRISTMAS '77; on the rear wrapper in the lower left corner in black: 50p

Publication date: December 1, 1977

Price: 50p

Number of copies: 2,500

Contents: "A waking dream" p. [26].

Note: This poem appears here in print for the first time.

B45   ANNE SEXTON: THE ARTIST AND HER   1978
                            CRITICS

Anne | Sexton | *The Artist* | *and Her Critics* | EDITED BY J. D. McCLATCHY | Indiana University Press | Bloomington and London

Collation: [1–10]¹⁶ = 160 leaves; 208 × 139 mm.

B. BOOKS AND PAMPHLETS

Binding: Bound in moderate red (15) imitation-cloth paper and lettered across the spine in gold: McClatchy | Anne Sexton | [decorative device] | INDIANA; in the lower right corner of the upper cover blind stamped [publisher's logo]; white wove paper; all edges trimmed; white wove endpapers; dust wrapper white paper with shiny exterior surface printed in black and vital red (11).

Publication date: July 31, 1978

Price: $12.95

Number of copies: "approximately 2,300"

Contents: Review of *All my pretty ones* by Anne Sexton, pp. 124–126.

Note: This review is an excerpt from a group review (C 174).

C

CONTRIBUTIONS BY THOM GUNN
TO PERIODICALS

This section attempts to include all of Thom Gunn's contributions, *i.e.*
poems, prose, letters to periodicals or newspapers when they appeared there
prior to publication in a book. Other contributions first appearing in media
other than books will be found under separate sections in this book, *i.e.*
interviews, prose on the sleeve of a recording, radio broadcasts, *etc.* If the
poem is untitled, the first line is used for identification. All poems or prose
not signed "Thom Gunn" are noted as such. The items are listed chronologically and then alphabetically if several poems appear in one issue of a
periodical or newspaper. Instead of using Roman numerals to indicate the
volume of a particular issue, Arabic numerals are used and separated by a
colon from the issue number. If only one number is given after the name of
the periodical, it is the issue number and it can be assumed that there is no
volume number. In some cases, *e.g. The Observer,* an individual issue is
indicated only by the date. The place of publication of a periodical or newspaper has been listed only one time and that is when it first was the recipient
of a contribution by Thom Gunn. Titles of reviews and letters are purposely
omitted because it could not be ascertained as to whether Thom Gunn or the
editor assigned the title to the individual item. Following each entry is a
notation that indicates where the item was published in book(s). The term
"uncollected" is used to indicate that the bibliographers have been unable to
locate a book in which the item was reprinted. Abbreviations for Thom
Gunn's books are those previously listed. B followed by a number is a cross
reference to the B section of this bibliography.

C1 [Poem] A THOUSAND CHEERS FOR AUTHORS. *The Gower* (University College School, London), 28: 6 (July 1940) 402.
Signed: T. W. Gunn.
Uncollected (see Appendix I).

C2 [Story] RAIN. *Bedales Chronicle* (Bedales School, Petersfield, Hampshire, England), 28: 4 (March 1942) 6.
Signed: Tommy Gunn.
Uncollected (see Appendix I).

C3 [?] *Editions Trois* (Bedales School, Petersfield, Hampshire, England), 1 (spring term 1943) [?].
Uncollected.

C4 [?] *Editions Trois* 2 (summer term 1943) [?].
Uncollected.

C5 [?] *Editions Trois* 3 (autumn term 1943) [?].
Uncollected.
Note: The preceding three entries were not seen by the bibliographers. Michael Wishart writes:
"My small periodical was called 'Editions Trois'. There were 3 copies of 3 issues. All have vanished without trace. The three issues appeared during the spring, summer, and autumn terms of 1943. The covers were 'repeated monotypes' an invention of my own involving repainting the glass panel from which the print was taken for each printing and resulting inevitably in minute textural and other differences. Most of the articles and poems were typed in triplicate. Each issue included at least one poem by Thom Gunn, as well as articles of criticism and linocuts and original drawings by myself. The most important individual contribution was Gunn's . . . poem on the death of his mother . . . I considered this so exceptional that I set it on the school press. It was printed on paper with a black border—*i.e.* conventional mourning paper, but the paper was PINK."

C6 [Poem] THE HEIGHTS. *The Gower*, 31: 1 (December 1944) 8.
Signed: T. W. Gunn (Vs).
Uncollected (see Appendix I).

C. POEMS AND PROSE

C7 [Poem] POEM. *Cambridge Today* (*Varsity* supplement) (Cambridge, England), 4: 16 (June 1951) 15.
(Retitled "The soldier" in *TMB*.)

C8 [Poem] THE FABLE IS DIFFERENT. *Cambridge Today*, [5]: [17] (Michaelmas term 1951) 17.
Signed: Thom. Gunn.
Uncollected (see Appendix I).

C9 [Poem] MOTHER LOVE. *Cambridge Today*, [5]: [17] (Michaelmas term 1951) 5.
Signed: Thom. Gunn.
Uncollected (see Appendix I).

1952

C10 [Poem] TWO GHOSTS. *Oasis* (Cambridge, England), 5 (February 1952) 8.
Uncollected (see Appendix I).

C11 [Poem] THE MODERN MUSIC. *Workshop* (a subsidiary of *Oasis*) (Cambridge, England), 1 (February 16, 1952) 4.
Signed: Thom. Gunn.
Uncollected (see Appendix I).

C12 [Poem] A MIRROR FOR POETS. *Granta* (Cambridge, England), 55: 1131 (February 23, 1952) 16.
B1, *FT, P 50–66*.

C13 [Essay] *"Oasis"*: an experiment in selling poetry. *The Bookseller* (London), 2412 (March 15, 1952) 782–785.
Uncollected.

C14 [Poem] HELEN'S RAPE. *Cambridge Today*, 5: 18 (Lent term 1952) 7.
B1, *FT*.

C15 [Poem] TO HIS CYNICAL MISTRESS. *Cambridge Today*, 5: 18 (Lent term 1952) 2.
B1, *FT, P 50–66*.

C16 [A review of] *The common pursuit* by F. R. Leavis. *Cambridge Today*, 5: 18 (Lent term 1952) 14.
Uncollected.

C17 [Poem] ARISTOTELIAN LOVE-SONG. *The Trinity Magazine* (Cambridge, England), (May term 1952) 27.
Signed: T. G.
Uncollected (see Appendix I).

C18 [Poem] CHANCE OR CALCULATION? *The Trinity Magazine*, (May term 1952) 10.
Signed: T. G.
Uncollected (see Appendix I).

C19 [Poem] CONTENTEDNESS. *The Trinity Magazine*, (May term 1952) 10.
Signed: T. G.
Uncollected (see Appendix I).

C20 [Poem] LAZARUS NOT RAISED. *The Trinity Magazine*, (May term 1952) 9.
Signed: T. G.
B1, *FT, P 50–66.*

C21 [A review of] *Romantic landscape* by Paul Dehn. *Granta*, 56: 1136 (November 1, 1952) 26.
Uncollected.

C22 [Poem] ROUND AND ROUND. *The Cambridge Review* (Cambridge, England), 74: 1797 (November 8, 1952) 106.
FT.

C23 [Profile] TONY WHITE. *Varsity* (Cambridge, England), 17: 5 (November 8, 1952) 4.
Signed: T. W. G.
Uncollected.

C24 [Poem] CARNAL KNOWLEDGE. *Granta*, 56: 1137 (November 15, 1952) 19.
B2, *FT.*

C25 [A review of] *Collected poems 1934–1952* by Dylan Thomas. *The Cambridge Review*, 74: 1799 (November 22, 1952) 158, 160.
B31.

C26 [Poem] LA PRISONNIÈRE. *The Cambridge Review*, 74: 1800 (November 29, 1952) 185.
FT.

C26a [Poem] JEKYLL AND HYDE. *Spy* (Cambridge, England), 1 [? 1952]?
(Retitled "Secret sharer" in G1)
FT.

Note: The compilers have been unable to locate a copy of this periodical. Mention is made of publication and the retitled poem in a letter from Thom Gunn to John Lehmann dated Cambridge, June 30, 1952.

1953

C27 [Poem] BIRTHDAY POEM. *Trio* (Oxford, England), 2 (January 1953) 18.
TSOM.

C28 [Poem] THE BIRTHPLACE REVISITED. *Trio*, 2 (January 1953) 20.
Uncollected (see Appendix I).

C29 [Poem] THE WOUND. *Trio*, 2 (January 1953) 19.
TG, FT, SP, TE, P 50–66.

C30 [Poem] *first line*: O do not calculate your kiss *Chequer* (Cambridge, England), 1 (February 1953) 1.
Uncollected (see Appendix I).

C31 [Poem] THE COURT REVOLT. *Chequer*, 1 (February 1953) 24.
FT.

C32 [Poem] WIND IN THE STREET. *New Poems* (Swinford, Eynsham, Oxon.), 1: 3 (spring 1953) 3.
TG, FT.

C33 [Poem] THE BEACH HEAD. *Granta*, 56: 1139 (February 7, 1953) 20.
TG, FT, SP, P 50–66.

C34 [Poem] A VILLAGE EDMUND. *Granta*, 56: 1141 (March 7, 1953) 18.
*TG, FT*a.

C35 [A review of] *Hunter* by J. A. Hunter. *Granta*, 56: 1141 (March 7, 1953) 23.
Signed: T. W. G.
Uncollected.

C36 [Poem] LERICI. *The Trinity Magazine*, (May term 1953) 17.
Signed: T. G.
FT.

C37 [Poem] THE OWNER. *The Trinity Magazine*, (May term 1953) 2.
Signed: T. G.
Uncollected (see Appendix I).

C38 [Poem] THE FURIES. *Chequer*, 2 (May 1953) 14–15.
Uncollected (see Appendix I).
Note: One portion of a much longer poem "The furies" that was never published.

C39 [Poem] LOOKING GLASS. *Gadfly* (Cambridge, England), 2: 2 (May 30, 1953) 16.
FT.

C40 [A review of] *Springtime* edited by G. S. Fraser and Ian Fletcher. *Gadfly*, 2: 2 (May 30, 1953) 27.
Signed: APEMANTUS.
Uncollected.

C41 [Poem] THE WHEEL OF FORTUNE. *The Cambridge Review*, 74: 1815 (May 30, 1953) 537.
TSOM.

C. POEMS AND PROSE

C42 [Poem] INCIDENT ON A JOURNEY. *Chance* (London), 3 (April–June 1953) 70.
Uncollected (see Appendix I).

C43 [Poem] HERE COME THE SAINTS. *Delta* (Cambridge, England), 1 ([autumn 1953]) [7].
FT, P 50–66.

C44 [Poem] HIDE AND SEEK. *Delta*, 1 ([autumn 1953]) [8].
Uncollected.

C45 [Poem] LOFTY IN THE PALAIS DE DANSE. *The Paris Review* (New York), 3 (autumn 1953) [92–93].
FT.

C46 [Poem] THE DEATH OF A STRANGER. *The Cambridge Review*, 75: 1818 (October 17, 1953) 44.
B31.

C47 [A review of] *Poems 1953* by Robert Graves. *Gadfly*, 3: 3 (October 31, 1953) 35–36.
Uncollected.

C48 [Poem] TAMER AND HAWK. *The New Statesmen and Nation* (London), 46: 1184 (November 14, 1953) 604.
FT, SP.

C49 [A review of] *John Masefield* by Muriel Spark. *The New Statesman and Nation*, 46: 1185 (November 21, 1953) 651.
Unsigned (ref. T.G.).
Uncollected.

C50 [Poem] ELIZABETH BARRETT BARRETT. *Gadfly*, 4: 4 ([November 1953]) 11.
B26.

C51 [Poem] MATTER AND SPIRIT. *Gadfly*, 5: 5 ([November 1953]) 14.
B3.

C52 [Poem] CAPTAIN IN TIME OF PEACE. *New Poems*, 2: 2 ([late 1953?]) 3.
FT.

1954

C53 [Poem] EARTHBORN. *The London Magazine* (London), 1: 1 (February 1954) 64.
B3.

C54 [Poem] WORDS IN ACTION. *The Spectator* (London), 192: 6559 (March 12, 1954) 288.
Uncollected.

C55 [Poem] TERMS. *The Spectator*, 192: 6562 (April 2, 1954) 398.
Uncollected.

C. POEMS AND PROSE

C56 [Poem] HUNGRY. *The London Magazine*, 1: 4 (May 1954) 26.
Uncollected.

C57 [Poem] PALINODE. *The London Magazine*, 1: 4 (May 1954) 25–26.
Uncollected.

C58 [Poem] AT THE BACK OF THE NORTH WIND. *The Spectator*, 192:
6570 (May 28, 1954) 646.
TSOM.

C59 [Response to questionnaire] *Granta*, 57: 1147 (June 8, 1954) [20–21]
[24–25].
Uncollected.

C60 [A review of] *Brother to dragons, a tale in verse and voices* by Robert
Penn Warren. *The Spectator*, 192: 6574 (June 25, 1954) 795.
Signed: T. W. G.
Uncollected.

C61 [A group review of] *Shakespeare survey: an annual survey of Shake-
spearean study and production no. 7, The poetry of Shakespeare's plays* by
F. E. Halliday, and *The complete works of Shakespeare* edited by Charles
Jasper Sisson. *The Spectator*, 193: 6575 (July 2, 1954) 32–33.
Uncollected.

C62 [Poem] APOCRYPHAL. *Botteghe Oscure* (Rome), 14 ([autumn] 1954)
173–174.
B39.

C63 [Poem] EXCURSION. *Botteghe Oscure*, 14 ([autumn] 1954) 174–175.
B39, *TMB.*

C64 [Essay] LETTER FROM CAMBRIDGE. *The London Magazine*, 1: 7
(August 1954) 66–69.
Uncollected.

C65 [Poem] JESUS AND HIS MOTHER. *The Times Literary Supplement*
(London), 2740 (August 6, 1954) xix.
B4, *TSOM, TE, P 50–66.*

C66 [A review of] *The romantic movement and methodism* by Frederick C.
Gill. *The Spectator*, 193: 6581 (August 13, 1954) 211.
Signed: TWG
Uncollected.

C67 [Poem] THE SEPARATION. *The Spectator*, 193: 6582 (August 20, 1954)
231.
TSOM.

C68 [Poem] THE SILVER AGE. *The Spectator*, 193: 6585 (September 10,
1954) 304.
B6.

C. POEMS AND PROSE

C69 [A review of] *The world in the evening* by Christopher Isherwood. *The London Magazine*, 1: 9 (October 1954) 81–85.
Uncollected.

1955

C70 [Poem] RALPH'S DREAM. *The London Magazine*, 2: 1 (January 1955) 48–51.
Uncollected.
Note: One portion of a much longer poem "The furies" that was never published.

C71 [Poem] LIGHT SLEEPING. *New World Writing* (New York), 7 (April [March 25] 1955) 115–116.
B7, *TMB*.

C72 [Poem] BEFORE THE CARNIVAL. *The Paris Review*, 9 (summer 1955) [68–69].
TSOM.

C73 [Poem] ST MARTIN AND THE BEGGAR. *The Paris Review*, 9 (summer 1955) [66–68].
TSOM.

C74 [Poem] AUTUMN CHAPTER IN A NOVEL. *Poetry* (Chicago), 86: 3 (June 1955) 136–137.
B5, *TSOM*, *P 50–66*.

C75 [Poem] THE CORRIDOR. *Poetry*, 86: 3 (June 1955) 137–139.
B6, *TSOM*.

C76 [Poem] DURING AN ABSENCE. *Poetry*, 86: 3 (June 1955) 125–126.
SP, *P 50–66*.

C77 [Poem] HIGH FIDELITY. *Poetry*, 86: 3 (June 1955) 139.
TSOM.

C78 [Poem] HUMAN CONDITION. *Poetry*, 86: 3 (June 1955) 127–128.
B5, *TSOM*.

C79 [Poem] LEGAL REFORM. *Poetry*, 86: 3 (June 1955) 134–135.
TSOM.

C80 [Poem] LINES FOR A BOOK. *Poetry*, 86: 3 (June 1955) 130.
TSOM.

C81 [Poem] MERLIN IN THE CAVE: HE SPECULATES WITHOUT A BOOK. *Poetry*, 86: 3 (June 1955) 131–134.
B5, *TSOM*.

C82 [Poem] A PLAN OF SELF SUBJECTION. *Poetry*, 86: 3 (June 1955) 128–129.
(Retitled "A plan for self-subjection") in B5, *TSOM*.

C83 [Poem] A DISTRICT IN ROME. *The London Magazine*, 2: 7 (July 1955) 14.
Uncollected.

C84 [Poem] THE PARAPLEGIC LYING ON HIS BACK. *The London Magazine*, 2: 7 (July 1955) 13–14.
Uncollected.

C85 [Poem] ON THE MOVE. *Encounter* (London), 5: 6 (December 1955) 50.
B5, *TSOM, SP, TE, P 50–66*.

1956

C86 [A review of] *Collected poems* by William Empson. *The London Magazine*, 3: 2 (February 1956) 70–75.
Uncollected.

C87 [Poem] JULIAN THE APOSTATE. *The Paris Review*, 12 (spring 1956) [100].
TSOM.

C88 [Poem] THE NATURE OF AN ACTION. *The Paris Review*, 12 (spring 1956) [101–102].
TSOM.

C89 [A review of] *Collected poems* by Wallace Stevens. *The London Magazine*, 3: 4 (April 1956) 81–84.
Uncollected.

C90 [Letter to the editor] *The London Magazine*, 3: 4 (April 1956) 64–65.
Uncollected.

C91 [Poem] TO YVOR WINTERS, 1955. *The London Magazine*, 3: 5 (May 1956) 30–31.
TSOM, P 50–66.

C92 [Introduction and notes] Young American poets 1956. *The London Magazine*, 3: 8 (August 1956) 21–22, 34–35.
Uncollected.

C93 [Poem] THE ALLEGORY OF THE WOLF BOY. *The Times Educational Supplement* (London), 2150 (August 3, 1956) 995.
TSOM, P 50–66.

1957

C94 [A group review of] *The form of loss* by Edgar Bowers, *The battlement* by Donald F. Drummond, *A world of saints* by Thomas Cole, *Three priests in April* by Stephen Stepanchev, *Poets of today III. The floating world and other poems* by Lee Anderson, *My father's business and other poems* by Spencer Brown, *The green town* by Joseph Langland, and

C. POEMS AND PROSE

Villa narcisse by Katherine Hoskins. *Poetry*, 89: 4 (January 1957) 244–252.
Uncollected.

C95 [Poem] FIRST MEETING WITH A POSSIBLE MOTHER-IN-LAW.
Listen (Hessle, East Yorkshire), 2: 2 (spring 1957) 4.
TSOM.

C96 [Poem] THOUGHTS ON UNPACKING. *The London Magazine*, 4: 4 (April 1957) 38.
TSOM.

C97 [Poem] THE UNSETTLED MOTORCYCLIST'S VISION OF HIS DEATH.
Poetry, 90: 1 (April 1957) 32–33.
TSOM, SP, P 50–66.

C98 [Poem] WAKING IN A NEWLY-BUILT HOUSE, OAKLAND. *Poetry*,
90: 1 (April 1957) 34.
(Retitled "Waking in a newly-built house") in *MSC, M & MSC.*

C99 [Poem] VOX HUMANA. *The Nation* (New York), 184: 17 (April 27, 1957) 365.
TSOM, SP, TE, P 50–66.

C100 [Essay] Thom Gunn writes. . . . *Poetry Book Society Bulletin* (London), 14 (May 1957) [1–2].
Uncollected.

C101 [Letter to the editor] *The London Magazine*, 4: 6 (June 1957) 65–66.
Uncollected.

C102 [A group review of] *The modern poet's world* edited by James Reeves
and *Introducing modern poetry* by W. G. Bebbington. *The Spectator*,
199: 6735 (July 26, 1957) 140, 142.
Uncollected.

C103 [A review of] *Collected poems 1930–1955* by George Barker. *The Spectator*, 199: 6736 (August 2, 1957) 167.
Uncollected.

C104 [A review of] *Collected poems* by Louise Bogan. *The Spectator*,
199: 6739 (August 23, 1957) 254.
Uncollected.

C105 [A review of] *The romantic survival: A study in poetic evolution* by John Bayley. *The London Magazine*, 4: 9 (September 1957) 76–79.
Uncollected.

C106 [A review of] *Robert Graves: poems selected by himself* by Robert Graves. *The Spectator*, 199: 6741 (September 6, 1957) 311.
Uncollected.

1958

C107 [A group review of] *The poetry of experience* by Robert Langbaum and *Romantic image* by Frank Kermode. *The London Magazine*, 5: 2 (February 1958) 62–65.
Uncollected.

C108 [Poem] THE FEEL OF HANDS. *Listen*, 2: 4 (spring 1958) 3.
MSC, M & MSC.

C109 [Poem] THE BYRNIES. *The London Magazine*, 5: 3 (March 1958) 12–13.
B9, *MSC, SP, TE, P 50–66, M & MSC.*

C110 [Poem] FROM THE HIGHEST CAMP. *The London Magazine*, 5: 3 (March 1958) 13.
MSC, P 50–66, M & MSC.

C111 [Poem] INTERROGATED TO INTERROGATOR. *The London Magazine*, 5: 3 (March 1958) 11–12.
B10.

C112 [Poem] THE VALUE OF GOLD. (Printed program for Phi Beta Kappa ceremony, Stanford University) (Palo Alto, California) (June 14, 1958).
MSC, M & MSC.

C113 [A review of] *Poetry today* by Geoffrey Moore. *The Spectator*, 200: 6778 (May 23, 1958) 661.
Uncollected.

C114 [A group review of] *The triumph of the muse and other poems* by John Heath-Stubbs, *A crackling of thorns* by John Hollander, and *The two freedoms* by Jon Silkin. *The Spectator*, 201: 6789 (August 8, 1958) 200.
Uncollected.

C115 [A group review of] *Brutus's orchard* by Roy Fuller, *The open sea and other poems* by William Meredith, *Home truths* by Anthony Thwaite, and *The forever young and other poems* by Pauline Hanson. *Poetry*, 92: 6 (September 1958) 378–384.
Uncollected.

C116 [Poem] THE ANNIHILATION OF NOTHING. *Poetry*, 93: 1 (October 1958) 4.
MSC, SP, P 50–66, M & MSC.

C117 [Poem] BLACK JACKETS. *Poetry*, 93: 1 (October 1958) 2–3.
MSC, M & MSC.

C118 [Poem] IN SANTA MARIA DEL POPOLO. *Poetry*, 93: 1 (October 1958) 1–2.
MSC, SP, TE, P 50–66, M & MSC.

C. POEMS AND PROSE

C119 [Poem] CLAUS VON STAUFFENBERG, 1944. *The Spectator*, 201: 6797 (October 3, 1958) 447.
(Retitled "Claus Von Stauffenberg") in *MSC, SP, M & MSC*.

C120 [A group review of] *Poems* by Anthony Cronin, *Errors of observation* by Gordon Wharton, and *A winter talent and other poems* by Donald Davie. *Listen*, 3: 1 (winter 1958) 12–14, 19–22.
Uncollected.

C121 [A group review of] *Paterson* (*Book five*) by W. C. Williams, *95 poems* by E. E. Cummings [sic.], *Body of waking* by Muriel Rukeyser, *Selected poems and new* by Jose Garcia Villa, *Poems of a Jew* by Karl Shapiro, *I marry you: a sheaf of love poems* by John Ciardi, *A place to stand* by David Wagoner, *The dark houses* by Donald Hall, and *The sum* by Alan Stephens. *The Yale Review* (New Haven, Connecticut), 48: 2 (December 1958) 297–305.
Uncollected.

1959

C122 [Poem] THE BOOK OF THE DEAD. *The London Magazine*, 6: 2 (February 1959) 30.
B12, *MSC, TE, M & MSC*.

C123 [Poem] THE MONSTER. *The London Magazine*, 6: 2 (February 1959) 31.
B12, *MSC, M & MSC*.

C124 [A group review of] *In defense of the earth* by Kenneth Rexroth, *The next word* by Thomas Blackburn, *The cocks of Hades* by C. A. Trypanis, *The man who told his love* by Christopher Logue. *The Spectator*, 202: 6816 (February 13, 1959) 234–235.
Uncollected.

C125 [Essay and a group review of] *The new poets of England and America* edited by Donald Hall, Robert Pack and Louis Simpson, *Good news of death* by Louis Simpson, and *The form of loss* by Edgar Bowers. *The Spectator*, 202: 6822 (March 27, 1959) 443.
Uncollected.

C126 [Poem] ALL-NIGHT BURLESQUE. *The Observer* (London), (April 26, 1959) 22.
B11.

C127 [A review of] *No further west: California visited* by Dan Jacobson. *The Spectator*, 202: 6831 (May 29, 1959) 783.
Uncollected.

C128 [A group review of] *Seeing is believing* by Charles Tomlinson, *The dark houses* by Donald Hall, *Mirrors & windows: poems* by Howard

Nemerov. *The American Scholar* (Washington, D.C.), 28: 3 (summer 1959) 390, 392, 394, 396.
Uncollected.

C129 [A group review of] *John Betjeman's collected poems* compiled by the Earl of Birkenhead, *Oddments, inklings, omens, moments: poems* by Alistair Reid, *A sense of the world: poems* by Elizabeth Jennings, *The wilderness and other poems* by Louis O. Coxe, *The green chapel* by Barbara Gibbs, *The night of the hammer* by Ned O'Gorman, and *Words for the wind* by Theodore Roethke. *The Yale Review*, 48: 4 (June 1959) 617–626.
Uncollected.

C130 [Poem] MAP OF THE CITY. *The Observer*, (August 9, 1959) 10.
B13, (retitled "A map of the city") in *MSC, M & MSC*.

C131 [Poem] NOTES ON THE FRENCH. *The Critical Quarterly* (London), 1: 3 (autumn 1959) 207.
Note: This poem has been revised and becomes two poems in *MSC* and *M & MSC*. The first "Baudelaire among the heroes" is part 1 of "Notes on the French" and the second, "Readings in French", which first appears in *MSC* and *M & MSC* consists of revised text and renumbered parts 2, 3, 5, 6 and 7 from "Notes on the French".

C132 [A group review of] *Vision and rhetoric: Studies in modern poetry* by G. S. Fraser and *The chequer'd shade: reflections on obscurity in poetry* by John Press. *The London Magazine*, 6: 10 (October 1959) 61–64.
Uncollected.

C133 [Poem] PLEASURE. *The Observer* (Christmas book section), (November 29, 1959) 1.
(Retitled "Modes of pleasure") in *MSC, P 50–66, M & MSC*.

C134 [A group review of] *Summer knowledge* by Delmore Schwartz, *Saint Judas* by James Wright, *A dream of governors* by Louis Simpson, *Light and dark* by Barbara Howes, *Apples from Shinar* by Hyam Plutzik, *The self-made man* by Reed Whittemore, *The crow and the heart* by Hayden Carruth, *Of the festivity* by William Dickey, and *Life studies* by Robert Lowell. *The Yale Review*, 49: 2 (December 1959) 295–305.
Uncollected.

1960

C135 [Essay] DISCIPLINED RICHNESS. *Poetry Northwest* (Seattle, Washington), 1: 3 (winter 1960) 19.
Uncollected.

C136 [Poem] A TRUCKER. *The Observer*, (April 24, 1960) 23.
MSC, M & MSC.

C137 [Poem] THE SNAIL. *The Observer*, (April 24, 1960) 23.
(Retitled "Considering the snail") in *MSC, SP, P 50–66, M & MSC.*

C138 [Poem] AN INHABITANT. *The London Magazine*, 7: 5 (May 1960) 14–15.
Uncollected.

C139 [Poem] THE MIDDLE OF THE NIGHT. *The London Magazine*, 7: 5 (May 1960) 15–16.
MSC, M & MSC.

C140 [A group review of] *Thrones, 96–109 de los cantares* by Ezra Pound, *Bone thoughts* by George Starbuck, *Ko, or a season on earth* by Kenneth Koch, *A water walk by Villa d'Este* by Jean Garrigue, *Portrait of your niece* by Carol Hall, *In an iridescent time* by Ruth Stone, *The summer anniversaries* by Donald Justice. *The Yale Review*, 49: 4 (June 1960, 589–598.
Uncollected.

C141 [Poem] WITH GOOD HUMOR. *The Paris Review*, 24 (summer–fall 1960) [79].
(Retitled "Modes of pleasure") in *MSC, M & MSC.*

C142 [Poem] ADOLESCENCE. *The Spectator*, 205: 6888 (July 1, 1960) 30.
MSC, TE, P 50–66, M & MSC.

C143 [A group review of] *The exclusions of a rhyme* by J. V. Cunningham, *Collected poems* by Lawrence Durrell, *A winter come, a summer gone* by Harold Moss, *An eye in the sky* by Louis Grudin, and *Homage to Clio* by W. H. Auden. *The Yale Review*, 50: 1 (September 1960) 125–135.
Uncollected.

C144 [Poem] SIGNS OF AN UNDERTAKING. *The Spectator*, 205: 6899 (September 16, 1960) 409.
Uncollected.

C145 [A review of] *In defense of reason* by Yvor Winters. *The London Magazine*, 7: 10 (October 1960) 64–66.
Uncollected.

C146 [Poem] BLACKIE, THE ELECTRIC REMBRANDT. *The Spectator*, 205: 6909 (November 25, 1960) 845.
MSC, SP, P 50–66, M & MSC.

1961

C147 [Poem] BONHEUR. *The Paris Review*, 25 (winter–spring 1961) [53].
(Revised and retitled "L'epreuve") in *MSC, M & MSC.*

C148 [Poem] A SCHOOL OF RESISTANCE. *The Paris Review*, 25 (winter–spring 1961) [52].
Uncollected.

C149 [A group review of] *Collected poems* by J. C. Squire, *The prodigal son* by James Kirkup, *Collected poems* by William Plomer, *Ballad of the Mari Lwyd* by Vernon Watkins, *Cypress and acacia* by Vernon Watkins, *The forests of Lithuania* by Donald Davie, and *Lupercal* by Ted Hughes. *Poetry*, 97: 4 (January 1961) 260–270.
Uncollected.

C150 [Poem] DAS LIEBESLEBEN. *Encounter*, 16: 3 (March 1861) [5].
B17.

C151 [Poem] FLYING ABOVE CALIFORNIA. *Encounter*, 16: 3 (March 1961) 3.
MSC, P 50–66, M & MSC.

C152 [Poem] HOTBLOOD ON FRIDAY. *Encounter*, 16: 3 (March 1961) [4].
MSC, M & MSC.

C153 [Poem] LIGHTS AMONG REDWOOD. *Encounter*, 16: 3 (March 1961) [4].
MSC, M & MSC.

C154 [Poem] LOOT. *Encounter*, 16: 3 (March 1961) [5].
MSC, M & MSC.

C155 [Poem] RASTIGNAC AT 45. *Encounter*, 16: 3 (March 1961) [4].
MSC, M & MSC.

C156 [Poem] TELEGRAPH AVENUE. *Encounter*, 16: 3 (March 1961) 3.
Uncollected.

C157 [Poem] INNOCENCE. *The London Magazine*, 8: 3 (March 1961) 19.
MSC, SP, P 50–66, M & MSC.

C158 [A group review of] *New and selected poems* by Howard Nemerov, *The drunk in the furnace* by W. S. Merwin, *Horatio* by Hyam Plutzik, *Stills and movies* by Ralph Pomeroy, *Say pardon* by David Ignatow, and *The distances* by Charles Olson. *The Yale Review*, 50: 4 (June 1961) 585–596.
Uncollected.

C159 [Poem] MY SAD CAPTAINS. *The Paris Review*, 26 (summer–fall 1961) [67].
MSC, SP, TE, P 50–66, M & MSC.

C160 [Poem] FROM AN ASIAN TENT. *The Observer*, (September 24, 1961) 28.
TMB.

C161 [Poem] THE GODDESS. *The Observer*, (September 24, 1961) 28.
B19, *AG, T, P 50–66.*

C. POEMS AND PROSE

C162 [Poem] KNOWLEDGE. *The Observer*, (September 24, 1961) 28.
Uncollected.

C163 [Poem] KURFÜRSTENDAMM. *The Observer*, (September 24, 1961) 28.
Uncollected.
Note: Almost all of this poem is rewritten and included in a longer
poem "Back to life" (C195).

1962

C164 [Poem] OUT OF BREATH. *Encounter*, 18: 1 (January 1962) 96.
Uncollected.

C165 [Response to questionnaire] *The London Magazine*, N.S. 1: 11
(February 1962) 40.
Uncollected.

C166 [Poem] A CRAB. *The London Magazine*, N.S. 1: 11 (February 1962)
6–7.
B19.

C167 [A group review of] *Imitations* by Robert Lowell, *Advice to a prophet*
by Richard Wilbur, *Solstices* by Louis MacNeice, *Halfway* by Maxine
W. Kumin, *West of your city* by William Stafford, *Poems and transla-
tions* by Thomas Kinsella, and *Garland for the winter solstice* by Ruthven
Todd. *The Yale Review*, 51: 3 (March 1962) 480–489.
Uncollected.

C168 [A review of] *Between Mars and Venus* by Robert Conquest. *The
Spectator* 208: 6984 (May 4, 1962) 596.
Uncollected.

C169 [A group review of] *The Jacob's ladder* by Denise Levertov, *For love
(poems 1950–1960)* by Robert Creeley, *Drowning with others* by James
Dickey, *A paper horse* by Robert Watson, *Medusa in Gramercy Park* by
Horace Gregory, *Between Mars and Venus* by Robert Conquest, *Movie-
going and other poems* by John Hollander, and *New and selected poems* by
Donald Davie. *The Yale Review*, 52: 1 (October 1962) 129–138.
Uncollected.

C170 [Essay] In nobody's Pantheon. *Shenandoah* (Lexington, Virginia),
13: 2 (winter 1962) [34]–35.
Uncollected.

1963

C171 [Poem] DRIVING TO FLORIDA. *The Observer*, (March 31, 1963) 27.
B22.

C172 [Poem] BREAKFAST. *The Observer*, (July 14, 1963) 24.
AG, T.

C173 [Poem] THIRD AVENUE. *The Observer*, (July 28, 1963) 21.
Uncollected.

C174 [A group review of] *Torse 3* by Christopher Middleton, *Poems, 1954–1962* by Adrienne Rich, *Arrivals and departures* by Charles Gullans, *All my pretty ones* by Anne Sexton, *Collected poems* by Weldon Kees, and *Silence in the snowy fields* by Robert Bly. *The Yale Review*, 53: 1 (October 1963) 135–144.
B45 (excerpted).

C175 [Essay] What hope for poetry? *Granta*, 68: 1229 (October 19, 1963) 8.
Uncollected.

C176 [Poem] THE DOCTOR'S OWN BODY. *The Observer*, (December 15, 1963) 25.
Uncollected.

1964

C177 [Poem] THE DYING LADY. *The Observer*, (February 9, 1964) 26.
Uncollected.

C178 [Poem] BERLIN IN RUINS. *The Critical Quarterly*, 6: 1 (spring 1964) 33.
B21, *AG, T*.

C179 [Poem] TENDING BAR. *The Critical Quarterly*, 6: 1 (spring 1964) 33–34.
Uncollected.

C180 [Statement] *Motley* (Davis, California) 1: 2 (spring 1964) 20.
Uncollected.

C181 [A group review of] *Between matter and principle* by Alan Stephens, *On the edge* by Philip Levine, *The burning perch* by Louis MacNeice, *The branch will not break* by James Wright, and *At the end of the open road* by Louis Simpson. *The Yale Review*, 53: 3 (March 1964) 447–458.
Uncollected.

C182 [Letter to the editor] *The Times Literary Supplement* (London), 3237 (March 12, 1964) 215.
Uncollected.

C183 [Poem] THE GIRL OF LIVE MARBLE. *The Observer*, (April 19, 1964) 28.
T.

C184 [Poem] VIGIL OF CORPUS CHRISTI. *The Observer*, (April 19, 1964) 28.
(Retitled "The vigil of Corpus Christi") in *AG, T, P 50–66*.

C. POEMS AND PROSE

1965

C185 [Essay] Poets in control. *Twentieth Century* (London), 173: 1024 (winter 1964/65) 102–106.
Uncollected.

C186 [Poem] CONFESSIONS OF THE LIFE ARTIST. *New Statesman* (London), 69: 1783 (May 14, 1965) 768–769.
AG, T.

C187 [Essay] William Carlos Williams. *Encounter*, 25: 1 (July 1965) 67–74.
B24.

C188 [Poem sequence] MISANTHROPOS. *Encounter*, 25: 2 (August 1965) 19–25.
T.
Note: Part V of "Misanthropos" is titled "A geography" and appears separately in *AG* but is untitled in *T*.
Note: Part IX of "Misanthropos" is later titled "Memoirs of the world" and appears separately in *P 50–66* but is untitled in *T*.
Note: Part X of "Misanthropos" is later titled "A snow vision" and appears separately in *P 50–66* but is untitled in *T*.
Note: Part XI of "Misanthropos" is separately titled (as an individual poem) "(Epitaph for Anton Schmidt)" and appears as "*Epitaph for Anton Schmidt*" in *T*, and as "Epitaph for Anton Schmidt" in *TE* and *P 50–66*.
Note: Part XII of "Misanthropos" is separately titled (as an individual poem and as a section title) "Elegy on the Dust" and appears as such in *T* and *P 50–66*.

C189 [Poem] BURNING. *Occident*, (Berkeley, California), (fall 1965) [58].
(Untitled) in *P*.

C190 [Poem] CANNING TOWN PUB. *Occident*, (fall 1965) [58].
(Untitled) in *P*, (retitled "Canning town") in *P 50–66*.
Note: An early version which differs considerably appeared in B24 titled "The night out".

C191 [Poem] AN OLD MAN. *Occident*, (fall 1965) [58].
(Untitled) in *P*, (retitled "Two old men") in *TE*, (retitled "The conversation of old men") in *P 50–66*.

1966

C192 [Letter to the editor] *The Times Literary Supplement*, 3346 (April 14, 1966) 327.
Uncollected.

C193 [A review of] *A range of poems* by Gary Snyder. *Agenda* (London), 4: 3 & 4 (summer 1966) 39–44.
Uncollected.

C194 [Poem] PIERCE STREET. *New Statesman*, 72: 1845 (July 22, 1966) 132.
B25, *T, P 50–66*.

C195 [Poem] BACK TO LIFE. *The Critical Quarterly*, 8: 3 (autumn 1966) 198–199.
B25, *T*.
Note: This is a later version, revised and expanded of "Kurfürstendamm" (C163).

C196 [Poem] BRAVERY. *Agenda*, 4: 5 & 6 (autumn 1966) 31.
T.

C197 [Poem] TOUCH. *Agenda*, 4: 5 & 6 (autumn 1966) 29–30.
T, TE, P 50–66.

C198 [Poem] NO SPEECH FROM THE SCAFFOLD. *Poetry*, 109: 2 (November 1966) 71.
T.

C199 [Poem] THE OLD MAN IN THE BRITANNIA. *Poetry*, 109: 2 (November 1966) 70.
Uncollected.

C200 [Poem] THE PRODUCE DISTRICT. *Poetry*, 109: 2 (November 1966) [73]–74.
T.

C201 [Poem] SNOWFALL. *Poetry*, 109: 2 (November 1966) 72.
T.

C202 [Poem] TAYLOR STREET. *Poetry*, 109: 2 (November 1966) 69–70.
T.

1967

C203 [Poem] FILLMORE AUDITORIUM. *Occident*, N.S. 1 (spring–summer 1967) 60–61.
Uncollected.

C204 [Essay] The new music. *The Listener* (London), 78: 2001 (August 3, 1967) [129]–130.
Uncollected.

C205 [Essay] Thom Gunn writes. . . . *Poetry Book Society Bulletin*, 54 (September 1967) [1].
Uncollected.

C206 [Poem] THE ROOFTOP. *The Listener*, 78: 2006 (September 7, 1967) 310.
Mo, M & MSC.

C. POEMS AND PROSE

C207 [Poem] THE COLOUR MACHINE. *Art and Artists* (London), 2: 7
(October 1967) 27.
Su, Mo, M & MSC.

C208 [Poem] FROM THE WAVE. *The Gower*, 41: 6 (October 1967) 293–294.
TE, Mo, M & MSC.

C209 [Poem] APARTMENT CATS. *The Listener*, 78: 2015 (November 9,
1967) 610.
Mo, M & MSC.

C210 [Poem] SUNLIGHT. *The Listener*, 78: 2015 (November 9, 1967) 610.
Su, Mo, M & MSC.

1968

C211 [Poem] NORTH KENT. *The Listener*, 79: 2030 (February 22, 1968) 231
Uncollected.

C212 [Poem] AQUEDUCT. *The Critical Quarterly*, 10: 1 & 2 (spring &
summer 1968) 56.
B27, *TMB.*

C213 [Statement] *the Review* (London), 18 (April 1968) 34–35.
Uncollected.

C214 [Poem] FLOODED MEADOWS. *The Listener*, 79: 2036 (April 4, 1968)
432.
Mo, M & MSC.

C215 [A group review of] *The back country* by Gary Snyder and *Six sections
from mountains and rivers without end* by Gary Snyder. *The Listener*,
79: 2040 (May 2, 1968) 576–577.
Uncollected.

C216 [Poem] THREE. *The Listener*, 80: 2053 (August 1, 1968) 149.
Su, Mo, M & MSC.

C217 [Statement] *Per/Se* (Stanford, California), 3: 3 (fall 1968) 40.
Uncollected.

C218 [Poem] THE LIGHT. *Chirimo* (Salisbury, Rhodesia), 2 (October 1968)
22.
B33.

1969

C219 [Poem] THE NAKED PEACE MARCHER. *Journal for the Protection of all
Beings* (This issue called "Green Flag") (San Francisco, California), 3
(1969) [29].
Uncollected.

C220 [Letter to the editor] *The Listener*, 81: 2097 (June 5, 1969) 789.
Uncollected.

C221 [Poem] AT THE CENTER. *The Free You* (Menlo Park, California), 3: 8
(July 1969) 44.
Su, Mo, M & MSC.

C222 [Poem] FOR SIGNS. *The Southern Review* (Baton Rouge, Louisiana),
N.S. 5: 3 (July 1969) 749–750.
Mo, M & MSC.

C223 [Poem] JUSTIN. *The Southern Review*, N.S. 5: 3 (July 1969) 748.
Mo, M & MSC.

C224 [Poem] RITES OF PASSAGE. *The Southern Review*, N.S. 5: 3 (July
1969) 746–747.
Su, Mo, M & MSC.

C225 [Poem] WORDS. *The Southern Review*, N.S. 5: 3 (July 1969) 747.
Mo, M & MSC.

C226 [Letter to the editor] *Hierophant* (Los Angeles, California), 3 (December 1969) 44.
Uncollected.

1970

C227 [Poem] BEING BORN. *Poetry*, 116: 1 (April 1970) 3–4.
Mo, M & MSC.

C228 [Poem] THE DISCOVERY OF THE PACIFIC. *Poetry*, 116: 1 (April
1970) 5.
B34, *Mo, M & MSC.*

C229 [Poem] THE MESSENGER. *Poetry*, 116: 1 (April 1970) 1–2.
Mo, M & MSC.

C230 [Poem] GRASSES. *The Listener*, 83: 2143 (April 23, 1970) 539.
B32, *Mo, M & MSC.*

C231 [Poem] TO NATTY BUMMPO [*sic*.]. *The Listener*, 83: 2143 (April 23,
1970) 539.
(Title corrected to "To Natty Bumppo") in *Mo, M & MSC.*

C232 [Response to questionnaire] *Tracks* (Coventry, England), 8 (summer
1970) 9–10.
Uncollected.

C233 [Poem] MOLY. *London Magazine*, N.S. 10: 4 & 5 (July–August 1970)
58–59.
Mo, M & MSC.

C234 [Poem] TOM-DOBBIN. *London Magazine*, N.S. 10: 4 & 5 (July–
August 1970) 59–61.
Mo, M & MSC.

C235 [Poem] PHAEDRA IN THE FARM HOUSE. *Poetry Review* (London), 61: 3 (autumn 1970) [188]–189.
Mo, M & MSC.

1971

C236 [Poem] RITA. *Sebastian Quill* (San Francisco, California), 2 (spring 1971) [12].
So.

C237 [Essay] Thom Gunn writes. . . . *Poetry Book Society Bulletin*, 68 (spring 1971) [1–2].
Uncollected.

C238 [Poem] SPARROW. *Workshop* (London), 13 ([autumn] 1971) 18.
So, JSCx.

C239 [Statement] *Workshop*, 13 ([autumn] 1971) 31.
Uncollected.

C240 [Poem] HITCHING INTO FRISCO. *Antaeus* (Tangier, Morocco), 3 (autumn 1971) 105.
So, JSCx.
Note: This poem and the following two poems appear under the author's collective title "Three songs".

C241 [Poem] BABY SONG. *Antaeus*, 3 (autumn 1971) 106.
So, JSCx.

C242 [Poem] ENCOLPIUS. *Antaeus*, 3 (autumn 1971) 107.
So.

1972

C243 [Poem] THE PLUNGE. *Isthmus* (San Francisco, California), 1 (spring 1972) 44–45.
Ma, JSCx.

C244 [Essay] Hardy and the ballads. *Agenda*, 10: 2 & 3 (spring–summer 1972) 19–46.
Uncollected.

C245 [Poem] FAUSTUS TRIUMPHANT. *Blackfish* (Burnaby, British Columbia, Canada), 3 (summer 1972) [18–19].
Ma, JSCx.

C246 [Poem] THE STREAM (Cobb). *Blackfish*, 3 (summer 1972) [20].
Uncollected.

C247 [Response to questionnaire] *Agenda*, 10: 4/11: 1 (autumn–winter 1972–1973) 23–24.
Uncollected.

C. POEMS AND PROSE

1973

C248 [Poem] THE BED. *Antaeus*, 12 (winter 1973) 50.
TTA, JSCx.

C249 [Poem] AUTOBIOGRAPHY. *The Iowa Review* (Iowa City, Iowa), 4: 1 (winter 1973) 88.
B41, *JSCx.*

C250 [Poem] TO THE GEYSERS. *The Iowa Review*, 4: 1 (winter 1973) 89. (Retitled "Sleep by the hot stream") in *TTA, JSC.*

C251 [Statement] *The Iowa Review*, 4: 1 (winter 1973) 89.
Uncollected.

C252 [A review of] *Florida East coast champion* by Rod Taylor. *Poetry*, 121: 4 (January 1973) 239–241.
Uncollected.

C253 [A group review of] *Thomas Hardy and British poetry* by Donald Davie and *Collected poems 1950–1970* by Donald Davie. *The New York Times Book Review* (New York), (January 7, 1973) 5, 26.
Uncollected.

C254 [Poem] AN AMOROUS DEBATE/LEATHER KID AND FLESHLY. *Open Reading* (Sonoma, California), Second Series 3 (spring 1973) 30–31.
Ma, JSCx.

C255 [Poem] DIAGRAMS. *The Listener*, 90: 2311 (July 12, 1973) 48.
TTA, JSCx.

C256 [Poem] THE GEYSER. *The Listener*, 90: 2311 (July 12, 1973) 48.
TTA, JSCx.

C257 [Poem] SETTING OUT. *The Listener*, 90: 2311 (July 12, 1973) 48.
Uncollected.

C258 [Poem] METAL LANDSCAPES (AND THE STATUE OF LIBERTY). *The Listener*, 90: 2320 (September 13, 1973) 350.
(Retitled "Iron landscapes (and the Statue of Liberty)") in *TTA, JSCx.*

1975

C259 [Poem] BRINGING TO LIGHT. *Agenda*, 12: 4/13: 1 (winter–spring 1975) 22–24.
B42, *JSCx.*

C260 [Letter to the editor] *The American Poetry Review* (Philadelphia, Pennsylvania), 4: 2 (March/April 1975) 47.
Uncollected.

C261 [Poem] BEHIND THE MIRROR. *Chicago Review* (Chicago, Illinois), 27: 1 (summer 1975) 127.
JSCx.

C. POEMS AND PROSE

C262 [Poem] THE RELEASE. *Gay News* (London), 74 ([July 2, 1975]) 12.
JSCx.

C263 [Poem] THE BATH HOUSE. *New Departures* (Piedmont, Bisley, near Stroud, Gloucestershire), 7/8, 10/11 [September 1975] 78–80.
TTA, JSC.
Note: This is an earlier version of the poem that appears as part 4 of "The geysers", however because of a delay in the publication of the issue of *New Departures* the revised version appeared first in *TTA*.

C264 [Poem] THE CHERRY TREE. *The New Yorker* (New York), 51: 31 (September 22, 1975) 36.
JSCx.

C265 [Poem] JACK STRAW'S CASTLE. *Manroot* (South San Francisco, California), 10 (late fall–winter 1975) 52–54.
JSC.
Note: This version bears very little resemblance to the final version of "Jack Straw's castle".

1976

C266 [Poem] DOLLY. *Thames Poetry* (London), 1: 1 (winter 1975–6) 3.
JSCx.

C267 [Poem] HAMPSTEAD: THE HORSE CHESTNUT TREES. *Thames Poetry*, 1: 1 (winter 1975–6) 1–2.
JSCx.

C268 [Poem] THE OUTDOOR CONCERT. *Thames Poetry*, 1: 1 (winter 1975–6) 7.
JSCx.

C269 [Poem] THE ROADMAP. 1963. *Thames Poetry*, 1: 1 (winter 1975–6) 4. (Retitled "The roadmap") in *JSCx.*

C270 [Poem] YOKO. *Thames Poetry*, 1: 1 (winter 1975–6) 5–6.
JSCx.

C271 [A review of] *In the distance* by Dick Davies. *Thames Poetry*, 1: 2 (summer 1976) 59–62.
Uncollected.

C272 [Essay] Thom Gunn writes. . . . *Poetry Book Society Bulletin*, 90 (autumn 1976) [1].
Uncollected.

C273 [Poem] THE CONVERSATION. *Words Broadsheet* (London), 21 ([October 13, 1976]) (single sheet, French folded, making eight panels, unpaged).
Uncollected.

C274 [Poem] NEW YORK. *The New Yorker*, 52: 42 (December 6, 1976) 185.
Uncollected.

1977

C275 [Poem] ADULTERY. *Canto* (Andover, Massachusetts), 1: 1 (spring 1977) 14–15.
Uncollected.

C276 [Poem] ELEGY. *The Southern Review*, 13: 3 (July 1977) 583–584.
Uncollected.

C277 [Poem] HIDE AND SEEK. *The Southern Review*, 13: 3 (July 1977) 582–583.
Uncollected.

C278 [Poem] WALKER. *Christopher Street* (New York, N.Y.), 2: 4 (October 1977) 50.
Uncollected.

C279 [Essay] THE OPENNESS OF DONALD DAVIE. *Sequoia* (Stanford, California), 22: 2 (winter 1977) 30–32.
Uncollected.

C280 [Poem] 3 AM. *London Magazine*, N.S. 17: 6 (December 1977) 15–16.
Uncollected.

C281 [Poem] THE SAD SATANIST. *The Berkeley Review* (Berkeley, California), 6 & 7 (spring 1978) 109.
Uncollected.

C282 [Poem] THE EXERCISE. *The Listener*, 100: 2587 (November 23, 1978) 683.
Uncollected.
Note: This poem and the following poem appear under the author's collective title "Two poems about the wind".

C283 [Poem] SMALL PLANE IN KANSAS. *The Listener*, 100: 2587 (November 23, 1978) 683.
Uncollected.

C284 [Poem] THE CAT AND THE WIND. *The New Yorker*, 54: 41 (November 27, 1978) 188.
Uncollected.

C285 [Response to questionnaire] *The Sentinel* (San Francisco, California), 5: 25 (December 15, 1978) [9].
Uncollected.

D

TRANSLATIONS

This list of translations, although undoubtedly incomplete, is a result of as extensive a search of available sources as was possible. Entries are arranged alphabetically according to language and then in three subsections, *i.e.* books, anthologies, and periodicals. Only the English titles of the translated works are listed; bilingual translations are indicated. The Japanese names and titles have been Romanized.

CZECH

PERIODICAL

D1 Smylsl pohybu. *Světova literatura* (Prague), 4 (1958) 107–111.

Translations by Jiří Konůpek of "On the move," "The nature of an action," "St Martin and the beggar," "Human condition," and "The corridor".

GERMAN

ANTHOLOGIES

D2 *Gedichte Philip Larkin, Thom Gunn, Ted Hughes*. Karl Heinz Berger (editor). Berlin: Verlag Volk und Welt, 1974.

Translations by Helmut Heinrich, Klaus-Dieter Sommer and Karl Heinz Berger of "A kind of ethics," "Without a counterpart," "For a birthday," "Incident on a journey," "At the back of the North wind," "Human condition," "A plan of self subjection," "In praise of cities," "St Martin and the beggar," "In Santa Maria del Popolo," "Rastignac at 45," "My sad captains," "The feel of hands," "Confessions of the life artist," "Taylor Street," "Touch," "Epitaph for Anton Schmidt," "For signs," and "Sunlight".

D3 *Heiligenlob Moderner Dichter*. Gisbert Kranz (editor). Regensburg: Verlag Friedrich Pustet, [September 3] 1975.

Translation by Gisbert Kranz of "St Martin and the beggar".

2,500 copies published at DM 9.80.

D4 *Moderne Englische Lyrik*. Willi Erzgräber (editor). Stuttgart: Philipp Reclam Jun., [July] 1976.

Translations by Ute and Werner Knoedgen of "Without a counterpart," "On the move," "Jesus and his mother," "The annihilation of nothing," "Black jackets," and "My sad captains". English and German texts.

6,500 copies paperbound, 1,000 copies hardbound, published at DM 11.20.

PERIODICALS

D5 Considering the snail. *Neue Zürcher Zeitung* (Zurich), 2909 (75), July 5, 1964, p. 4.

Translation by Ursula Spinner. English and German texts.

D. TRANSLATIONS

D6 *Ensemble 4 Lyrik Prosa Essay* Internationales Jahrbuch für Literatur. Munich: Langen–Müller, [March 27] 1973.

Translations by Helmut Winter of "Snowfall," "Breakfast," and "Considering the snail". English and German texts.

2,500 copies published at DM 19.80.

ITALIAN

BOOK

D7 Thom Gunn *I Miei tristi capitani e altre poesie*, prefazione di Agostino Lombardo. [Milan]: Arnoldo Mondadori Editore, [1968]. 189 × 125 mm., pp. [1–8], 9–321, [322], 323, [324–332].

Translations by Camillo Pennati of "The wound," "Lofty in the palais de danse," "Round and round," "Helen's rape," "Here come the saints," "La prisonnière," "The court revolt," "The right possessor," "Looking glass," "Lerici," "The beach head," "Tamer and hawk," "Captain in time of peace," "Incident on a journey," "For a birthday," "On the move," "At the back of the North wind," "The nature of an action," "Human condition," "A plan of self subjection," "Autumn chapter in a novel," "The silver age," "The unsettled motorcyclist's vision of his death," "Market at Turk," "In praise of cities," "The allegory of the wolf boy," "Jesus and his mother," "To Yvor Winters, 1955" "The inherited estate," "During an absence," "High fidelity," "Legal reform," "Merlin in the cave: he speculates without a book," "The corridor," "Vox humana," "In Santa Maria del Popolo," "The monster," "The byrnies," "Black jackets," "The middle of the night," "Readings in French," "Innocence," "A map of the city," "The book of the dead," "Waking in a newly-built house," "Flying above California," "Considering the snail," " 'Blackie, the electric Rembrandt'," "The feel of hands," "Rastignac at 45," "Lights among redwood," "Loot," "My sad captains," "Hotblood on Friday," "L'epreuve," "Adolescence," "A trucker," "A crab," "The goddess," "Confessions of the life artist," "In the tank," and "Back to life". English and Italian texts.

Published January 1968, in an impression of 2,000 copies at L. 2500.

ANTHOLOGIES

D8 *Poesia Inglese del Dopoguerra*. Roberto Sanesi (editor). Milan: Schwarz Editore, [April] 1958.

Translations by Roberto Sanesi of "Here come the saints," "Lerici," "A kind of ethics," "Human condition," and "To Yvor ˉWinters, 1955". English and Italian texts.

2,000 copies published at L. 2500.

D. TRANSLATIONS

D9 *Poesia Inglese del '900*. Contesto a fronte introduzione, versioni e note di Carlo Izzo. [Parma]: [Ugo] Guanda [editore], Third edition, [February 24] 1967.

Translations by Carlo Izzo of "The wound," "For a birthday," "Incident on a journey," "Considering the snail," and "Jesus and his mother". English and Italian texts.

1,500 copies published at L. 6500.

Note: The first and second editions did not contain translations of poems by Thom Gunn.

PERIODICAL

D10 Riti di passagio e altri versi. *Almanacco dello specchio* (Milan), 3 ([February] 1974) 148–175.

Translations by Camillo Pennati of "Rites of passage," "Moly," "The sand man," "Three," "From the wave," "Tom-Dobbin," "The roof top," "The colour machine," "Flooded meadows," "Being born," and "Sunlight". English and Italian texts.

3,000 copies published at L. 4000.

JAPANESE

BOOK

D11 Thom Gunn *Fighting Terms*. Kyoto: Etude Group, publication number 3, 1977. 212 × 142 mm., pp. [i–iv], [1]–57, [58–60].

Translations of the Faber and Faber paperback issue of *Fighting Terms* (A2e) by members of the Etude Group of "The wound," "Here come the saints," "To his cynical mistress," "Wind in the street," "Lazarus not raised," "Lofty in the palais de danse," "Round and round," "Helen's rape," "The secret sharer," "La prisonnière," "Carnal knowledge," "The court revolt," "The right possessor," "Looking glass," "Lerici," "A mirror for poets," "The beach head," "A kind of ethics," "Tamer and hawk," "Captain in time of peace," "Without a counterpart," "For a birthday," and "Incident on a journey". Japanese text.

Note: The author's "Note on the text" is not included in this translation. Published November 1, 1977, in an impression of 250 copies, none of which were for sale.

D. TRANSLATIONS

ANTHOLOGY

D12 *Gendai Shishū*. Hajime Shinoda (compiler). Tokyo: Shueisha Publishing Co., Ltd., [April 30] 1968.

[Not seen].

Translations by Satoshi Nakagawa of "Helen's rape," "Carnal knowledge," "Jesus and his mother," "The separation," "To Yvor Winters, 1955," "The annihilation of nothing," and "My sad captains".

10,000 copies published at ¥520.

SPANISH

ANTHOLOGY

D13 *Poesia Ingelesa Contemporanea*. Estudio preliminar, selectión, traducción y notas by E. L. Revol. Buenos Aires: Ediciones Librerias Fausto, [December 15] 1974.

Translations by E. L. Revol of "The annihilation of nothing," and "The secret sharer". English and Spanish texts.

4,000 copies published at 150,000 pesos.

SWEDISH

ANTHOLOGY

D14 *Åtta Engelska Poeter*. Petter Bergman and Göran Printz-Påhlson (editors). Stockholm: FIB:s Lyrikklub, [August 1] 1957.

Translations by Göran Printz-Påhlson of "For a birthday," and "Lerici" and "The corridor" by Petter Bergman.

5,000 copies published in paperback and hardback editions.

E

INTERVIEWS

This list of interviews is confined to those interviews in which Thom Gunn discusses his poetry or philosophy in direct response to an individual interrogator or interrogators. It does not include prose responses to questionnaires or other solicited prose statements (included in sections B and C). Minor prose statements, *e.g.* those on dust wrappers *etc.* are listed in section H.

E1 Kitay, Michael, Julian Jebb, R.[onald] H.[ayman]. Interview. *Chequer*, 6 (summer 1954) 17–19.

E2 Hamilton, Ian. Four conversations. *The London Magazine*, N.S. 4: 6 (November 1964) 64–70.

E3 Love me, love my poem. *The Observer*, (March 7, 1965) 23.

E4 Morrish, Hilary. Violence and energy, an interview. *The Poetry Review*, 57: 1 (spring 1966) 32–35.

E4a Coulette, Henri (editor). Thom Gunn *The unstrung lyre: interviews with fourteen poets*. n.p. [Washington, D.C.], [National Endowment for the Arts], (n.d.) [1971], C4–C27.

E5 Newer, Hank. *Brushfire* interview Thom Gunn. *Brushfire* (Reno, Nevada), 25 (1975–76) [155–159].

E6 Iyer, Pico. Thom Gunn and the Pacific drift. *Isis* (Oxford), 1971 (June 2, 1977) 20–21.

E7 Sarver, Tony. Thom Gunn. *The Advocate* (San Mateo, California), 220 (July 27, 1977) 39–40.
    Note: This interview is reprinted, with the addition of different photographs in *Gay News*, 134 (January 12–25, 1978) 16, 26.

E8 Scobie, W. I. Gunn in America: A conversation in San Francisco. *London Magazine*, N.S. 17: 6 (December 1977) [5]–15.

F

RECORDINGS

This list attempts to describe the commercially published recordings of Thom Gunn reading his own poems either alone or in company with other poets. Each entry includes an abstract of the record (or videotape) label, a description of the recording, a list of contents, and the circumstances of recording and publication. No attempt has been made to list recordings made at readings or on other occasions that are in institutional archives or owned privately.

F1 *Listen presents Thom Gunn reading "On the move"* [and other poems].
The Marvell Press, Hessle, Yorkshire, 1962, LPV4.

One 12 in., 33⅓ r.p.m., monaural disc. Matrix: side 1: MAR/LP-113-A-10; side 2: MAR/LP-113-B-10.

Contents: Side 1: "In praise of cities," "Claus von Stauffenberg," "The byrnies," "Black jackets," "A plan of self subjection," "During an absence," "The feel of hands," "On the move," "Lofty in the palais de danse," "The corridor," "Market at Turk," and "The beaters". Side 2 : "Interrogated to interrogator," "Here come the saints," "The beach head," "Tamer and hawk," "Captain in time of peace," "For a birthday," "The silver age," "A mirror for poets," "The wound," "From the highest camp," "Lazarus not raised," "Vox humana," "The value of gold," and "Waking in a newly-built house," read by Thom Gunn.

Notes: Recorded January 20, 1959, Oakland, California, and released in 1962. On the front cover of the sleeve is reproduced photograph of Thom Gunn by Bill Marshall leaning against a lamppost. On the back cover of the sleeve is a 65 line autobiographical essay by Thom Gunn commenting on his poetry and his own personal history.

F2a *The Jupiter anthology of 20th century English poetry, part III* edited by Anthony Thwaite.
Jupiter Recordings Ltd., London, 1963, JUR 00A8.

One 12 in., 33⅓ r.p.m., monaural disc. Matrix: side 1: v A v 1//420; side 2: v B v 1//421 11.

Contents: Side 2: "The annihilation of nothing" and "Innocence" read by Thom Gunn.

b *Anthology of 20th century English poetry, part III* [edited by Anthony Thwaite].
A Jupiter Recording issued by Folkways, Folkways Records & Service Corporation, New York, N.Y., 1967, FL 9879.

One 12 in., 33⅓ r.p.m., monaural disc. Matrix: side 1: FL 9879A; side 2: FL 9879B.

Contents: Same as F2a.

c *The Jupiter Anthology Part Three 00A8* [edited by Anthony Thwaite].
Audio-Visual Productions, 15 Temple Sheen Road, London SW14 7PY, Telephone 01-876 0064 [February 1975], 00A8.

One two track standard cassette.

Contents: Same as F2a.

F. RECORDINGS

F3 *The poet speaks, Record five, Ted Hughes, Peter Porter, Thom Gunn, Sylvia Plath*, edited by Peter Orr.

Argo Record Company Ltd., London, 1965, RG 455.

One 12 in., 33⅓ r.p.m., monaural disc. Matrix: side 1: ARG-2713-1A; side 2: ARG-2714-1A.

Contents: Side 2: "Epitaph for Anton Schmidt," "Elegy on the dust," "The allegory of the wolf boy," "The unsettled motorcyclist's vision of his death," "Thoughts on unpacking," "A map of the city," "Considering the snail," "The book of the dead," and "Misanthropos-IX" read by Thom Gunn.

Notes: Recorded May 26, 1965, and "in association with the British Council and the Poetry Room in the Lamont Library of Harvard University". There are at least two issues of this recording; the first has a sleeve with a drawing by Arthur Wragg of three figures in the foreground and outlines of houses in the background. The subsequent sleeve has each word of the title "The poet speaks" printed in different colors, *i.e.* gray, purple, and gold. The reissue has a different recording identification number, *i.e.* PLP 1085, however the matrix numbers are the same for both sides.

F4 *Thom Gunn reading his own poetry 820/6.*

Audio-Visual Productions, 15 Temple Sheen Road, London SW1X 7PY, Telephone 01-876 0064, [June 1971], 820/6.

One single track standard cassette.

Contents: "Lines for a book," "On the move," "At the back of the North wind," "Elvis Presley," "Lofty in the palais de dance," "Breakfast," "The goddess," "The vigil of Corpus Christi," "Rastignac at 45," "The byrnies," and "Flying above California".

Note: These poems were recorded in London in 1959 and on January 27, 1965, by the British Council in association with the Poetry Room in the Lamont Library at Harvard University and leased to Audio-Visual Productions for commercial distribution.

F5 *British poets of our time Thom Gunn*, poems read by the author, edited by Peter Orr.

Argo, The Decca Record Company, London, 1975, PLP 1203.

One 12 in., 33⅓ r.p.m., monaural disc. Matrix: side 1: ARG-4235-1K; side 2: ARG-4236-1K.

Contents: Side 1: "The wound," "To his cynical mistress," "Incident on a journey," "Autumn chapter in a novel," "The silver age," "Jesus and his mother," "Vox humana," "In Santa Maria del Popolo," "Innocence," "The feel of hands," "Considering the snail," "My sad captains,"

"Flying above California," and "The value of gold". Side 2: "The byrnies," "The book of the dead," "The goddess," "Touch," "Pierce Street," "Grasses," "The messenger," "The fair in the woods," "Words," "Rites of passage," "From the wave," "Moly," and "Sunlight".

Note: Recorded for Argo Records by The British Council in their studio at Albion House, London, June 5, 1974.

G

RADIO AND TELEVISION APPEARANCES

The programs in this section are limited to those in which poems and prose first appeared on radio or television. Radio or television programs that constituted readings of poems or prose previously printed are not included.

G1 *New soundings number 7.* 1952.

A program edited and introduced by John Lehmann on which "The secret sharer" was read.

Broadcast on B.B.C. Third Programme, September 24, 1952.

G2 *New soundings number 11.* 1953.

A program edited and introduced by John Lehmann on which "Incident on a journey" was read.

Broadcast on B.B.C. Third Programme, February 4, 1953.

G3 *New poetry.* 1953.

A program introduced by G. S. Fraser on which "A mirror for poets" was read.

Broadcast on B.B.C. Third Programme, September 16, 1953.

G4 *First reading number 6.* 1953.

A program edited and introduced by John Wain on which "For a birthday," "A kind of ethics," "Matter and spirit," and "Cameleon" were read.

Broadcast on B.B.C. Third Programme, September 24, 1953.

G5 *New Verse.* 1954.

A program introduced by Anthony Hartley on which "A plan of self subjection" and "Light sleeping" were read.

Broadcast on B.B.C. Third Programme, April 8, 1954.

G6 *Thom Gunn talks to Al Alvarez.* 1964.

A program produced by George Walton Scott. Excerpts of this program were used in *Poetry Today* (*vide infra*).

Broadcast on B.B.C. Third Programme, July 20, 1964.

G7 *Poetry today 3. Thom Gunn.* 1964.

A program produced by George Walton Scott on which six poems by Thom Gunn were read and on which three prose statements commenting on his poems were inserted and first broadcast here.

Broadcast on B.B.C. Third Programme, October 15, 1964.

G8 *"Misanthropos" A poem in four parts by Thom Gunn.* 1965.

A program produced by Douglas Cleverdon with an introduction titled "Argument" by Thom Gunn (not printed in any other place than in the script produced for the broadcast).

Broadcast on B.B.C. Third Programme, March 8, 1965.

G. RADIO AND TELEVISION APPEARANCES

G9 *Poets of the sixteenth century 10. Poems and songs of Fulke Greville, Lord Brooke.* 1968.

A program compiled by Thom Gunn and Douglas Cleverdon.
Broadcast on B.B.C. Third Programme, June 2, 1968.

G10 *The living poet: Thom Gunn.* 1968.

A program produced by Douglas Cleverdon on which Thom Gunn introduces and comments on his own poetry. The prose comments and poems "Sunlight," and "The sand man" were first read on this program.
Broadcast on B.B.C. Third Programme, December 19, 1968.

G11 *Hardy and the ballads.* 1976.

A program read by Thom Gunn and prepared for Open University Arts Faculty, Level III Course, Twentieth Century Poetry, A.306/1.
Broadcast on B.B.C. Open University, February 14, 1976. It was rebroadcast on February 21, 1977, and February 26, 1977.
Note: This is less an original work than an abridgement of the article with the same title published in *Agenda* (C244).

H

MISCELLANY

This section attempts to list odds and ends that do not obviously fit into other sections of the book. It is intended to record the existence of these ephemeral items but not to place undue emphasis on their importance.

H1 [autobiographical statement] [untitled] on the back of the sleeve for the recording *Listen presents Thom Gunn reading "On the move"* [and other poems] (F1). A 65 line autobiographical statement that is identical to the statement in the *Poetry Book Society Bulletin* (C100) with the addition of sections titled "Life" and "Publications [to date]". The Marvell Press, Hessle, Yorkshire, 1962.

H2 [Introduction to "Misanthropos"] Argument. (G8). A 2 page statement that Thom Gunn read for the broadcast of "Misanthropos" on the B.B.C. Third Programme, March 8, 1965. Pages [1] and 2 of the mimeographed B.B.C. script (of which "about 20" are produced). British Broadcasting Company, London, 1965.

Note: Douglas Cleverdon excerpted this introduction in an article in *Radio Times* (London), 166: 2156 (March 4, 1965) 2.

Note: The Argument was not included when the poem sequence was published in *Encounter* (C188).

H3 [statement on dust wrapper] Nemerov, Howard. *The Winter Lightning*. London, Rapp & Whiting, 1968.

Contains, on front flap a quotation by Thom Gunn "One of the best poets writing in English". This is excerpted from a review by Thom Gunn of another of Nemerov's books (C158).

H4 [statement on dust wrapper] Conquest, Robert. *Arias from a love opera and other poems*. London, Macmillan and Co. Ltd., 1969 New York, The Macmillan Company, 1969.

Contains on the inner front flap of the dust wrapper a statement by Thom Gunn "A strong and individual voice talking about things that matter".

H5 [excerpt from a manuscript] Sotheby & Co. *Catalogue of 19th century and modern first editions, presentation copies, autograph letters and literary manuscripts*. London, December 14–15, 1970, 145.

Contents: excerpt from notation in Thom Gunn's manuscript notebook dated March 31, 1964.

H6 [statement on dust wrapper] Peck, John. *Shagbark*. Indianapolis/New York, The Bobbs-Merrill Company, Inc., 1972.

Contains on rear panel of dust wrapper a statement by Thom Gunn "A good description of John Peck's book could be taken from his own lines: *Doors in this termless morning | Sills, thresholds | and the firmness beyond.* It is poetry both of intimation and fulfillment. Sensory richness ties you down to a reality. However, if the richness is what you first encounter, the next is an oddity of the poem's structure that seems to lift you disconcertingly away from that firmness (as in "Cider and Vesalius," "For the Engraver," or "The Bracelet"). Then you realize that, disconcerting as such a lift may be, it is not discordant with the palpable firmness after all, but a direct extension of it. The structure that at first seemed merely odd turns out to be the subject of the poem. This is a very beautiful book."

Note: In the printing of the dust wrapper for the hardcover issue and the rear wrapper of the paperback issue of the book the source of the statement is not identified. Later copies of the dust wrapper have a white paper label pasted on below the quotation identifying the source, *i.e.* "—Thom Gunn".

H7 [statement on rear wrapper] Taylor, Rod. *Florida East Coast Champion*. San Francisco, Straight Arrow Books, second printing, December 1972.

Contains, on the rear wrapper, a quotation by Thom Gunn "For me, Rod Taylor is simply the best poet to turn up in the last fifteen years. His poetry is the real thing . . . whole poetry, in which the writer is fully living . . ." This is excerpted from a review by Thom Gunn of this book in *Poetry* (C252).

H8 [autobiographical statement] Thom Gunn on Thom Gunn. A 2 page, 280 × 216 mm., autobiographical statement issued as a press release called "BOOK NEWS" printed by offset lithography on Farrar, Straus and Giroux letterhead. Dated at the end on the second page "November 1972", but issued in 1973, at about the same time that Farrar, Straus and Giroux published *Moly and My Sad Captains*.

Note: This is a revision of a similar statement written for Faber and Faber Ltd. in *ca.* 1957, but never published.

H9 [statement on dust wrapper] Nemerov, Howard. *Gnomes & Occasions*. Chicago and London, The University of Chicago Press, 1973.

Contains, on the front flap of dust wrapper, a quotation by Thom Gunn "One of the best poets writing in English." This is excerpted from a review by Thom Gunn of another of Nemerov's books (C158).

H10 Videotape. Thom Gunn/Nathaniel Tarn/Joanne Kyger. American Peotry Archive & Resource Center, The Videotape Collection of The Poetry Center at San Francisco State University [San Francisco, California], First Series: 1975. Catalog number V-T 63/65.
½ inch color reel to reel; ¾ inch color cassette.

Contents: "The cherry tree," "Touch," "The idea of trust," and "Jack Straw's castle."

Note: Recorded November 20, 1974, in the home of John and Margot Doss, San Francisco, California.

Note: This videotape is available for lease and showing for "non-commercial, educational purposes only, and will be without charge to the viewers and/or listeners".

H11 Videotape [Thom Gunn introducing Ted Hughes].

American Poetry Archive & Resource Center, The Videotape Collection of The Poetry Center at San Francisco State University [San Francisco, California], Third Series: 1978. Catalog number V–T 218.

½ inch color reel to reel; ¾ inch color cassette.

Contents: Introduction of Ted Hughes.

Note: Recorded July 20, 1977, at the San Francisco Museum of Art San Francisco, California.

Note: This videotape is available for lease and showing for "non-commercial, educational purposes only, and will be without charge to the viewers and/or listeners".

H12 [excerpt from a letter] Sotheby Parke Bernet & Co.

Catalogue of autograph letters and historical documents. London, February 20–21, 1978, 94.

Contents: short excerpt from a letter from Thom Gunn to Ronald Hayman concerning Thom Gunn's contribution to MY CAMBRIDGE (B43).

H13 [drawing on poster] MICHAEL McCLURE | & & & | ∷ THOM GUNN ∷ | [rectangular panel, 158 × 252 mm. created by a single rule, in which a face has been drawn in black ball-point pen (outline of face by Thom Gunn) and felt-tip pen (features of face by Michael McClure)] | together giving a reading at | gill theater in campion hall | university of san francisco | *golden gate avenue between masonic and parker* | 8 pm thurs. february 23, 1978 | *tickets $2.50 available at the door and city lights book store* | THIRTY COPIES PRINTED BY WESLEY B. TANNER & DRAWN ON BY MICHAEL McCLURE & THOM GUNN. | [holograph signatures with black ball-point pens] Michael McClure Thom Gunn.

Note: These 30 copies, 534 × 375 mm., were printed on white American hand-made laid paper with a butterfly watermark (Oakland, California) in August 1978. Of these 30 copies, 22 were offered for sale at $25.00 each. This edition was preceded by an edition of 300 copies of the poster, 435 × 278 mm., printed on coated white light weight commercial card stock in February 1978. These copies contain a printed face drawn wholly by Michael McClure in the rectangular panel.

APPENDIX I

JUVENILIA

This appendix starts with two poems and a piece of prose from school magazines. They are thus the earliest work that Thom Gunn published. It also contains poems written and published as an undergraduate which he chose not to include in his first book and which have not appeared in book form anywhere. They are here reprinted, with his permission, to make them available to interested scholars. In most instances the publications in which they originally appeared were fugitive and are difficult to get hold of. Publishing them here in no way implies that the poet considers them to possess any literary quality.

A THOUSAND CHEERS FOR AUTHORS

The earliest authors, by the cave fire,
   They told stories all about dragons;
They told stories of peasant and squire;
   They told stories, jogging in wagons;
They sang stories to the tune of the lyre;
   They told stories, drinking from flagons.
      A thousand cheers for authors!

Then the clever printers came,
   With cunning in their hands.
Then reading gained a wider fame
   In near and distant lands.
Then many men could read the same,
   A book with chains and leather bands.
      A thousand cheers for authors!

In Mister Bumpus' bookshop—
   Oh, there is my delight!—
Of books he has a monster crop;
   They are a lovely sight.
I hope that authors never stop,
   For reading gives the "wisdom-light."
      A thousand cheers for authors!

I love to think of books of old
   The great Greeks wrote so long ago.
Chaucer the first English stories told;
   Sweet Shakespeare came and stout Defoe,
With Jonathan Swift and Bunyan bold,
   Till Dumas—he's the best I know!
      A thousand cheers for authors.

—T. W. Gunn

RAIN

Rain! It came down. I went out. I *had* to do some shopping. Not a crumb to eat. I heard it come down—"Plop! Plop." It fell onto the house. It slid down the roof and trickled into the gutter and ran down the drain. I stood at the end of the red-brick garden path. It was wet and slippery! It was on the old beech tree. It slithered down its trunk and gathered into a dark, murky puddle at the bottom of the tree, by its roots.

It was raining harder now. It beat upon the ground—"tap-a-tap-a-tap-tap." It was slowly trickling down my neck. Ugh—what a horrid feeling. It cracked the ground like a whip. "Crack, slash-crack."

Poor flowers! Dashed to the ground as the rain-god bent his fury on them. But it was soothing, too. After that hot room—Phew! it was hot!

But, oh! I must hurry. I must if I want to get any food for my husband and the friends he said he was bringing home.

          ★   ★   ★   ★

I trotted back up the garden path . . . soaked and wet.

I took out the door-key. The plants drooped to the ground, and there was only a drizzle now.

That is right; leave the wet umbrella on the ground to dry itself out. Do not put the wet clothes by the fire, but hang them on the back of a chair and let them dry. Now, the fire; I must put some more coal on. That's right—roaring fire! Now, lay the table—lovely food—salmon—(I pinched a little bit to taste.)

          ★   ★   ★   ★

Ah! The table laid at last; now for a rest in a soft arm-chair!

A ring at the door bell. That's Dick, my husband.

I went to answer it.

"This is Mr. and Mrs. Jackson; this is my wife." Hasty introductions. . . . Dinner directly.

"Nice dinner."

Air-raid siren.

"We needn't take any notice of it—need we?"

"What's the time?"

"Half-past nine."

          ★   ★   ★   ★

Boom! Boom!

The thud of guns.

The drone of a plane.

Booo—oomp—crash.

Darkness. Where are we?

APPENDIX I: JUVENILIA

"Dickie," I called.
No answer.
"Dickie!" frantically.
"Dickie!"
I called again and again.
I stumbled about the room.
I felt blood on my face.
"Mr. and Mrs. Jackson."
No answer.
I nearly went frantic.
I ran outside, and the rain was cool on my blood-spattered cheek.

—Tommy Gunn

THE HEIGHTS

We loved to walk the lower slopes,
   Smooth but interspersed with rocks.
Of higher steeps we kept wild hopes
   And envied the adventurous fox.

We heard the sound of distant falls,
   And watched the rushing foam below,
Imagined we caught hollow calls
   That from tall rocks leap to and fro.

We dreamed of those high-domed ruins
   Where veiled kings keep their ghostly courts,
Of dim halls filled with white birds' cooings,
   Turrets where tangling ivy sports.

We hoped for caverns walled with ice,
   Inlets to undiscovered seas:
We climbed the long-mysterious heights.
   We climbed—but we found none of these.

—T. W. Gunn (Vs)

APPENDIX I: JUVENILIA

THE FABLE IS DIFFERENT

"Their blood is cak'd, tis cold, it seldom flows,
Tis lack of kindly warmth they are not kind."

—Timon, of the Senators

They live in a respectable Underworld
Where persons have little connection with persons or things,
And if an outrageous event or bereavement brings
Them near to the entrance they never clamour for blood.
They fear Odysseus' shining eyes
And prefer no statement at all to the risk of lies.

Their houses with shelves of fragile vases are crammed
Which are for the duster not for human touch:
So they travel heavy when they travel, which isn't much
For if they went far it might be they'd get damned
Like the runners in the unlit streets
Whom they hear at midnight indignantly from quiet sheets.

They hate and despise the rough and crazy boys
Who wait in jeering gangs at corner to snatch
At the waists of passing girls, or keep insolent watch,
Who drink, shout, love, in places of dirt and noise
In a certain quarter of the town
That any responsible magistrate would pull down.

They are the wicked step mothers who lock up
The child while it is still young with pliable bone
In basement between known rules they clamp it down
Till it as well emerges afraid to lap
From the horny cup of Odysseus' hand
And afraid of his ships which come from a definite land.

—Thom. Gunn

APPENDIX I: JUVENILIA

MOTHER LOVE

The mother takes the child, the one whom she adores,
Strengthens to cartilage the umbilical cord,
The train and carriages of jealous love to bear.

Main or branch line traffic, this is the only track:
Each act or thought a departure, reaction a journey back.
Any and every thing done for each other's sake.

She is an egotist (he is her favourite limb),
He is selfish (was she not born to care for him?)
—Journeys are frequent, needful, along the narrow line.

One day a bitter freight slowly steams across.
Later repenting, to prove she had not meant to aggress,
She steps up cheap excursions (but he uses them the less).

The fatal load was bluff, had only been to show
That she was strongest and best, she pleads, how might she know
It could not be withdrawn: later the line's marked Closed.

At night a coup d'état: she sends an armoured train
Packed with careful reproaches which are to tie him down
With railway network, as lifelong province of her own.

But the puzzled Gulliver who rouses shakes them off
Breaks the exclusive line without meaning to be rough
Turns on his other side and gives a sleepy laugh.

And it is not till later that he can comprehend
The finality of his action. He can't be wholly blamed
Though he might have seen how little long-distance call can mend.

Though ready to acknowledge the filial link, her sanction
He demanded to extend and be proclaimed a junction.
This she refused: their quarrels brought the line's extinction.

Founded on safe impulse, his mother's love was simple
But he, unconscious of difficulties, an ambitious rebel,
Plans popular lines from himself to crowds of the nicest people.

Financial troubles follow, the architect resigns,
Materials are faulty, and crashes litter those lines
Finished; the project fails; loneliness all he finds.

Indeed he began to find it everywhere as soon
As the old line of his mother's was permanently closed down.
Remains now derelict station; and this she had always known.

—Thom. Gunn

TWO GHOSTS

I was told this house was still inhabited
By two sisters an indefinite long since dead
Unpossessive part-owners hardly deserving the name
Of ghosts, for in their lives they had been the same
Flitting among the polished knobs of furniture,
But only their voices now.

I resolved to know the friendly double essence
Imagined I found their comfortable presence
In spinster concord together picking pears
In the garden, or whispering on the cellar stairs,
Or flitting among the polished knobs of furniture,
But only their voices now.

A harmless tale with which to charm a guest
This of two gentle sisters who could not rest
In effortless cramping dark inside the tomb
But continued to busy themselves from room to room,
Flitting among the polished knobs of furniture,
But only their voices now.

One rainy night, my hand on the kitchen door,
I heard two voices I had not heard before:
Item by item one droned an accusation,
The other spat back furious protestation.
(Flitting among the polished knobs of furniture,
But only their voices now).

168

rule] | THOM GUNN; white laid paper; all edges trimmed; white wove endpapers; dust wrapper strong red (12) laid paper printed in black. [same as A22a]

Publication date: July 12, 1976

Price: $15.00

Number of copies: 120

Note: There were 20 over-run copies bound; these were lettered after the colophon on page [29]: [holograph in red ink] Author's copie | [holograph number in red ink] [i–xx] | [holograph signature in blue ink] Thom Gunn

Pagination: Same as A22a, except after the colophon on page [29] appears: [holograph number in red ink] | [holograph signature in blue ink] Thom Gunn

Contents: Same as A22a.

A23   THE MISSED BEAT   1976

a. *First edition:*

THOM GUNN The Missed Beat WITH | A WOOD ENGRAVING BY SIMON BRETT | [engraving of aqueduct in moderate yellow (87)] | THE JANUS PRESS NEWARK VERMONT | 1976

Collation: [1]⁸ French fold = 8 French fold leaves; 228–231 × 158 mm.

Binding: Quarter bound in dark gray (266) cloth and vertically striped moderate greenish yellow (102) and light olive (106) Fabriano Ingres paper covered boards; lettered down the spine in black on a 6 × 71 mm. moderate greenish yellow (102) laid paper label: THOM GUNN THE MISSED BEAT; toned Okawara handmade paper, French fold; top edges uncut, fore-edges untrimmed, bottom edges trimmed and untrimmed; dark greenish yellow (103) laid endpapers; issued in a slipcase, the sides of which are covered with vertically striped moderate greenish yellow (102) and light olive (106) Fabriano Ingres paper (as on the boards of the book), and the spine, top and bottom edges of the slipcase are covered with dark gray (266) cloth; lettered down the spine of the slipcase in black on a 7.5 × 88 mm. moderate greenish yellow (102) laid paper label: THOM GUNN: THE MISSED BEAT

Note: The paper used on the endpapers, boards and sides of the slipcase is variously watermarked with: INGRES COVER FABRIANO; however, this watermark does not appear on all copies, nor necessarily in all three places on the same copy.

Publication date: May 1, 1976

Price: $35.00

c   65

A. BOOKS PAMPHLETS AND BROADSIDES

Number of copies: 50

Note: There were about 20 copies of the complete sheets with The Janus Press imprint, with the signature of both the author and the artist on the colophon page, which were sewn into dark greenish yellow (103) laid paper wrappers and were divided between the publisher of The Janus Press and the publisher of The Gruffyground Press. These copies were not offered for sale.

Also, five incomplete copies, sewn into dark greenish yellow (103) laid paper wrappers, were sent to Thom Gunn at the time that the edition was published. These copies lack the title page, copyright page, "The Missed Beat" and the colophon page. On the next to last page, which is blank in these copies, Gunn has written out in holograph in black ink "The Missed Beat" poem and added in holograph, in red ink, his own colophon, number and signature at the bottom of the same page.

Pagination: [1] half-title; [2] blank; [3] title page; [4] [in moderate yellow (87)] eight lines of acknowledgements, including the copyright notice; [5–10] text; [11] engraving of aqueduct (same as on title page) printed in black; [12–13] text; [14] [in moderate yellow (87)] The wood engraving was printed from Simon Brett's | original block; the text is handset Times New Roman | printed on Okawara at The Janus Press in Newark, West | Burke, Vermont in the United States of America by Claire | van Vliet for Anthony Baker at The Gruffyground Press, | Ladram, Sidcot, Winscombe, Somerset in England. The | cover is Fabriano Ingres. | The edition is limited to two hundred & twenty copies | of which fifty are for The Janus Press and one hundred | and seventy are for The Gruffyground Press. | [holograph signature in pencil] Thom Gunn | [15–16] blank.

Contents: The Soldier—Light Sleeping—Excursion—From an Asian Tent —The Clock—Aqueduct—The Missed Beat.

b. *First English edition, first state:*   1976

THOM GUNN The Missed Beat WITH | A WOOD ENGRAVING BY SIMON BRETT | [engraving of aqueduct in moderate yellow (87)] | SIDCOT · THE GRUFFYGROUND PRESS | 1976

Collation: [1]⁶ French fold = 6 French fold leaves; 230–233 × 159 mm.

Binding: Sewn into wallet-edged French fold dark greenish yellow (103) Fabriano Ingres laid paper wrappers and printed on the upper wrapper in black: THOM GUNN: THE MISSED BEAT; toned Okawara handmade paper, French fold; top edges uncut; fore-edges untrimmed, bottom edges trimmed and untrimmed.

Publication date: May 24, 1976

A. BOOKS, PAMPHLETS AND BROADSIDES

Price: £6.00

Number of copies: "about 70"

Note: In "about 70" copies the space between the first and second lines on the title page is 16 mm. Thereafter, the title page was "tightened" and in all remaining copies, including those with The Janus Press imprint, the space between the first and second lines of the title page is 11 mm.

Pagination: [1] title page; [2] [in moderate yellow (87)] eight lines of acknowledgements, including the copyright notice; [3–8] text; [9] engraving of aqueduct (same as on title page) printed in black; [10–11] text; [12] [colophon in moderate yellow (87), same as in first edition, A24a, but with the addition below the author's holograph signature of:] [holograph signature in pencil] Simon Brett. | [holograph rule]

Contents: Same as A24a.

Note: There was a press over-run of about ten additional copies. In addition, one copy with The Gruffyground Press imprint was bound into a cloth and paper covered board binding similar to The Janus Press edition, but without a slipcase, and this copy bears only Thom Gunn's signature on the colophon.

c. *First English edition, second state:*   1976

These copies are the same in every respect as A24b except for the spacing on the title page. In these copies the space between the first and second lines on the title page is 11 mm. [see note after *Number of copies* in A24a]

Number of copies: "about 100"

A24   JACK STRAW'S CASTLE   1976
                            [and other poems]

a. *First edition, hardcover issue:*

THOM GUNN | Jack Straw's Castle | FABER AND FABER | 3 Queen Square, London

Collation: [1–5]⁸ = 40 leaves; 217 × 137 mm.

Binding: Bound in vital reddish orange (34) cloth and lettered down the spine in gold: JACK STRAW'S CASTLE [solid square] THOM GUNN [solid square] FABER; white wove paper; all edges trimmed; white wove endpapers; dust wrapper pale yellow (89) wove paper printed in black, vital ornage (48) and strong blue (178).

Publication date: September 20, 1976

Price: £3.25

Number of copies: 750; second printing, May 24, 1977, 350 copies.

Pagination: [1–2] blank; [3] half-title; [4] by the same author | MOLY | POEMS 1950–1966: A SELECTION | TOUCH | POSITIVES | SELECTED POEMS (with Ted Hughes) | FIGHTING TERMS | MY SAD CAPTAINS | THE SENSE OF MOVEMENT; [5] title page; [6] *First published in 1976* | *by Faber and Faber Limited* | *3 Queen Square London WC1* | *Printed in Great Britain by* | *Latimer Trend & Company Ltd Plymouth* | *All rights reserved* | *ISBN 0 571 10974 8 (hardbound edition)* | *ISBN 0 571 11010 x (Faber Paperbacks)* | © *Thom Gunn, 1976*; [7] To the memory of | Tony White; [8] blank; 9–10, Contents; [11] section title; [12] blank; 13–30, text; [31] section title; [32] blank; 33–58, text; [59] section title; [60] blank; 61–77, text; 78, Acknowledgements; [79–80] blank.

Contents: The Bed—Diagrams—Iron Landscapes—The Corporal—Fever—The Night Piece—Last Days at Teddington—All Night, Legs Pointed East—The Geysers: Sleep by the Hot Stream; The Cool Stream; The Geyser; The Bath House—Three Songs: Baby Song; Hitching into Frisco; Sparrow—The Plunge—Bringing to Light—Thomas Bewick—Wrestling—The Outdoor Concert—Saturnalia—Faustus Triumphant—Dolly—Jack Straw's Castle 1–11—An Amorous Debate—Autobiography—Hampstead: the Horse Chestnut Trees—The Roadmap—The Idea of Trust—Courage, a Tale—Behind the Mirror—The Cherry Tree—Mandrakes—Yoko—The Release—Breaking Ground.

Note: There were an unknown number of advance proof copies issued in gray reddish orange (39) wove paper wrappers; lettered down the spine in black: JACK STRAW'S CASTLE; and with the same information as appears on the title page printed in black on the upper wrapper with the additional imprint of: UNCORRECTED | PROOF COPY | Not for sale | Nor for review or serialization | without the publisher's permission | Publication date not yet settled

b. *First edition, paperback issue:* 1976

[The transcription of the title page is identical with that of the first edition, hardcover issue.]

Collation: [1–5]⁸ = 40 leaves; 217 × 135 mm.

Binding: Glued into stiff white wove paper wrappers, the exterior of which is shiny, and printed in black, pale yellow (89), vital orange (48) and strong blue (178); lettered down the spine in black: JACK STRAW'S CASTLE [solid strong blue (178) square] THOM GUNN [solid strong blue (178) square] [in pale yellow (89) on a vital orange (48) panel] FABER; on the upper wrapper: [in pale yellow (89) and strong blue (178) on a black panel] THOM | GUNN | [in black on vital orange (48) and pale yellow (89) panels] JACK | STRAW'S | CASTLE; on the rear wrapper, in black on pale yellow (89), is the price and the publisher's statement regarding the book; the inner upper wrapper lists other books by Thom Gunn; the inner rear wrapper lists other poets published by Faber and Faber; white wove paper; all edges trimmed.

Publication date: September 20, 1976

Price: £1.95

Number of copies: 4,000; second printing, April 15, 1977, 2,500 copies.

Pagination: Same as A24a, except for page [6], where lines seven and eight are reversed, and with the addition between line eight and the final line of: CONDITIONS OF SALE | [followed by six lines of conditions of sale, printed in italics].

Contents: Same as A24a.

c. *First American edition:* 1976

THOM GUNN | Jack Straw's Castle | *and Other Poems* | [publisher's logo] | FARRAR, STRAUS AND GIROUX NEW YORK

Collation: [1]¹⁶ + [2]⁸ + [3]¹⁶ = 40 leaves; 208 × 136 mm.

Binding: Bound in moderate reddish purple (241) cloth; lettered down the spine in silver; Thom Gunn JACK STRAW'S CASTLE *Farrar Straus Giroux*; yellow white (92) laid paper; all edges trimmed; light gray (264) wove textured endpapers; dust wrapper white wove paper printed in black, gray purplish red (256) and brilliant greenish blue (168).

Publication date: October 29, 1976

Price: $7.95

Number of copies: Publisher prefers not to reveal the number of copies printed.

Pagination: [1] half-title; [2] blank; [3] By Thom Gunn | *Fighting Terms* | *The Sense of Movement* | *Selected Poems* (with Ted Hughes) | *Positives* (with Ander Gunn) | *Touch* | *Poems 1950–1966: A Selection* | *Moly and My Sad Captains* | *Jack Straw's Castle and Other Poems*; [4] blank; [5] title page; [6] Copyright © 1971, 1973, 1974, 1975, 1976 by Thom Gunn | All rights reserved | First published in 1976 by Faber & Faber Limited | First American printing, 1976 | Printed in the United States of America | Library of Congress Cataloging in Publication Data | Gunn, Thom. | Jack Straw's castle and other poems. | I. Title. | PR6013.U65J34 1976 821'.9'14 76–40937; [7] To the memory of | Tony White; [8] blank; 9–10, Contents; [11] section title; [12] blank; 13–30, text; [31] section title; [32] blank; 33–58, text; [59] section title; [60] blank; 61–77, text; [78] Acknowledgements; [79–80] blank.

Contents: Same as A24a.

Note: There were an unknown number of advance proof copies issued in strong greenish yellow (99) wove paper wrappers with the same information as appears on the title page printed on the upper wrapper with the additional imprint of: UNCORRECTED PAGE PROOF

d. *First American paperback edition:*   1977

[The transcription of the title page is identical with that of the first American edition.]

Collation: 40 single leaves; 209 × 136 mm.

Binding: A perfect binding glued into stiff white wove paper wrappers, the exterior of which is shiny, printed in black, gray purplish red (256) and brilliant greenish blue (168); lettered down the spine: [in gray purplish red (256)] Thom Gunn [in black] JACK STRAW'S CASTLE [publisher's logo] N 568; on the upper wrapper in black: [surrounded by a frame of panels in gray purplish red (256) and brilliant greenish blue (168)] Jack | Straw's | Castle | and | Other | Poems | [single rule of 62 mm.] | Thom Gunn; on the rear wrapper in black [in the upper left] N 568 | ISBN 0-374-51417-8 | [in the upper right] $3.45 | [in gray purplish red (256)] THOM GUNN | [five line quotation from a review by Raymond Oliver] | [in gray purplish red (256)] Jack Straw's Castle | [eleven line publisher's statement] | *Cover design by Charles Skaggs* | THE NOONDAY PRESS | A division of Farrar, Straus and Giroux | 19 Union Square West | New York 10003; white wove and white laid paper; all edges trimmed.

Publication date: September 9, 1977

Price: $3.45

Number of copies: Publisher prefers not to reveal the number of copies printed.

Pagination: Same as A24c.

Contents: Same as A24a.

A25   A CRAB   1978

a. *First edition:*

[in deep red (13)] A Crab | Thom Gunn

Collation: [1]² = 2 leaves; 242 × 190 mm.

Binding: Leaflet; white laid paper; all edges trimmed; issued in white wove paper envelope.

A. BOOKS, PAMPHLETS AND BROADSIDES

Publication date: May 1978

Price: Not for sale

Number of copies: 30

Pagination: [1] title page; [2] blank; [3] text; [4] Number [holograph number in red ink] of 30 copies handset & handprinted, May 1978 [publisher's logo: skull and crossbones]

Note: Only 26 copies were numbered; four were unnumbered.

Contents: A crab.

Note: Laid into copies, a photocopied letter on white wove paper, 172 × 127 mm. the text of which is as follows: Dear [ribbon typed name of recipient and comma] | Enclosed is a piracy of an | uncollected Thom Gunn poem. | We hope you like it. It's a | gift, but it's also a small | reminder that we still live | in a country where secret | underground presses aren't | usually necessary. We'd like | to keep it that way. | If you believe in press | freedom, maybe you'd consider | sending the equivalent of | what this poem would cost in | a bookshop (about $10—or | more if you can afford it) | for 'The Body Politic Free | the Press Fund' in Canada to: | Lynn King in Trust for The Body Politic, | 111 Richmond St. W., | Suite 320, | Toronto, | CANADA M5H 3N6. | Thanks, | THE PIRATES.

B

BOOKS AND PAMPHLETS EDITED,
OR WITH CONTRIBUTIONS BY
THOM GUNN

In this section, books and pamphlets in which a contribution by Thom Gunn appears either for the first time in a book or for the first time in print are listed chronologically. Any material which was previously unpublished is identified.

POETRY FROM CAMBRIDGE 1951–52   1952

POETRY | FROM | CAMBRIDGE | 1951–1952 | A selection of verse by members of the University. | *Edited by* | THOM GUNN | THE FORTUNE PRESS | LONDON, S.W. 1.

Collation: [1–3]⁸ = 24 leaves; 188–190 × 124–128 mm.

Binding: Quarter bound in black cloth with imitation snake-skin grained black paper covered boards and lettered up the spine in gold: *POETRY FROM CAMBRIDGE* 1951–52; white wove paper; top edges trimmed, other edges untrimmed; white wove endpapers; dust wrapper medium gray (265) printed in deep red (13).

Publication date: 1952, sometime after June during 1952.

Price: 6s

Number of copies: unknown

Contents: "Introduction", p. 5; "To his cynical mistress", p. 27, collected in *FT*; "Helen's rape", pp. 27–28, collected in *FT*; "A mirror for poets", pp. 28–29, collected in *FT*; "Lazarus not raised", pp. 29–30, collected in *FT, P 50–66*.

Note: The prose introduction appears here for the first time in print.

B2   SPRINGTIME   1953

SPRINGTIME | *An Anthology of Young Poets* | *and Writers edited by* | *G. S. Fraser and* | *Iain* [*sic.*] *Fletcher* | PETER OWEN LIMITED | *London*

Collation: [1]⁴ + [2–9]⁸ = 68 leaves; 210 × 135 mm.

Binding: Bound in dark purplish red (259) cloth and lettered down the spine in gold: *Springtime Peter Owen;* white wove paper; all edges trimmed; white wove endpapers; dust wrapper white wove paper printed in dark purplish red (259) and deep blue (179).

Note: Ian Fletcher's name is consistently misspelled on the title page and on the upper dust wrapper.

Note: An unrecorded number of the total edition were bound in black cloth. The publisher's records do not record which binding takes precedence. In a conversation with the publisher, he stated that the dark purplish red (259) was probably first.

B. BOOKS AND PAMPHLETS

Publication date: March 30, 1953

Price: 12s 6d

Number of copies: 1,500

Contents: "Carnal knowledge", pp. 48–49, collected in *FT*.

Note: The contents also include "A mirror for poets" and "Helen's rape" which were previously collected.

B3   POETRY FROM CAMBRIDGE 1952–4   1955

Poetry from Cambridge | 1952–4 | [rule with an open triangular space in the center] | Edited by Karl Miller | Fantasy Press

Collation: [1]²² = 22 leaves; 191 × 117 mm.

Binding: Stapled into a moderate blue (182) wove paper wrapper lettered across the upper wrapper in black: POETRY | FROM | CAMBRIDGE | 1952–4 | [three solid dots 3 mm. in diameter in moderate reddish brown (43)] | EDITED BY KARL MILLER | FANTASY PRESS; white wove paper; all edges trimmed; dust wrapper moderate blue (182) wove paper printed in black and moderate reddish brown (43).

Publication date: May 10, 1955

Price: 5s

Number of copies: 100

Note: Another 199 copies were published on May 26, 1955, and are indistinguishable from the first 100.

Contents: "Matter and spirit", pp. 22–23; "Earthborn", p. 24; and "Cameleon", p. 26.

Note: The poem "Cameleon" appears here for the first time in print.

Note: The contents also include "The beachhead", "Tamer and hawk", and "For a birthday", all of which were previously collected.

B4   NEW POEMS 1955   1955

New Poems | [interrupted rule with decorative circle in center] [within decorative circle] 1955 | *Edited by* | PATRIC DICKINSON | J. C. HALL | ERICA MARX | *with an introduction* | [publisher's logo] | *London* | MICHAEL JOSEPH

Collation: [1–7]⁸ + [8]⁶ = 62 leaves; 202 × 130 mm.

Binding: Quarter bound in dark reddish brown (44) cloth with white and moderate reddish brown (43) decorative paper covered boards and lettered across the spine in gold: *New* | *Poems* | [rule interrupted with dot in center] | *1955* | [rule interrupted with dot in center] | *a* | *P.E N.* | *Anthology* | [publisher's logo] | MICHAEL | JOSEPH; white wove paper; all edges trimmed; top edges stained dark reddish brown (44); white wove endpapers; dust wrapper moderate reddish orange (37) wove paper printed in dark purplish blue (201).

Publication date: October 17, 1955

Price: 12s 6d

Number of copies: 2,500

Contents: "Jesus and His mother", pp. 16–17, collected in *TSOM*, *TE* and *P 50–66*.

Note: The contents also contain "Earthborn" which was previously collected.

B5   NEW LINES   1956

NEW LINES | [decorative rule] | *An Anthology* | *edited by* | ROBERT CONQUEST | LONDON | MACMILLAN & CO LTD | NEW YORK · ST MARTIN'S PRESS | 1956

Collation: [1–7]⁸ = 56 leaves; 227× 137 mm.

Binding: Bound in moderate green (145) cloth and lettered across the spine in gold: NEW | LINES | [decorative rule] | *An* | *Anthology* | *Macmillan*; white wove paper; all edges trimmed; white wove endpapers; dust wrapper white wove paper printed in moderate bluish green (164).

Publication date: June 28, 1956

Price: 12s 6d

Number of copies: 1,500; second printing, September 24, 1956, 750 copies; third printing, April 23, 1957, 1,000 copies; fourth printing, October 25, 1961, 1,000 copies; fifth printing, January 26, 1967, 500 copies in cloth and 3,000 copies in paper wrappers.

Contents: "On the move", pp. 31–33, collected in *TSOM, SP, TE, P 50–66*; "Human condition", pp. 33–34, collected in *TSOM*; "Merlin in the cave: he speculates without a book", pp. 34–37, collected in *TSOM*; "Autumn chapter in a novel", pp. 37–38, collected in *TSOM, P 50–66*; "A plan of self-subjection", pp. 38–39, collected in *TSOM*; "Puss in boots to the giant", pp. 39–40, collected in *TSOM*; "The inherited estate", pp. 40–42, collected in *TSOM*.

Note: The poems "Puss in boots to the giant" and "The inherited estate" appear here for the first time in print.

Note: The contents also include "Lerici" which was previously collected.

B6   NEW POEMS 1956   1956

New Poems | [rule interrupted with decorative circle in center] [within decorative circle] 1956 | *Edited by* | STEPHEN SPENDER | ELIZA-BETH JENNINGS | DANNIE ABSE | [publisher's logo] | *London* | MICHAEL JOSEPH

Collation: [1–7]⁸ + [8]¹⁰ = 66 leaves; 202 × 130 mm.

Binding: Quarter bound in dark yellowish pink (30) cloth with white, light yellowish pink (28), light olive gray (112) and deep purple (219) decorative paper covered boards and lettered across the spine in white: *New* | *Poems* | [rule interrupted with dot in center] | *1956* | [rule interrupted with dot in center] | *a* | *P. E N.* | *Anthology* | [publisher's logo] | MICHAEL JOSEPH; white wove paper; all edges trimmed; top edges stained dark yellowish pink (30); white wove endpapers; dust wrapper moderate greenish blue (173) wove paper printed in dark blue (183).

Publication date: July 2, 1956

Price: 12s 6d

Number of copies: 2,500; second printing, September 7, 1956, 500 copies.

Contents: "The silver age", p. 113; and "The corridor", pp. 113–114, collected in *TSOM*.

B7   POETRY NOW   1956

POETRY NOW | *an anthology* | *edited by* | G. S. FRASER | FABER AND FABER | 24 Russell Square | London
Collation: [1–12]⁸ + [13]⁴ = 100 leaves; 202 × 132 mm.

Binding: Bound in dark yellowish pink (30) cloth and lettered across the spine in gold: *POETRY* | *NOW* | an | anthology | edited | by | G. S. FRASER | Faber | and | Faber; white wove paper; all edges trimmed; white wove endpapers; dust wrapper light blue gray (190) wove paper printed in black and vital red (11).

Publication date: October 12, 1956

Price: 15s

Number of copies: 3,390

Contents: "Light sleeping", pp. 81–82, collected in *TMB*.

Note: Contents also contain "Helen's rape" which was previously collected.

B8   NEW POEMS 1957   1957

New Poems | [rule interrupted with decorative circle in center] [within decorative circle] 1957 | *Edited by* | KATHLEEN NOTT | C. DAY LEWIS | THOMAS BLACKBURN | [publisher's logo] | *London* | MICHAEL JOSEPH

Collection: [1–8]⁸ + [9]⁶ = 70 leaves; 202 × 132 mm.

Binding: Quarter bound in brilliant greenish yellow (98) cloth with black and white decorative paper covered boards and lettered across the spine in black: *New* | *Poems* | [rule interrupted with a dot in center] | 1957 | [rule interrupted with a dot in center] | *a* | *P. E N.* | *Anthology* | [publisher's logo] | MICHAEL JOSEPH; white wove paper; all edges trimmed; white wove endpapers; dust wrapper pale green (149) wove paper printed in dark purplish blue (201).

Publication date: October 21, 1957

Price: 15s

Number of copies: 2,600

Contents: "Canzon: the flagellants", pp. 59–60 which is an earlier version of "The beaters" which was published in *TSOM* prior to the appearance of the earlier version in this book.

Note: The contents also contain "Vox humana" which was previously collected.

B9   NEW POEMS 1958   1958

New Poems | [rule interrupted with decorative circle in center] [within decorative circle] 1958 | *Edited by* | BONAMY DOBRÉE | LOUIS MacNEICE | PHILIP LARKIN | [publisher's logo] | *London* | MICHAEL JOSEPH

Collation: [1–7]⁸ + [8]⁶ = 62 leaves; 200 × 132 mm.

Binding: Quarter bound in vital red (11) cloth with white, strong red (12), dark gray (266) and light olive (106) decorative paper covered boards and lettered across the spine in white: *New* | *Poems* | [rule interrupted with dot in center] | *1958* | [rule interrupted with dot in center] | *a* | *P. E N.* | *Anthology* | [publisher's logo] | MICHAEL | JOSEPH; white wove paper; all edges trimmed; white wove endpapers; dust wrapper light gray (264) wove paper printed in dark reddish orange (38).

Publication date: November 10, 1958

Price: 13s 6d

Number of copies: 2,600

Contents: "The byrnies", pp. 44–45, collected in *MSC, SP, TE, P 50–66, M & MSC.*

B10   THE GUINNESS BOOK OF POETRY   1959
1957/58

THE GUINNESS | BOOK OF POETRY | 1957/58 | [publisher's logo] | PUTNAM | 42 GREAT RUSSELL STREET | LONDON MCMLIX

Collation: [1–9]⁸ = 72 leaves; 215 × 140 mm.

Binding: Bound in moderate blue (182) cloth and lettered across the spine in gold: [block of five rules] | *The | Guinness | Book of | Poetry* | [block of five rules] | *2* | [block of three rules] | *PUTNAM* | [block of three rules]; white wove paper; all edges trimmed; top edges stained pale blue (185); white wove endpapers; dust wrapper white wove paper printed in black and light blue (181).

Publication date: May 4, 1959

Price: 10s 6d

Number of copies: 3,000

Contents: "Interrogated to interrogator", p. 69.

B11   THE GUINNESS BOOK OF POETRY   1960
1958/59

THE GUINNESS | BOOK OF POETRY | 1958/59 | [publisher's logo] | PUTNAM | 42 GREAT RUSSELL STREET | LONDON

Collation: [1–7]⁸ + [8]¹⁰ + [9]⁸ = 74 leaves; 215 × 139 mm.

Binding: Bound in moderate blue (182) cloth and lettered across the spine in gold: [block of five rules] | *The | Guinness | Book of | Poetry* | [block of five rules] | *3* | [block of three rules] | *PUTNAM* | [block of three rules]; white wove paper; all edges trimmed; top edges stained pale blue (185); white wove endpapers; dust wrapper white wove paper printed in black and brilliant orange yellow (67).

Publication date: April 11, 1960

Price: 10s 6d

Number of copies: 3,000

Contents: "All-night burlesque", p. 65.

B12   45–60 AN ANTHOLOGY OF ENGLISH   1960
POETRY 1945–60

45–60 | AN ANTHOLOGY OF | ENGLISH POETRY | 1945–60 | Chosen by | THOMAS BLACKBURN | [publisher's logo] | PUTNAM | 42 GREAT RUSSELL STREET | LONDON

Collation: [1–11]⁸ = 88 leaves; 185 × 110 mm.

Binding: Bound in strong red (12) cloth and lettered on the spine in gold: [across] BLACKBURN | [down] 45–60 AN ANTHOLOGY OF ENGLISH POETRY | [across] PUTNAM; white wove paper; all edges trimmed; top edges stained strong red (12); dark red (16) wove endpapers; dust wrapper white wove paper printed in black, light gray (264), strong red (12) and brilliant greenish yellow (98).

Publication date: November 14, 1960

Price: 18s

Number of copies: 3,500

Contents: "The book of the dead", p. 87, collected in *MSC, TE,* and *M & MSC*; "The monster", pp. 89–90, collected in *MSC* and *M & MSC*.

Note: The contents also include "The corridor" which was previously collected.

B13   THE GUINNESS BOOK OF POETRY   1961
1959/60

THE GUINNESS | BOOK OF POETRY | 1959/60 | [publisher's logo] | *PUTNAM | 42 GREAT RUSSELL STREET | LONDON*

Collation: [1–7]⁸ + [8]⁶ + [9]⁸ = 70 leaves; 216 × 138 mm.

Binding: Bound in moderate blue (182) cloth and lettered across the spine in gold: [block of five rules] | *The | Guinness | Book of | Poetry* | [block of five rules] | 4 | [block of three rules] | *PUTNAM* | [block of three rules]; white wove paper; all edges trimmed; top edges stained pale blue (185); white wove endpapers; dust wrapper white wove paper printed in black and strong purplish red (255).

Publication date: May 8, 1961

Price: 10s 6d

Number of copies: 3,000

Contents: "Map of the city", p. 69, collected in *MSC* and *M & MSC* as "A map of the city".

B14   COMMISSIONED POEMS 1962   1962

The Poetry Festival was held at the San Francisco | Museum of Art from June 21 through June 24, 1962. | The Festival was dedicated to the memory of Dag | Hammarskjold and the Cause of World Peace. | [in simulated open face type] COMMISSIONED POEMS | 1962 | POETRY FESTIVAL | the POETRY CENTER, San Francisco State College

Collation: One gathering of 17 leaves; 276 × 210 mm.

Binding: Stapled into a heavy white wove paper wrapper printed on the upper wrapper in black and vital orange (48) and on the spine in vital orange (48); the rear wrapper remains white. Lettered across the upper wrapper, as part of a block print of a man holding a poster: POETRY | FESTIVAL. Beneath the lettering is a 15 × 83 mm. portion of the upper wrapper that has been cut out and COMMISSIONED POEMS | 1962 from the title page shows through; white wove paper; all edges trimmed.

Publication date: "late spring 1962"

Price: distributed free

Number of copies: "two hundred and fifty to five hundred copies, no more"

Note: Publication details were provided by James Schevill who edited the publication.

Contents: "In the tank", p. 12, collected in *T*.

Note: The poem "In the tank" appears here for the first time in print.

B15   POET'S CHOICE   1962

a. *First edition:*

POET'S CHOICE | [rule with a simple knot in its center] | EDITED BY | Paul Engle and Joseph Langland | [publisher's logo] | THE DIAL PRESS NEW YORK 1962

Collation: [1–8]^{16} + [9]^4 + [10–11]^{16} = 164 leaves; 230–232 × 154–156 mm.

Binding: Bound in strong reddish brown (40) cloth and lettered across the spine in gold: [decorative device] | [down] POET'S CHOICE | [across] [decorative device] | EDITED BY | ENGLE | AND | LANGLAND | [publisher's logo] | DIAL; white wove paper, top edges trimmed, other edges untrimmed; deep reddish orange (38) wove endpapers; dust wrapper shiny pale orange yellow (73) wove paper printed in black, gold, and deep reddish orange (38).

Publication date: October 29, 1962

Price: $6.00 until December 31, 1962, and after that $6.95.

B. BOOKS AND PAMPHLETS

Number of copies: Data unavailable from the publisher.

Contents: Prose statement with reproduction of Thom Gunn's signature explaining why he chose "My sad captains" as his choice for inclusion in this book, p. 279.

Note: The prose statement appears here in print for the first time.

b. *First paperback edition:*

POET'S | CHOICE | [rule with a single knot in its center] | EDITED BY | Paul Engle and Joseph Langland | [publisher's logo] A DELTA BOOK · 1966

Collation: 160 single leaves; 202 × 134 mm.

Binding: A perfect binding glued into a white heavy wove paper wrapper printed in shiny black, medium gray (265) and vital green (139) and lettered on the spine: [across] [in vital green (139)] 6982 [down] [in black] POET'S CHOICE edited by Engle and Langland [across] [in vital green (139)] [publisher's logo]; the upper wrapper is lettered across [in medium gray (265)] $1.95 $2.25 IN CANADA | [surrounded by a vital green (139) border connecting with the lower panel] [in black] POET'S | CHOICE | [on a vital green (139) panel] [in white] edited by Paul Engle and Joseph Langland | [in black] over one hundred great poets choose their | favorite poem from their own work | and give the reasons for their choices. | [in white] Robert Frost / William Carlos Williams | Marianne Moore / Conrad Aiken | E. E. Cummings / Archibald MacLeish | Robert Graves / Langston Hughes | Ogden Nash / Robert Penn Warren | John Betjeman / Theodore Roethke | Stephen Spender / Karl Shapiro | Randall Jarrell / John Ciardi / Allen Tate | Robert Lowell / Howard Nemerov | Allen Ginsberg / Alistair Reed | con't on back cover | [in dark gray (266)] [publisher's logo] | DELTA; on the rear wrapper [on a vital green (139) panel] [in dark gray (266)] [publisher's logo] | [in white] E. J. Pratt / Edmund Blunden / Louise Bogan | Leonine Adams / Oscar Williams / Robert Francis | Brewster Ghiselin / Earle Birney / Richard Eberhart | John Holmes / Patrick Kavanagh / Stanley Kunitz | E. L. Mayo / Phyllis McGinley / William Empson | Richmond Lattimore / Vernon Watkins / Elizabeth Bishop | J. V. Cunningham / Josephine Miles | Kenneth Patchen | Roy Fuller / Irving Layton / George Barker | John Frederick Nims / Delmore Schwartz / John Berryman | Barbara Howes / William Stafford / Henry Rago | John Malcolm Brinnin / Peter Viereck / Gwendolyn Brooks | Charles Causely / Joseph Langland / John Heath-Stubbs | William Jay Smith / Lawrence Ferlinghetti | William Meredith / Reed Whittemore / James Schevill | Richard Wilbur / Kingsley Amis / Donald Davie | Anthony Hecht / Philip Larkin / Howard Moss | Daniel G. Hoffman / Denise Levertov / William H. Matchett | Louis Simpson / Edgar Bowers / Michael Hamburger | Vassar

B. BOOKS AND PAMPHLETS

Miller / Donald Justice / John Wain | Elizabeth Jennings / James Merrill / W. D. Snodgrass | David Wagoner / Henri Coulette / Galway Kinnell | W. S. Merwin / Charles Tomlinson / Phyllis Webb | William Dickey / Donald Hall / Thomas Kinsella | Philip Levine / Anne Sexton / Thom Gunn / John Hollander | X. J. Kennedy / Ted Hughes / Jay McPherson | Leonard Cohen / John Hall Wheelock / John Crowe Ransom | Mark VanDoren / C. Day Lewis / Paul Engle | Robinson Jeffers | [in dark gray (266)] Dell Publishing Co., Inc. Printed in U S A; white wove paper; all edges trimmed.

Publication date: January 1966

Price: $1.95

Number of copies: Data unavailable from publisher.

Contents: Same as B15a.

c. *Second paperback edition:*

POET'S CHOICE | *EDITED BY* | Paul Engle and Joseph Langland | *with a new introduction by Paul Engle* | [publisher's logo] | TIME Reading Program Special Edition | TIME INCORPORATED · NEW YORK

Collation: 168 single leaves; 202 × 130 mm.

Binding: A perfect binding glued into a card cover that has a wavy pattern in multiple shades of blue, green, tan, and gray with the title always in white, across the spine: POET'S | CHOICE | edited | by | Engle | and | Langland; on the upper wrapper: POET'S | CHOICE | edited by Paul Engle | and Joseph Langland; on the rear wrapper in the upper right corner there is the signature of "Frank Bozzo" and a publisher's logo in the lower left corner; white wove paper; all edges trimmed; inner front and inner rear wrappers moderate greenish yellow (102).

Publication date: August 9, 1966

Price: $1.25 to subscribers

Number of copies: 80,000

Contents: Same as B15a.

B16　　　　　FIVE AMERICAN POETS　　　　　1963

Five | *American Poets* | [rule] | EDGAR BOWERS | HOWARD NEMEROV | HYAM PLUTZIK | LOUIS SIMPSON | WILLIAM STAFFORD | *edited by* | *Thom Gunn and Ted Hughes* | FABER AND FABER | 24 Russell Square | London

Collation: [1–7]⁸ = 56 leaves; 216 × 137 mm.

B. BOOKS AND PAMPHLETS

Binding: Bound in gray purplish blue (204) cloth and lettered down the spine in gold: [enclosed in a ruled box] FIVE AMERICAN POETS *Faber and Faber*; white wove paper; all edges trimmed; white wove endpapers; dust wrapper pale yellow green (121) wove paper printed in black, deep purplish blue (197) and deep reddish orange (36).

Publication date: May 31, 1963

Price: 21s

Number of copies: 2,500

Contents: "Foreword", (signed "T.G. T.H.") p. 7; "Edgar Bowers", p. 13; "Howard Nemerov", p. 33; "Hyam Plutzik", p. [55]; "Louis Simpson", p. [71]; and "William Stafford", p. [95].

Note: The "Foreword" and all the introductory biographical notes were collaborative efforts of Thom Gunn and Ted Hughes and appear here in print for the first time.

B17   EROTIC POETRY   1963

[left-hand title page] [in black] Erotic Poetry | [in strong blue (178)] DECORATION BY WARREN CHAPPELL

[right-hand title page] [in black and strong blue (178)] [line drawing] | [in black] *The Lyrics, Ballads, Idyls | and Epics of Love— | Classical to Contemporary | Edited by WILLIAM COLE* | Forward by Stephen Spender | [in strong blue (178)] [publisher's logo] | [in strong blue (178)] [rule] | [in black] RANDOM HOUSE | [in strong blue (178)] 1963

Collation: [1–13]¹⁶ + [14]⁸ + [15–18]¹⁶ = 280 leaves; 238 × 157–160 mm.

Binding: Bound in moderate green (145) cloth and lettered across the spine in gold: [in deep red (13)] [three rules] | [in deep red (13)] [a band of scallop shell design] | Erotic | Poetry | [dot] | WILLIAM | COLE | [in deep red (13)] [a band of scallop shell design] | [publisher's logo] | RANDOM HOUSE | [in deep red (13)] [three rules]; on the upper cover in gold: EROTIC POETRY | [in deep red (13)] [line drawing]; white wove paper; top and bottom edges trimmed, fore-edges untrimmed; top edges stained deep pink (3); light gray brown (60) wove endpapers; dust wrapper white wove paper printed in black, brilliant yellow (83), strong yellow (84), deep red (13), deep green (142), strong yellowish green (131), brilliant greenish blue (168), pale orange yellow (73), moderate yellowish brown (77) and dark brown (59).

Publication date: September 1963

Price: $8.95

Number of copies: Publisher prefers not to reveal the number of copies printed.

Contents: "Das liebesleben", pp. 402–403.

Note: The contents also contain "Loot" previously collected.

B18   THE CONCISE ENCYCLOPEDIA OF   1963
ENGLISH AND AMERICAN POETS AND
POETRY

a. *First edition:*

The Concise Encyclopedia of | ENGLISH AND AMERICAN | Poets and Poetry | Edited by | STEPHEN SPENDER and | DONALD HALL | [publisher's logo] Hutchinson of London

Collation: [1–26]⁸ = 208 leaves; 246 × 185 mm.

Binding: Bound in moderate orange yellow (71) cloth and lettered across the spine in gold: [rule] | [title on dark red (16) panel] THE CONCISE | Encyclopedia of | English | and American | Poets & Poetry | [rule] | Edited by | STEPHEN SPENDER | & DONALD HALL | [publisher's logo] | HUTCHINSON; in the lower right hand corner of the upper cover blind stamped [publisher's series logo]; white wove paper and white shiny paper; all edges trimmed; top edges stained moderate orange (53); white wove endpapers with shiny composite photograph of books of poetry displayed on bookshelves; dust wrapper heavy white wove paper printed with the same photograph as used on endpapers with additional printing in black and brilliant greenish yellow (98).

Note: Of this edition the title page of all copies examined is tipped in.

Publication date: October 28, 1963

Price: £5.00

Number of copies: Publisher prefers not to reveal the number of copies printed.

Contents: "Thomas Chatterton", pp. 72–73; "Hart Crane", pp. 101–102; "Sir Walter Raleigh", pp. 270–271; "Theodore Roethke", pp. 277–278; "[Arthur] Yvor Winters", p. 359; and "Thomas Wyatt", pp. 362–363.

Note: The six prose statements appear here in print for the first time.

b. *First American edition:*

The Concise Encyclopedia of | ENGLISH AND AMERICAN | Poets and Poetry | Edited by | STEPHEN SPENDER and | DONALD HALL | HAWTHORN BOOKS INC · *Publishers* · NEW YORK

Collation: [1–26]⁸ = 208 leaves; 247 × 187 mm.

Binding: Bound in moderate blue (182) cloth and lettered across the spine in gold: [title and editors within a gold rule border] THE CONCISE | ENCYCLOPEDIA OF | ENGLISH AND | AMERICAN | POETS & POETRY | EDITED BY | STEPHEN SPENDER | AND DONALD HALL | HAWTHORN; white wove paper and white shiny paper; all edges trimmed; top edges stained dark blue gray (192); end-papers the same as in the first edition; dust wrapper the same as for the first edition with the substitution of: [in white] HAWTHORN [instead of HUTCHINSON] at the foot of the spine panel of the dust wrapper.

Publication date: 1963

Note: The publisher does not have more precise information on the date of publication of the first printing or subsequent reprints.

Price: $17.95

Note: $17.95 was the price supplied by the publisher, however the one copy of the dust wrapper found for examination was printed with the price $12.95/ $15.00 on the front inner flap.

Number of copies: The publisher does not have data on the number of copies printed in the first printing or subsequent reprints.

Note: On the verso of the title page of the first printing of the American edition there is a statement "Printed in England" which is not present in the second printing.

Contents: Same as B18a.

B19   NEW POEMS 1963   1963

a. *First edition:*

[abstract floral design] | NEW POEMS | 1963 | A P.E.N. Anthology of | Contemporary Poetry | [abstract floral design] | *Edited by* | LAWRENCE DURRELL | HUTCHINSON OF LONDON

Collation: [1–10]⁸ = 80 leaves; 200 × 133 mm.

Binding: Quarter bound in black imitation-cloth paper with white paper covered boards printed in dark gray (266) and vital red (11) and lettered across the spine: [in gold] New | Poems | [in white] [bulging rule] | [in gold] 1963 | [in white] [publisher's logo] | [in white] HUTCHINSON; white wove paper; all edges trimmed; white wove endpapers; dust wrapper white wove paper printed in black and vital red (11).

Publication date: November 18, 1963

Price: 21s

Number of copies: Publisher prefers not to reveal the number of copies printed.

Contents: "A crab", p. 57; "The goddess", p. 58, collected in *AG, T, P 50–66*.

b. *First American edition:*

[abstract floral design] | NEW POEMS | 1963 | A British | P.E.N. Anthology | [abstract floral design] | *Edited by* | LAWRENCE DURRELL | HARCOURT, BRACE & WORLD, INC. | NEW YORK

Collation: [1–10]⁸ = 80 leaves; 198 × 132 mm.

Binding: Quarter bound in black imitation-cloth paper with white paper covered boards printed in dark gray (266) and vital red (11) and lettered across the spine: [in gold] New | [in gold] Poems | [in white] [bulging rule] | [in gold] 1963 | [in white] HARCOURT | [in white] BRACE; white wove paper; all edges trimmed; white wove endpapers; dust wrapper shiny white wove paper printed in black and moderate blue (182).

Publication date: April 8, 1964

Price: $3.95

Number of copies: 1,030

Contents: Same as B19a.

B20   15 POEMS FOR WILLIAM   1964
                     SHAKESPEARE

a. *First trade edition:*

[entire text of title page is enclosed within a double rule border] 15 *Poems* | *for William* | *Shakespeare* | [rule] | *edited by* Eric W. White | *with an introduction by* | Patrick Garland | John Lehmann & | William Plomer | [rule] | 1964: *Stratford-upon-Avon* | The Trustees & Guardians | of Shakespeare's Birthplace

Collation: [1]¹² = 12 leaves; 249 × 148 mm.

Binding: Sewn into a lighter shade of light yellowish brown (76) wallet-edge wove paper wrapper; on the upper wrapper: [ornamental floral border printed in very dark green (147) serving as a border surrounding the title] [in decorative type] 15 | [in decorative type] POEMS | *for William* | *Shakespeare* | Edmund Blunden Dom Moraes | Charles Causley Peter Porter | Roy Fuller W. J. Snodgrass | Thom Gunn Stephen Spender | Randall Jarrell Derek Walcott | Thomas Kinsella Vernon Watkins | Laurie Lee

David Wright | Hugh MacDiarmid | [thick ornamental floral rule in very dark green (147)]; white wove paper; all edges trimmed.

Publication date: June 1964

Price: 3s 6d

Number of copies: 1,000

Contents: "The kiss", p. [15], later collected and retitled "The kiss at Bayreuth" in *AG* and *T*.

Note: The poem "The kiss" appears here for the first time in print.

b. *First limited edition:*

[The transcription of the title page is identical to that of the first trade edition.]

Collation: [1]¹² = 12 leaves; 247 × 149 mm.

Binding: Bound in paper vellum covered boards stamped in gold on the upper cover: [portrait of William Shakespeare surrounded by a rule and then surrounded by] ∧ WILLIAM SHAKESPEARE ∧ STRATFORD UPON AVON | 1564 ∧ 1964 | 15 POEMS | *for William* | *Shakespeare*; white wove paper; all edges trimmed; white wove endpapers; the verso of the title page carries a statement of limitation and the copy number.

Publication date: June 1964

Price: 10s 6d

Number of copies: 100

Contents: Same as B20a.

B21   NEW POETRY 1964   1964

[cover title] [top left side of the upper wrapper] [in black] Sylvia Plath | Philip Larkin | R. S. Thomas | Thom Gunn | Ted Hughes | Karen Gershon | Jon Stallworthy | William Stafford | Louis Simpson | Theodore Roethke | Adrienne Rich | Robert Bly | James Wright | Anne Sexton | [top right side of the upper wrapper] [in white] New | Poetry | 1964 | [in black] PRICE ONE SHILLING | CRITICAL QUARTERLY POETRY SUPPLEMENT NUMBER 5 | [graphic design lower half of upper wrapper]

Collation: [1]¹² = 12 leaves; 219 × 132 mm.

Binding: Stapled into a white card wrapper printed in black and deep greenish yellow (100); the rear wrapper gives information about The Critical Quarterly Society; white wove paper; all edges trimmed.

Publication date: autumn 1964

B. BOOKS AND PAMPHLETS

Price: 1s

Number of copies: 9,000

Contents: "Berlin in ruins", p. 10, collected in *AG* and *T*.

B22   THE OBSERVER REVISITED   1964

THE | OBSERVER | REVISITED | 1963–64 | *Compiled by* | CYRIL DUNN | [publisher's logo] HODDER AND STOUGHTON

Collation: [1–16]⁸ = 128 leaves; 216 × 135 mm.

Binding: Bound in dark purplish red (259) imitation-cloth paper covered boards and lettered across the spine in gold: *The* | *Observer* | *Revisited* | * * | compiled by | CYRIL | DUNN | [publisher's logo]; white wove paper; all edges trimmed; top edges stained moderate red (15); white wove endpapers; dust wrapper shiny white paper printed in black and vital green (139).

Publication date: October 26, 1964

Price: 21s

Number of copies: 4,000

Contents: "Driving to Florida", p. 256.

B23   MOMENTS OF TRUTH   1965

[decorative rule: hourglass alternating with abstract floral design] | Moments of Truth | Nineteen Short Poems | by Living Poets | [decorative rule: (as above)] | London | The Keepsake Press | 1965 | [decorative rule: (as above)]

Collation: [1]¹⁴ = 14 leaves; 171 × 108 mm.

Binding: Stapled into a lighter shade of light gray yellowish brown (79) card wrapper printed in dark yellowish brown (78) on the right side of the upper wrapper: MOMENTS | OF TRUTH | George Barker | Martin Bell | John Betjeman | Edwin Brock | Robert Conquest | Gavin Ewart | Roy Fuller | Thom Gunn | Bernard Gutteridge | Francis Hope | Ted Hughes | Edward Lowbury | Kathleen Nott | Peter Porter | Peter Redgrove | James Reeves | Peter Russell | David Wevill | Hugo Williams; the left side of the upper wrapper and the entire rear wrapper have an applied serigraph of a wavy pattern in multiple shades of gray and purplish blue; white wove paper; top edges untrimmed, other edges trimmed.

Publication date: autumn 1965

Price: 5s

Number of copies: 328

Note: The colophon states "Of this edition each contributor receives 12 copies as keepsakes; 100 are for sale."

Contents: "The night out", p. 7, collected in *P* (untitled) and in *P 50–66* (as "Canning town").

Note: The poem "The night out" appears here for the first time in print.

B24 WILLIAM CARLOS WILLIAMS 1966

a. *First edition, hardcover issue:*

WILLIAM CARLOS | WILLIAMS | A COLLECTION OF CRITICAL ESSAYS | Edited by | *J. Hillis Miller* | Prentice-Hall, Inc. [publisher's logo] *Englewood Cliffs, N.J.*

Collation: [1–6]^{16} = 96 leaves; 203 × 140 mm.

Binding: Bound in black cloth and lettered down the spine in gold: WILLIAM CARLOS WILLIAMS *Edited by* J. Hillis Miller Prentice-Hall; white wove paper; all edges trimmed; white wove endpapers; dust wrapper white wove paper printed in shiny black and very light bluish green (162).

Publication date: June 17, 1966

Price: $3.95

Number of copies: 5,000

Contents: "William Carlos Williams", pp. 171–173.

Note: This reprint contains only the final seven paragraphs of the original essay.

b. *First edition, paperback issue:*

[The transcription of the title page is identical with that of the first edition, hardcover issue.]

Collation: 96 single leaves; 202 × 137 mm.

Binding: A perfect binding glued in heavy white wove paper wrappers printed in shiny black and very light bluish green (162); lettered down the spine in light bluish green (162): [in two lines] TWENTIETH | CENTURY VIEWS | [in one line] WILLIAM CARLOS WILLIAMS | [in two lines] *Edited by* | J. Hillis MILLER | [across the spine] S-TC-61 | [publisher's series logo] | A SPECTRUM BOOK; on the upper wrapper printed in light bluish green (162): TWENTIETH CENTURY VIEWS | WILLIAM CARLOS | WILLIAMS | *A Collection of Critical Essays* | *Edited by* J. HILLIS MILLER | [abstract illustration] |

A SPECTRUM BOOK [publisher's series logo] S-TC-61 $1.95; on the rear wrapper [in black] there is a publisher's statement.

Publication date: June 17, 1966

Price: $1.95

Number of copies: 8,000

Note: The book was reprinted but the publisher does not have the date of reprinting or the number of copies of the reprint edition.

Contents: Same as B24a.

B25 NEW POEMS 1966 1966

[cover title] [in black] CRITICAL QUARTERLY POETRY SUPPLEMENT NUMBER 7 | [rule in white] | [in white] *New Poems 1966* | [rule in white] | [in black] Thom Gunn, Robert Lowell, R. S. Thomas, Gary Snyder, Ted Hughes | Randall Jarrell, Seamus Heaney, Donald Davie, Louis Simpson | Charles Tomlinson, Edward Braithwaite, Sylvia Plath | Iain Crichton Smith, David Holbrook, Elizabeth Jennings | [in white] [illustration of leaves] | [in black] PRICE | ONE SHILLING

Collation: [1]^{12} = 12 leaves; 218 × 137 mm.

Binding: Stapled into a white card wrapper printed in black and vital purple (216); the rear wrapper gives information about The Critical Quarterly Society; white wove paper; all edges trimmed.

Publication date: autumn 1966

Price: 1s

Number of copies: 9,000

Contents: "Back to life", pp. 2–3, collected in *T*; "Pierce Street", pp. 3–4, collected in *T* and *P 50–66*.

B26 THE BEST OF GRANTA 1967

THE BEST OF | *Granta* | 1889–1966 | Edited by | JIM PHILIP | JOHN SIMPSON | NICHOLAS SNOWMAN | LONDON | SECKER & WARBURG

Collation: [1–7]^{16} = 112 leaves; 196 × 167 mm.

Binding: Bound in dark purplish red (259) imitation-cloth paper covered boards and lettered down the spine in gold: THE BEST OF *GRANTA* 1889–1966 SECKER & WARBURG; white wove paper; all edges trimmed; white wove endpapers; dust wrapper shiny white paper printed in black, vital red (11), and very light bluish green (162).

Publication date: June 5, 1967

Price: 25s

Number of copies: 4,000

Contents: "Elizabeth Barrett Barrett", pp. [127]–128.

B27   **WORD IN THE DESERT**   1968

WORD | IN THE DESERT | *The Critical Quarterly* | *Tenth Anniversary Number* | edited by | C. B. Cox and A. E. Dyson | *London* | OXFORD UNIVERSITY PRESS | NEW YORK TORONTO | 1968

Collation: [1–13]⁸ = 104 leaves; 216 × 137 mm.

Binding: Bound in deep reddish orange (36) cloth and lettered across the spine in gold: [double rule] | [title on a dark olive green (126) panel] Word | in the | Desert | [double rule] | OXFORD; white laid paper; all edges trimmed; white wove endpapers; dust wrapper white wove paper printed in shiny vital yellow (82), moderate olive brown (95) and vital reddish orange (34).

Publication date: July 25, 1968

Price: 35s

Number of copies: 1,978

Contents: "Aqueduct", p. 56, collected in *TMB.*

B28   SELECTED POEMS OF FULKE   1968
                             GREVILLE

a. *First edition:*

Selected Poems of | FULKE GREVILLE | Edited with an Introduction by | THOM GUNN | FABER AND FABER | 24 Russell Square | London

Collation: [1–10]⁸ = 80 leaves; 200 × 132 mm.

Binding: Bound in moderate blue (182) cloth and lettered across the spine in gold: [title on a black panel surrounded by a gold rule] *Selected | Poems | of | Fulke | Greville | Faber*; white wove paper; all edges trimmed; white wove endpapers; dust wrapper very light greenish blue (171) wove paper printed in black and strong reddish orange (35).

Publication date: September 30, 1968

Price: 21s

Number of copies: 4,000

Contents: "Note on text", p. 7; "Life and Works", pp. 9–12; "Introduction", pp. 13–41; footnotes throughout the book; all appear here for the first time in print.

b. *First American edition:*

Selected Poems of | FULKE GREVILLE | Edited with an Introduction by | THOM GUNN | [publisher's logo] | THE UNIVERSITY OF CHICAGO PRESS

Collation: [1–10]⁸ = 80 leaves; 200 × 132 mm.

Binding: Bound in moderate blue (182) cloth and lettered across the spine in gold: [title on a black panel surrounded by a gold rule] *Selected | Poems | of | Fulke | Greville* | CHICAGO; white wove paper; all edges trimmed; white wove endpapers; dust wrapper very light greenish blue (171) wove paper printed in black and strong reddish orange (35).

Publication date: April 29, 1969

Price: $4.75

Number of copies: 1,481

Contents: Same as B28a.

B29   RUTH PITTER: HOMAGE TO A POET   1969

a. *First edition:*

RUTH PITTER: | HOMAGE TO A POET | Edited by Arthur Russell | With an introduction | by | David Cecil | [initials within decorative oval] R P | rapp + whiting

Collation: [1–8]⁸ = 64 leaves; 215 × 137 mm.

Binding: Bound in white and dark greenish blue (174) linen-grained paper covered boards and lettered down the spine in gold: [across] [three rules] | Ruth Pitter: Homage to a poet [six-spoked decorative device] [across] [three rules]; on the upper cover in the lower left corner in gold: rapp + whiting; white laid paper; all edges trimmed; white wove endpapers; dust wrapper light blue gray (190) wove paper printed in black and strong blue (178).

Publication date: spring 1969

Price: 35s

Number of copies: 700

Contents: "Urania as poet", pp. 63–65.

Note: The prose statement "Urania as poet" appears here for the first time in print.

b. *First American edition:*

RUTH PITTER: | HOMAGE TO A POET | Edited by Arthur Russell | With an introduction | by | David Cecil | [initials within decorative oval] R P | Dufour Editions Inc.

Collation: [1–8]⁸ = 64 leaves; 215 × 137 mm.

Binding: Bound in white and dark greenish blue (174) linen-grained paper covered boards and lettered down the spine in gold: [across] [three rules] | Ruth Pitter: Homage to a Poet | [across] Dufour | [across] [three rules]; white laid paper; all edges trimmed; white wove endpapers; dust wrapper light blue gray (190) wove paper printed in black and strong blue (178).

Publication date: Data unavailable from publisher.

Price: $6.00

Number of copies: 300

Contents: Same as B29a

B30   CONTEMPORARY POETS OF THE   1970
ENGLISH LANGUAGE

CONTEMPORARY POETS | OF THE | ENGLISH | LAN-GUAGE | WITH A PREFACE BY | C. DAY LEWIS | EDITOR | ROSALIE MURPHY | DEPUTY EDITOR | JAMES VINSON | ST JAMES PRESS | CHICAGO LONDON

Collation: [1]¹⁰ + [2–39]¹⁶ + [40]¹⁴ = 632 leaves; 245 × 173 mm.

Binding: Bound in brown black (65) cloth and lettered across the spine in gold: Contemporary | Poets | of the | English | Language | St. James Press; and across the upper cover in gold: Contemporary | Poets | of the | English | Language; white wove paper; all edges trimmed; white wove endpapers; dust wrapper of a linen finish gray yellowish brown (80) paper printed in gold.

Publication date: August 1970

Price: $25.00, £8.50

Number of copies: 3,000

Note: The book was retitled "CONTEMPORARY POETS" in the second printing, June 1, 1973, 1,000 copies; third printing, March 15, 1974, data on the number of copies of this reprint unavailable from the publisher. A second edition titled "CONTEMPORARY POETS" with different editors and design was published in June 1975 (St. James Press, London), August 1975 (St. Martin's Press, New York, N.Y.), total imprint 7,000 copies.

Contents: [autobiographical statement] p. 455; [biographical and critical statement about Gary Snyder] pp. 1026–1027.

Note: Both prose statements appear here for the first time in print.

Note: In the second edition (1975) the autobiographical statement by Thom Gunn was omitted.

B31   THE CAMBRIDGE MIND   1970

a. *First edition:*

THE | CAMBRIDGE | MIND | Ninety years of the *Cambridge Review* | 1879–1969 | [rule] | *edited by* ERIC HOMBERGER, | WILLIAM JANEWAY *and* SIMON SCHAMA | [publisher's logo] | JONATHAN CAPE | THIRTY BEDFORD SQUARE LONDON

Collation: [1–9]⁸ + [10]¹² + [11–18]⁸ + [19]⁶ + [20]⁸ = 162 leaves; 216 × 139 mm.

Binding: Bound in pink gray (10) imitation-cloth paper covered boards and lettered across the spine in gold: THE | CAMBRIDGE | MIND | [decorative loop] | EDITED BY | ERIC | HOMBERGER | WILLIAM | JANEWAY | AND | SIMON | SCHAMA | [publisher's logo]; white wove and shiny paper; all edges trimmed; white wove endpapers; dust wrapper white wove paper printed in strong pink (2) and black.

Publication date: October 29, 1970

Price: 80s

Number of copies: 3,000

Contents: [prose] "The energy of Dylan Thomas", pp. 285–287; [poem] "The death of a stranger", p. 288.

b. *First American edition:*

THE | CAMBRIDGE MIND | *Ninety Years of the Cambridge Review* | *1879–1969* | *edited by Eric Homberger,* | *William Janeway and Simon Schama* | *with illustrations* | [publisher's logo] *Little, Brown and Company* | *Boston Toronto*

Collation: [1–3]¹⁶ + [4]⁴ + [5–11]¹⁶ = 164 leaves; 208 × 138 mm.

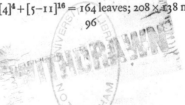